MY NATIONAL PARK DIET
LOSING WEIGHT, LEARNING, AND LAUGHING DURING 2011 TO 2014 INSIDE 47 OF AMERICA'S PUBLICLY OWNED NATURAL WONDERS

JEREMY WHITE

Petrified Forest NP: May 2011

Glacier NP: July 2014

CONTENTS

1. Developing a Park Plan   1
   February 2011
2. Petrified Forest National Park   11
   May 8th, 2011
3. Grand Canyon National Park   21
   May 10, 2011
4. Mesa Verde National Park   29
   May 12, 2011
5. Saguaro National Park   39
   October 30, 2011
6. Big Bend National Park   47
   January 14, 2012
7. Guadalupe Mountains National Park   53
   January 15, 2012
8. Carlsbad Caverns National Park   59
   January 16, 2012
9. Joshua Tree National Park   65
   February 4th, 2012
10. Zion and Bryce Canyon National Parks   71
    February 17-18, 2012
11. Death Valley National Park   83
    February 19, 2012
12. Shenandoah National Park   91
    May 20, 2012
13. Cuyahoga Valley National Park   95
    June 9, 2012
14. Pinnacles National Park   101
    June 30, 2012
15. Sequoia and Kings Canyon National Parks   109
    July 1, 2012
16. Yosemite National Park   117
    July 2, 2012
17. Redwood National Park   123
    July 4, 2012
18. Crater Lake National Park   131
    July 5, 2012
19. Lassen Volcanic National Park   135
    July 7, 2012

20. Acadia National Park   141
September 1, 2012

21. Great Sand Dunes National Park   147
September 29, 2012

22. Black Canyon of the Gunnison National Park   151
September 30, 2012

23. Great Basin National Park   155
October 2, 2012

24. Capitol Reef National Park   165
October 3, 2012

25. Arches National Park   171
October 4, 2012

26. Canyonlands National Park   177
October 5, 2012

27. Rocky Mountain National Park   183
October 6, 2012

28. Congaree National Park   187
November 10, 2012

29. Great Smoky Mountains National Park   191
November 11, 2012

30. Biscayne National Park   197
January 20, 2013

31. Everglades National Park   203
January 20-21, 2013

32. Isle Royale and Voyageurs National Parks   211
June 14, 2013

33. Wind Cave National Park   221
June 30, 2013

34. Badlands National Park   227
July 1, 2013

35. Theodore Roosevelt National Park   231
July 2-3, 2013

36. Yellowstone National Park   237
September 3-5, 2013

37. Grand Teton National Park   251
September 6, 2013

38. Olympic National Park   259
February 1-2, 2014

39. Hot Springs National Park   265
May 27, 2014

40. North Cascades National Park   271
July 4-5, 2014

41. Glacier National Park   281
July 7-9, 2014

42. Mount Rainier National Park *July 11-12, 2014*	293
43. Mammoth Cave National Park *August 9, 2014*	301
44. Channel Islands National Park *October 12, 2014*	309
45. Dry Tortugas National Park *December 15, 2014*	317
46. Closing My National Park Diet *From Late December 2014 to January 2015*	325
47. My Unfortunate Epilogue *2015 - 2023*	329
Author's Notes	343
Acknowledgments	345
Picture Sources	347

This book is a memoir of points in the author's life. The events and conversations in this book have been set down to the best of the author's ability.

Copyright © 2023 by Jeremy White

All rights reserved. No part of this book may be reproduced or used in any manner without written permission of the copyright owner except for the use of quotations in a book review.

ISBN 979-8-218-13730-4 (hardback)
ISBN 979-8-9879143-0-4 (ebook)

This book is dedicated to…

The American National Park system, without which my described travels would not have been possible.

My wonderful parents, Walter and Deanna White, without whom I would not have been possible.

ONE
DEVELOPING A PARK PLAN
FEBRUARY 2011

THANKFULLY THE TEARING noise that originated near my crotch as I sat on a conference room chair during a work meeting was not anatomical in origin. After a furtive glance southward, I could see that I had just heard a six-inch-long hole open in the left leg of my Dockers.

When I later sidled out of the room fervently hoping no co-workers who had also been in that meeting saw my khaki pants had a new vent, I did not know that walk of shame would become my first steps in a four-year journey during which I escaped a sucking mud hole, wild horses, and a German restroom critic; marveled at both a wall between the U.S. and Mexico for which geology paid and some millennia-old trees resembling bonsai cultivated by sadists; hiked on trails on which alligators dozed or bear spray was needed; and inadvertently initiated a guano avalanche with a kayak.

Because my pants ripped while I had sat in a cushy chair, my anatomy alone had pushed that fabric past its tensile limit. Alarmingly, these were not even old and worn pants. Just months before, I purchased a new lineup of 54-inch waist pants because the 50-inch waist ones I had been wearing for years had become overloaded sausage casings on my thighs. The new 54-inch-waist pants were already similarly stressed.

This pants size increase was just one sign that my weight was climbing. I needed a seat belt extender on recent business flights and often gasped after ascending the flight of stairs to my office cubicle. Nights in bed made my back so sore that I started sleeping on my recliner. For whatever reason, I had ignored those, but ripped pants convinced me my weight must again be on the rise. The next morning, I stepped out of the shower and onto a dust-bunny-covered scale to assess how much mass my ass had amassed.

348 pounds? That could not be right.

At 6-foot-2 with thick thighs, I weighed over 200 pounds in college when I scarcely had any fat. After college, my weight increased steadily, but I told myself that was caused by my shoulders filling out. When I passed 300 at age thirty, I finally acknowledged that more than my shoulders had expanded. By eating better, I stabilized at 320 for a while. Now at age 36, I had gained weight again, but I expected to see 330, not 348.

Since I was just out of the shower, nothing was on the scale but me and my glasses, without which my myopic eyes could not have read the digital display between my toes. Exhibiting signs of denial, I decided I must still be wet and toweled off again, methodically plumbing my belly button with the terry cloth this time. As an engineer who brilliantly and professionally designed beverage packaging, I should have known my navel would have to harbor two gallons of water to create the 18-pound discrepancy I sought.

When that second drying did not change the reading, I tried dusting and relocating the scale. None of those worked, so I ultimately accepted the accuracy of the scale reading and fell into a deep funk—the depressive kind, not the Bootsy Collins kind. Later in the day, I realized the real issue was not a number on a scale but the fact that I was huffing and puffing after a flight of stairs and too heavy to sleep in a bed. Those things were not healthy. I needed to make changes.

Coincidentally, at that moment, I also wanted to change what I did in my spare time.

Before 2011, I spent much of my life on trivia. I spent most of my free time answering trivia questions, preparing to answer trivia questions, writing trivia questions, and reading trivia questions to others at organized tournaments where I could not compete. Trivia competition had motivated me more than any other aspect of my life besides my equally beloved engineering job.

My primary trivia game of choice was quiz bowl, a competition style in which the members of two four-player teams vied to be first to "ring in" with a buzzer and give the correct answer to "pyramidal" style questions structured to reward depth of knowledge. Racing other players to the buzzer gave quiz bowl a sense of urgency that produced adrenaline rushes akin to playing physical sports, unlike Trivial Pursuit or pub quizzes where players have sufficient time to ponder a question and answer it relatively leisurely.

Over 22 years, I had played quiz bowl for the team at my high school in Clinton, Missouri, for the team at the University of Missouri-Rolla while studying chemical engineering there, and, during my gainfully employed adulthood, in open tournaments on teams with friends. For the past decade, I had played in five to ten tournaments every year, often volunteered to read questions for high school or college tournaments, wrote questions for an annual tournament I ran, and was a member of a team that won four pop culture quiz bowl national championships.

Early in 2011, that pop culture national championship tournament, my favorite event, closed shop. Other favorite tournaments of mine also ceased operations. My teammates called it quits due to a diminished slate of events and mounting real-life responsibilities. Single and without children or pets, I eschewed most responsibilities outside of those at work. Still it was time to use my vacation days to see more of the world instead of only traveling when on business trips, visiting my family, or playing games with a buzzer in hand.

My road to 348 pounds was, I reflected, paved in trivia. Quiz bowl games could be so exciting that they felt like a sport, but they never burned calories like an athletic sport. The game and other activities it inspired me to do primarily involved sitting. Many fit and trim people succeed at trivia games, so they do not automatically cause obesity. Quiz bowl had simply encouraged the inactivity exacerbating my weight issues.

My engineering job developing brand-new beverage packages or significantly improving old beverage packages for Gatorade required some active days in labs or factories. However, I spent far more days seated in conference rooms or writing spreadsheets, e-mails, and research reports in front of my computer. There was little I could do to change that. My diet had been healthier since I made significant adjustments in my early thirties, so I believed only a few calories were left to trim. If I could not reduce my calorie intake, weight loss required burning more calories.

If the key to a lighter me was more exercise, I should replace quiz bowl with a more calorie-burning hobby.

What activity? Most sports that burned significant calories were no longer within my physical capabilities. The two most stereotypical middle-aged-man sports were likely within my physical abilities. Still, to me, they looked dull and expensive (golf) or just barely more active than quiz bowl (bowling). My previous attempts to get exercise by running or jogging were swiftly abandoned because they caused joint pain. My past attempt to start bicycle riding had been scuttled after I found short stints on a bicycle seat caused temporary numbness in parts of my anatomy in which I preferred to retain feeling.

Walking was one physical activity I knew I could comfortably do for an extended time since I often walked long distances without issue, although always motivated by cheapness, not fitness. When I annually attended the three-day Lollapalooza summer music festival in Chicago's Grant Park, each day, I walked a mile from my home to the commuter train station and back to avoid paying to park, walked a mile-and-a-half from a Chicago Metra train station to the festival and back to avoid paying for an El ride or cab fare, and walked between the stages in the sprawling music festival to see different bands play because there was no other option. My feet ached the Monday after attending that festival, but otherwise, I walked roughly six miles a day for three days during Lollapalooza without significant difficulty.

Could I then walk my weight away? As an engineer and trivia nerd, I sought the answer in math and Internet searches. One website suggested burning 3,500 more calories than usual—without a change in diet—would cause one to shed a pound. Another site stated that walking a mile at my size burned roughly 100 calories.

At a minimum, I wanted to return to my old 320-pound equilibrium, but I decided to be bold and make a long-term goal of dropping to 300 pounds. If the above numbers were accurate, I needed to walk 1,680 miles to reach 300 pounds without decreasing my calorie intake. Losing that much weight in a year would require walking 4.7 miles daily. While I had walked that much in a single day, I doubted I could do it every day.

Averaging two miles a day seemed more feasible, but the math said losing 48 pounds at that rate would take four years. That was quite a long commitment. I felt no drive to walk apart from weight loss, so I suspected I would get bored or discouraged and then quit. How could I get excited about walking?

My ruminations about needing more exercise were underscored because they occurred during a blizzard-induced bout of sloth striking by my then-slovenly standards. Both my office and home at the time were in Barrington, Illinois, a northwest suburb of Chicago. Nearly twenty inches of snow hammered the area days before my pants split, then heavy winds piled giant flake drifts on my driveway higher than my waist. As a Chicagoland resident since 1997, I thought I was inured to heavy snow, but this was at another level.

Shoveling away multiple yards-long, four-foot-high ramparts of snow to get out of my house and get my car to the street left me sore and sapped of will to venture outside for anything but groceries and office work for two weeks, so I spent each night of the next fortnight burrowed beneath a blanket basking in a bevy of TV binge-watching so substantial that my DVR was soon bare but for a six-part documentary series twelve-hours long that had been there unwatched since it first aired on PBS in 2009.

The National Parks: America's Best Idea was directed by Ken Burns, best known for directing *The Civil War* and many other PBS history documentaries. I loved learning about history and enjoyed watching Burns' previous works, but for whatever reason, I assumed this documentary would be pretty landscape shots, not history. This erroneous perception and the length of the series kept me from starting it.

While finally watching it, I regretted my tardiness. This documentary was a history of how National Parks came to be, a more fascinating story than I would have ever expected. From it, I learned that most National Parks resulted from people recognizing a natural wonder was special and then initiating grassroots political efforts that prompted the federal government to protect that place for the enjoyment of current and future citizens.

Today there are National Parks in various nations all over the world. The phrase is now so immediately associated with the word wilderness that it is easy to forget that no place on Earth had ever been called a National Park until Yellowstone was declared one by the United States Congress in 1872. Even once America's earliest National Parks had been created, it was not immediately apparent what they should become. "Park" in other contexts connotes manicured lawns, playgrounds, and sports fields. In those early days, some thought that was what National Parks should be. Frederick Law Olmstead, New York's Central Park designer, was once brought to Yosemite and asked to recommend how to modify it to that kind of park.

It also needed to be made clear to what extent businesses would be allowed to operate or extract resources in National Parks. Ranchers tried to continue grazing their herds on park lands. The government approved building a dam across the beautiful Hetch Hetchy Valley in Yosemite National Park because San Francisco wanted to use the resulting lake as a water supply. Uranium was mined on the Grand Canyon's South Rim. Railroads built hotels and other attractions inside the parks.

In 1916, a federal National Park Service was finally created to run the parks. Under its leadership, the parks gradually assumed their current form of wilderness preserves and selected scenic areas developed with roads, trails, and facilities to accommodate visitors. Grazing, home developments, mineral extraction, and non-tourism business activities were generally barred, so creating a National Park often angered business interests. Then again, creating a National Park publicized its wonders and attracted tourists, so if government-built roads and facilities made parks more accessible, conservationists who thought parks should remain pure wildernesses were often rankled.

Burns' film showed that National Parks were not just plots of land but dynamically managed places at the crossroads of vigorous long-running debates like defining the appropriate roles of private enterprise and government and balancing commercialism and conservation. Burns asserted that National Parks were essentially small-d democratic both in execution because widespread efforts created them and in conception because America chose its most special natural places to be public lands, not privately owned.

While a federal government agency operates National Parks, Burns' film emphasized that the agency does so for the American people. Each American citizen was a co-owner of the National Parks and had a voice in how they were run. That would not be true if a tourism company like Disney owned National parks. If all Americans co-owned the National Parks, I was part owner of the Grand Canyon, Crater Lake, Old Faithful geyser in Yellowstone, and the mighty sequoias. All those places were terrific anomalies of geology and botany that had long been on my idle bucket list. At one point in the documentary, I smirked and thought, "If I am co-owner of the National Parks, I should check on my property."

While initially pleased that Burns' film was not just scenery, I found myself increasingly moved by the gorgeous scenery shots it often presented while making its points. Some stunning natural wonders it showed, despite being in my own country, were previously unfamiliar to me, underscoring just how little of my nation I had seen. The film also presented numerous interviews in which people talked breathlessly about making emotional connections with nature, having close encounters with wildlife, or simply finding moments of peace and joy in National Parks. I suddenly wanted to experience all of that.

When film enthusiasts discuss the most influential filmmakers, Ken Burns' name is unlikely to come up, but maybe it should. After watching Burns' film, this non-outdoorsy couch potato suddenly ached to visit some National Parks. As a borderline-compulsive list completer, I soon wanted to visit all of them.

While sometimes swayed by whims and emotions, as anyone can be, I am primarily rational. Thus, I immediately began rationalizing my desire to visit the National Parks. Doing so would scratch my itch to travel. Since the documentary and my subsequent reading suggested that some National Park features were best experienced on foot, perhaps National Parks were the incentive to walk I sought.

Maybe I could even lose my extra weight just by hiking in National Parks.

That last thought I knew was ridiculous as soon as I formed it. Even if I could walk ten miles a day, my earlier math suggested I would need to spend 168 days hiking in National Parks to reach my goal. That would take several years since I only had twenty vacation days from work a year, and most National Parks were far from Chicago.

So, I could not shed fifty pounds solely by vacationing in National Parks. Still, the more I thought about it, I believed National Park hiking could create a positive motivational feedback loop. Yes, I would burn more calories walking in National Parks than sitting in a chair playing quiz bowl, but more importantly, having memorable experiences hiking in National Parks might inspire me to walk more in my daily life so that I could become fitter and able to hike longer and see even more exciting spots on future National Park trips.

It was worth a try. If it did not work, at worst, I would stay fat while seeing amazing natural wonders.

One note of clarification is needed here. The National Park Service runs over 400 places in various categories like National Seashores, National Historic Sites, National Memorials, and National Battlefields. Each is a "National Park" in the broadest sense of the term, but when I set my goal in 2011, only 58 places had been officially designated a "National Park" by Congress. These were generally the system's marquee natural wonders. I decided to restrict my goal to them.

After more research, I developed doubts about visiting some of them. Two Alaska parks are vast tracts of wilderness with no roads or facilities, which would not work for me as I possessed zero wilderness survival skills. Yes, I wanted to see amazing things and burn calories, but I was not looking for extreme recreation. I wanted to drive to a park, walk well-maintained trails, and then leave to spend a night in a comfortable hotel.

As a tightwad, I swiftly ascertained that the National Parks in the contiguous 48 states were cheaper for me to visit than the eight parks in Alaska, the two in Hawaii, or the ones in American Samoa and the Virgin Islands. After considering everything, I resolved only to visit all 46 National Parks in the contiguous states, aka the "lower 48." These parks were all reachable by cheap flights and highway drives. All had developed facilities and nearby hotels, so camping was not needed.

With a list to complete, I can get obsessed and rush headlong to completion, forgetting to savor the process. To make sure I did not just pop into each park, nod twice, and go back to the car like Clark Griswold at the Grand Canyon, I decided to hold myself to walking at least five miles and spending at least eight hours in each park, a rule I dubbed my "workday standard" because eight hours is a typical workday.

After fiddling with Google Maps for hours, feeding my findings into an Excel spreadsheet, and cross-referencing that with my vacation time, I determined it would take four years to visit all 46 parks, which dovetailed nicely with the four years I had estimated that it would take me to drop to 300 pounds by walking. Of course, I calculated I would need to walk 1,680 miles in those four years to drop my weight by the desired amount, and, at five miles per park, only 230 of those miles would be hiked inside National Parks. The remaining 1,450 walking miles would have to slot into my daily life, which would test my motivational feedback loop hypothesis.

It was settled. From 2011 to 2014, my mission was to visit all 46 National Parks in the contiguous 48 states in 48 months and lose 48 pounds. I started calling this, with tongue in cheek, my "National Park Diet," even though I never had plans of eating meals exclusively made from things growing in the National Parks.

TWO
PETRIFIED FOREST NATIONAL PARK

MAY 8TH, 2011

WE WERE in a rented Ford Mustang, hurtling west on an interstate through the New Mexico desert, just east of the Arizona border and above the speed limit, when Robert Wright blurted, "Oh, crap!"

The car began beeping as if in distress after Robert, who was driving, uttered that mild interjection. Since I am a worry wart, a plethora of panic-provoking pictures promptly paraded through my mind, like this pony car plowing into opposing traffic or its engine petering out in a puff of smoke in this parched landscape.

"Is everything okay?" I asked Robert tentatively.

"Yeah," Robert sighed in reply, "but I must have hit the wrong button because the car can only go eighty now."

"Is the speed limited to eighty miles an hour, or is this a *Speed* situation where the Mustang must go eighty or it explodes?" I asked, hoping the latter option was a sarcastic one.

"No, smartass," Robert barked. "It's limited to eighty."

To demonstrate, Robert braked and then stomped on the gas. The car accelerated, beeped as it approached eighty, then held that speed no matter how long Robert pushed the pedal. When Robert began furiously poking buttons hoping to eliminate this new speed limit, paying little attention to the interstate, I suggested he drive and let me seek a solution in the owner's manual or on the Internet.

I learned that each key to this Mustang could be programmed with a unique speed limit, presumably so parents could give teenagers a key to the family car that prevented them from having fun with it. Robert had accidentally set ours to 80. Modifying this, once established, required an "admin key" that we did not have.

This happened after we had already driven 150 miles from the Albuquerque airport lot where we had rented this car the day before, so I did not want to return there. Ever an anal-retentive planner, any deviation from my carefully crafted itinerary would have pained my heart. Robert did not want to backtrack either and said he could live with the speed limit, so we kept driving west.

Since Robert had recently picked up a new hobby, amateur auto racing, this development seemed like a good thing. No roads on our trip had speed limits higher than 80. Our new speed restriction would prevent him from trying any newly acquired—and possibly not yet fully mastered—racing moves at excessively exuberant velocities. I kept that thought to myself.

This car had caused minor friction the day before when we met after making our separate morning flights to Albuquerque's airport—or Sunport as it is officially named. While planning the trip, I reserved all the hotel rooms, but Robert had booked the rental car. Although Robert reserved a mid-sized car, he was offered a low-cost upgrade to two different premium cars at the counter, one a big sedan and the other a Mustang.

Since we would log 1,500 miles on this trip, I wanted the sedan, but Robert insisted on the Mustang. My first car was a 1979 Mustang coupe, so I felt nostalgia for them, but as an obese 36-year-old, I no longer saw the charm in cramming my ample ass into a sports car if a more spacious option was available. We were also staying in a different city each night of this trip. I dreaded daily re-packing luggage into its minuscule trunk. However, Robert had reserved the car, making him the decider. We left in the Mustang to my chagrin.

Robert and I had been friends since we were roommates studying engineering at the University of Missouri-Rolla in the mid-1990s. He was now an aerospace engineer working near St. Louis, wearing thick glasses, voraciously reading science fiction, and playing *Dungeons and Dragons*. A casual observer might think him a stereotypical nerd not interested in hiking or even going outdoors, but Robert sprung to mind first when I started thinking about friends who might want to join me on a National Park trip.

Robert seemed ideal for several reasons. He was knowledgeable about parks and hiking because he had been a Boy Scout during his childhood in Virginia, done long hikes, and taken summer road trips to National Parks with his parents. Robert was a sensible sort and a little chubby, so he was not an uber-fit, gung-ho nut job who would want to engage in rock climbing, whitewater rafting, or other "extreme" recreation. Finally, like me, Robert was single and could travel without the approval of their significant other.

When I told Robert about my National Park goal, he said he was interested in joining me on a Southwestern trip. I thus sent Robert a proposed itinerary that involved flying to Phoenix and then driving two thousand miles stopping only to sleep and spend eight hours apiece in six National Parks over nine days.

"Look, I know you're hot and bothered to see some National Parks, but your whole itinerary is geology and Native American ruins," Robert said in an incredulous tone over the phone after reading my outline. "I want more variety if I'm going. You need to get other things in here, like some Old West or science stuff."

Negotiations ensued. To get Robert on board, I ultimately compromised on an itinerary that included only three National Parks. The other parks were dropped in favor of some museums, some natural wonders not in National Parks, and an all-day scenic train trip through southwestern Colorado that Robert insisted on taking.

Usually, I am not the compromising type when on a mission. Everyone else can get on board, get out of my way, or get flattened while I do it alone. "Flattened" was meant metaphorically, but I then weighed nearly 350 pounds, so a literal flattening was not inconceivable. A compromise was only tenable to me at that moment because I was nervous about hiking in National Parks alone. Parks were filled with natural wonders but also included natural risks, so it was good to go with someone who knew the places well.

We planned this trip in early April. By then, I had bought a treadmill to use indoors and had been walking ten miles a week outdoors for a month whenever the weather cooperated. My outdoor walking included walks to work, walks to the grocery store, and some weekend ambles on a 3.3-mile forest preserve trail. Still, all my walking to date was in flat, low-elevation Chicagoland.

Many National Parks, by contrast, were at high-altitude places with thin air and on hills or mountains, so most trails involved "elevation gain" in hiking jargon. The National Park Service's websites listed each trail's length, elevation gain, and surface material. They also classified their overall difficulty as "easy," "moderate," or "strenuous." I wanted no part of anything strenuous, but a few places I longed to see required hiking trails labeled "moderate" due to slowly climbing 400 vertical feet or more. I still needed to catch my breath after taking the stairs. Thus, it also seemed prudent to have someone along for my maiden voyage in case I found I had been too ambitious mid-trail and someone needed to call an ambulance…or a hearse.

After our destinations were chosen, it made more sense to start our trip by flying to Albuquerque, New Mexico. I had never been there before and until recently only knew it as where Bugs Bunny often makes wrong turns. However, I was excited to see Albuquerque as I had been obsessively watching *Breaking Bad*, a dramatic TV series set there. The series tells the fictional story of a middle-aged chemistry teacher who "cooks" methamphetamine to pay for necessary cancer treatments. It sustained my interest with its high quality, but it first hooked me with the prominence of chemistry in its plotlines and the fact that its main character was named Walter White, which is also my father's name.

Insanely detailed fan-created websites exist for most TV series. *Breaking Bad* was no exception, so it took minutes to find the addresses of every *Breaking Bad* filming location in Albuquerque. I most wanted to see the house used for exterior shots of Walter White's home, so I added it to our itinerary. It was close to the airport, so we went there first after leaving the rental car lot, meaning the first trip of my National Park Diet started not with a trek into a canyon but with a slow ride through a subdivision.

"It looks just like it does on the show!" I gushed as Robert drove past the house and I snapped a picture.

"What else would it look like?" Robert asked.

A man behind the wheel of an SUV parked across the street eyed us suspiciously as we passed, and I suppose I would look askance if two men in a car crept past my neighbor's house taking pictures. His suspicion made more sense when I later read that the home's owners, who allowed the series to film the house's exterior for a fee, had been dealing with rampant trespassing and vandalism since the series had become popular. Manners-deficient fans had even thrown pizzas on its roof to mimic a memorable scene.

I would never trespass or, as evidenced by my weight, throw pizza on a roof, but I was sufficiently obsessed with *Breaking Bad* that I would have driven around Albuquerque gaping at more locations used in the show if left to my own devices. However, Robert had yet to watch Breaking Bad, and I did not want to try his patience. Even without trying, though, I found some other spots.

At one point, we were stopped at a red light, and I pointed out my open window at a building and yelled, "That's the hotel where Jesse holed up with the hooker to establish an alibi!" When my exclamation caused the driver of a car in the next lane to stare at us quizzically, Robert looked back at him with a combination of head shake, shoulder shrug, and sigh with which he seemed to be trying to communicate, "I don't know him. I just volunteered to take a mentally disturbed individual on a car ride."

We spent most of that afternoon in Albuquerque's excellent Museum of Nuclear History. Its most impressive exhibit was a nine-acre outdoor display of missiles, airplanes, and other vehicles designed to deliver nuclear weapons, including an F-16, a B-52, a B-29, a Titan missile, a Minuteman missile, and part of a nuclear submarine. Given Robert's aerospace engineering career and interests in the field, he added fascinating tidbits about these vehicles to the information on the museum's already detailed interpretive signs.

Thus, we tarried long in the "missile gallery," as I dubbed it, and while there, the intense desert sun cooked my skin until it assumed a vermillion hue otherwise seen only on blushing lobsters. Sunburn is a hazard whenever I go outside because I have a pale complexion. I like to say I am so white that it is my last name. As such, I packed a bottle of SPF-high double digits for hikes but had not thought to bust it out for a museum.

Luckily for my skin, the Nuclear History Museum also had indoor exhibits, like scholarly displays on the Manhattan Project and nuclear waste disposal. I loved its quirkier artifacts, like radiation-based medical quackery, an X-ray machine once used to size shoes, and a display of atomic age popular culture. There was even an assembled 1950s home bomb shelter with its full complement of items intended to help one survive a nuclear apocalypse, like the barrel of high fructose corn syrup labeled "Carbohydrate Supplement."

After a night in a hotel, we left Albuquerque early the next morning after stopping at a grocery store to buy provisions. We planned on eating hotel continental breakfasts and restaurant dinners, but Robert recommended picnic lunches. This proved wise counsel. I followed it on later trips since most National Parks have no restaurants, and the eateries are often expensive and busy in those that do.

Robert had definite opinions on optimizing National Park picnics. He lectured me on his rationale for selecting each foodstuff he stuffed into our cart with an officious tone that begged mockery. Still, I let it go and only objected when Robert said we were done without having selected a dessert. Robert pointed out I was trying to lose weight, but I thought hiking merited some reward, so I added Little Debbie oatmeal cream pies to the cart. Upon returning to the car, I used a Sharpie to re-label them "Carbohydrate Supplement."

We drove 220 miles west on I-40 to Arizona's Petrified Forest National Park in only three hours, even though Robert accidentally limited our maximum possible speed during this drive. I-40 runs right through the middle of Petrified Forest, and its main visitor center is accessed via an interstate exit. Virtually every NPS unit has at least one visitor center, a building where one can get information on the park's trails, campgrounds, and facilities. Like most, this one had a small museum with exhibits on the park's biology, geology, and history. Naturally, this one had exhibits explaining the formation of the fossilized tree remains, or petrified wood, that was the park's namesake attraction.

The term Petrified Forest is misleading since that sounds like ancient stony trees still stand as if each tree in a prehistoric forest simultaneously peeked at Medusa. Petrified wood here is just tree trunks turned to fossilized stone with no branches or leaves, and they are lying flat on the ground—or still in the ground.

Although now an arid desert, this land was the lush, forested edge of a body of water during the Triassic period, the geologic period in which dinosaurs evolved that ended 200 million years ago. The Triassic trees that became these fossils died, fell, were washed downstream, and quickly buried in mud at the bottom of that body of water. Being buried helped the wood resist decay. Eventually, the buried pieces absorbed silica or other minerals that hardened into rock, with the rotting log acting as a mold. This lengthy process eventually produced a rocky facsimile of the original wood.

Before entering the park, we had to stop at an entrance station, basically a tollbooth with a park ranger inside collecting the twenty-dollars-per-car entry fee. After the money changed hands, the ranger handed us a map and reminded us that taking petrified wood from the park was illegal. We nodded acknowledgment, but I was thrown for a loop when he next asked if we had petrified wood in the car.

"Do you think we are smuggling petrified wood into the park?" I asked incredulously.

The ranger looked at me crossly and said, "No, but we do random searches at the exit to make sure no petrified wood is being removed, so if you have petrified wood with you, it needs to be declared now."

"Oh, that makes sense," I admitted sheepishly, fearing my smart-alecky question would prompt the ranger to flag us for full-body-cavity petrified wood searches on our way out.

Petrified Forest has a main road that directs visitors sequentially to its significant points of interest. It is a two-way road, so you do not have to visit things in that order if you want to be a maverick, but we followed the prescribed order since that was the most efficient way, and we were engineers who prized efficiency. Each stop had a short trail, ranging from a quarter mile long to 2.5 miles long. Those all led to artifacts or scenery of interest. I wanted to walk every single one, which would total about 6 miles.

We did not see one stick of petrified wood during our first ninety minutes in the park as the first few stops highlighted the general landscape here, called the Painted Desert, starkly beautiful badlands of undulating hills, steep-sided mesas, and conical buttes bare of plant life and composed of soft, crumbly sedimentary rock. These hills were horizontally banded with many layers colored vivid shades of red, yellow, and orange.

We finally found the park's namesake attraction by walking in an area called Blue Mesa, where the banded, undulating hills no longer sported warm colors but were muted shades of blue and violet. We hiked a one-mile trail from the top of a hill down to its base. While descending, we saw some huge, petrified logs protruding out of hillsides, partially exposed by erosion of the soft rock that once fully entombed them. At the base of the hills stood jumbles of petrified logs that erosion had entirely freed from the hillside.

We could more closely inspect petrified wood in The Crystal Forest, where enormous pieces of the stuff three feet or more in diameter lie fully exposed on the ground immediately adjacent to a short, paved trail. These giant fossil logs were, despite millions of years of geology between us and the death of the tree, still quite recognizable as a tree trunk with textured bark, knots, and grain.

Most petrified logs here were a swirl of red, orange, and purple colors like the surrounding hills. Some even shimmered from embedded quartz crystals. These looked more like blinged-up psychedelic art than fossils, so I was more drawn to the few comparatively drab pieces here colored like natural wood. They made it more tangible that we were looking at the fossilized remains of real trees that died in the age of dinosaurs.

A 2.5 mile-trail called Long Logs passed countless petrified tree trunks, most over one hundred feet long, and separated into roughly two-foot-long sections with vertical splits so clean they seemed to have been sawed by a dinosaur Paul Bunyan. These breaks were instead the natural result of erosion. As soft rock surrounding the petrified trunk erodes, one end of the trunk can be left unsupported while the rest is still buried, which can cause the heavy end to break off.

We drove from the park exit to our hotel for the night in Holbrook, Arizona. I had generally reserved Marriott hotels like Fairfield Inns or Courtyards because I had earned many Marriott points from my business travel and could use them to book rooms. No Marriott was near Petrified Forest, so I booked a room for this night at the Wigwam Motel on a silly impulse. At this old Route 66 tourist-trap motel, each room was a free-standing concrete cone painted to resemble a Native American teepee.

Our "wigwam" had dated furniture, a sketchy old TV with few channels, and, most distressingly, no Wi-Fi. I hated camping, so in my view, the

Wigwam was "roughing it." I was relieved to be in a Marriott the next night, but that said, I remember nothing specific about any individual Marriott on that trip since most Courtyards and Fairfield Inns were identical down to the Janet van Arsdale prints on the walls. By contrast, I recall small details of the Wigwam, like the oddly shaped shower necessitated by the cone's sloped walls.

While eating dinner that night, Robert asked if this first National Park had met my expectations.

"Well, I loved the fossils and those gorgeous colorful hills," I started, "but with the paved trails, it felt less like I was immersed in nature and more like we were in an outdoor museum like the missile gallery, but with petrified wood."

"You didn't want to camp. You didn't want to go into the backcountry. You didn't want to do anything strenuous," Robert reminded me. "You said you just want to walk to interesting stuff. Aren't outdoor museums what you want?"

"You're right," I conceded. "I suppose I do want to walk in curated nature. Still, many people interviewed in that Ken Burns documentary gushed about feeling rapturous connections with nature in National Parks. I want to feel that. I guess I just expected a National Park would feel…grander."

"The next National Park will feel grander," Robert reassured me. "It even has 'grand' in its name."

THREE
GRAND CANYON NATIONAL PARK

MAY 10, 2011

"IF THIS HAD BEEN in my backyard in third grade, I would have gone ape shit," I said to Robert Wright while gazing awestruck into the Grand Canyon from Mather Point.

Robert did not ask what I was talking about because he had known me long enough to know that asking me a question would prompt a long story. The tale he missed—or, more accurately, avoided—was how I had conducted a flawed geological survey in third grade, equipped only with a Snoopy ruler, a pencil, and a bucket.

During a third-grade geology unit at school, I learned about many different types of rocks and minerals, how they formed, and how to identify them via simple tests, like scratching them, rubbing them on tile, or observing how they broke when hit with a hammer. Fascinated, I read more about geology in books from the library and started using these techniques to classify stones I found in driveways or rock gardens.

As an engineer, I am ashamed to admit that science was my least favorite class in elementary school because so much of the curriculum was rote memorization of terms—like the names of bones or types of clouds—without any obvious application. In history, we learned how the world became the way it is. In math, we learned how to use numbers in ways handy for keeping track of money or designing a building. In reading and writing, we learned how to read or communicate better. Science just seemed to be vocabulary.

Science is not just facts about nature and the universe but the method of learning those facts. This geology unit was the first time I recall science being presented to me as a process and a tool kit one could use to learn about the world. I was soon hooked.

Identifying rocks in a rock garden was fun, but like solving a Sudoku—challenging but of little import. However, we were also taught that one professionally trained could study rock layers in situ and discern how that spot had changed over millions of years. As a third grader, I wanted to do that. Geological history was evidenced in rocks below my hometown, but flat Clinton, Missouri had no cliffs. I did not have a drill for taking core samples from rock layers far below the soil. I did, however, have private access to one site that I thought was promising.

At that time, my family lived on land once used for strip mining coal. Thus, behind our one-acre backyard was a "lake"—the original mine pit now filled with water—and the "hill"—a pile of dirt and rock dug from that pit. My maternal grandparents had purchased several acres of this formerly mined land decades ago, built a home on it, and had a huge garden and some livestock. Later, my grandparents gifted one acre to each of their three children. When I was five, we moved into a doublewide trailer my parents purchased and parked on my mother's acre.

In third grade, I knew none of that and assumed the hill and lake were natural. From playing on the hill, I knew its surface was studded with sedimentary rocks like limestone, sandstone, and shale. I thus resolved to study its origins one summer afternoon by, at one-foot increments on the slope, collecting, marking, and identifying rocks I pried from the hill's surface. The fact that I pulled these samples from the hill with my fingers should have been a tip-off that these were random mixes of loose rocks, not strata. The fact that we had such an anomalous hill should have been a tip-off that the hill was not natural, but I was in third grade.

When I proudly showed my parents my work, my father explained the hill's origin and that the rocks were no longer in their original order. My thoughts of an earth science "career" never recovered from this disappointment, but the enormous hole in the ground now before me brought my dormant geology fascination rushing back full force because the canyon's mile-high walls are composed of bare colorful rocks arranged neatly in horizontal bands that I imagined were each a page in a thick book of geological history.

Robert and I arrived here on Tuesday morning following our Petrified Forest visit. We spent the intervening Monday on a hodgepodge of activities near Flagstaff, Arizona that I dubbed "Outer Space Day" because we saw an enormous meteor crater west of Winslow, Arizona, and toured Lowell Observatory, the astronomical research facility that confirmed the redshift and found Pluto. I also made Robert photograph me standing on a corner in Winslow, Arizona. That was so I could re-enact a lyric from The Eagles' song "Take it Easy."

That had all been fun, but I had been restless throughout the day with thoughts of the Grand Canyon and made a swift beeline to Mather Point, the nearest spot on the canyon rim, as soon as our car was parked in the National Park. What I saw there astonished me more than anything I had ever beheld. One must see it to believe it. Even then, belief is a challenge.

It is tough to pinpoint why the Grand Canyon is so overwhelming since it does not own many superlatives. It is not the deepest, longest, or widest canyon in the world. It is, however, enormous in all those dimensions at roughly one mile deep, 270 miles long, and ten miles wide.

That said, if the Grand Canyon were an empty ditch of that size between two blandly colored cliffs, I doubt it would be a world-famous tourist destination. The Grand Canyon is thankfully far from empty or bland. The void between its rims is interrupted by vividly colored bare stone mesas and pyramidal mountain peaks separated by a maze of current and former channels of the Colorado River, the stream that has carved it.

Although not usually scared of heights, peering into a five-thousand-foot-deep abyss jangled my nerves, even with safety railings surrounding most of Mather Point. I noticed jet-black ravens perched on gnarled evergreen trees clinging to the canyon rim were watching the tourists. While they were probably waiting for dropped food, at that moment, I was sure those ravens were expecting one of us to provide their next meal by clumsily tumbling into the gulf below.

Before we knew it, we had spent thirty minutes at Mather Point gawking, marveling, and taking photos of the canyon. This was just one of many spots on the South Rim considered optimum viewpoints. The others have similar names, like Yavapai Point and Powell Point. Both a road and a hiking trail connect them in series. Cars are not allowed on the road along the South Rim for most of the year, so most visitors experience the Canyon by taking shuttle buses to some or all of those viewpoints.

Since hiking was part of my objective in National Parks, I wanted to eschew the buses and spend the day walking the South Rim Trail, which for most of its length, hugs the canyon rim. Shuttle riders would have brief canyon views punctuated by bus rides. We instead would have near-constant canyon views.

We soon learned that the Rim Trail only offers those constant canyon views when the weather cooperates. We could see buildings and people ten miles away on the opposite North Rim of the canyon when we arrived, but after only walking half a mile, thick clouds abruptly rolled in, and suddenly we could not even tell there was a North Rim. After a hard snow started, we could scarcely tell there was a canyon. Luckily, the snow only lasted a few minutes, the clouds dispersed, and the rest of the day was sunny and glorious.

In addition to the stupefying vistas, there were places on the South Rim Trail to learn more about its geology, like the excellent Yavapai Geology Museum and a stretch of the trail that had been dubbed The Trail of

Time. Along it, each meter represented a million years. Samples of each of the canyon's rock layers were displayed on plinths at distances along the trail corresponding to its date of formation. It was a little silly, perhaps, but The Trail of Time made the immense scale of geological time more tangible.

I learned from the Trail of Time that the "mile-thick book" of rock I imagined was missing some pages. The top layer of the canyon was 200 million years old, so everything since the dinosaurs was not represented in rocks here. Some of the intervening time had once been represented in rock layers that have already eroded. Lower down, an intersection of layers called the Great Unconformity represented where another 200 million years of rock had gone missing.

Near the end of the Trail of Time were samples of the canyon's bottom-most rock, metamorphic schist a mind-boggling 1.7-billion-years old. Because the bottom rock layer is that old, some make the mistake of saying the Grand Canyon is 1.7 billion years old, but the canyon, meaning the natural ditch itself and not the rocks in its walls, is much younger. The exact time is still debated, but most scientists think the Colorado River started cutting this channel in the last 70 million years. It took millions of years of incremental erosion for the Colorado River to slowly carve this canyon into something so grand.

The Trail of Time exhibit ended just before the Rim Trail entered Grand Canyon Village, a town of 2,000 people on the canyon rim replete with hotels, restaurants, gift shops, and other places looking to separate tourists from dollars. Robert and I had the canyon to ourselves most of the morning, even at some named viewpoints, but the village was abuzz with activity even on a weekday before the summer tourist season.

There was a striking building here that had been built in 1914 called Lookout Studio. It was perched on the canyon rim and, since it was made of rough-hewn local stone, almost appeared to be part of it. It had been constructed by the Santa Fe railroad, which was unsurprising since I knew it had once operated many tourist facilities here. However, I was surprised to read that this building had been designed, along with five other beautiful rustic buildings in the park, by a pioneering female architect named Mary Colter.

Another vintage building had once been a photography studio run by two brothers with Kolb as their surname. In addition to taking photos of tourists, they took artistic canyon shots in their spare time, often from precarious points. They made a film inside the canyon that they charged visitors to watch. Their studio is now a delightful museum displaying their equipment and photos. It still shows their movie on a screen.

The village was also the site of the junction of the Rim Trail and the Bright Angel Trail, the most famous and popular trail into the canyon. Robert had hiked to the bottom of the canyon and back to the top with his father as a teenager. During our trip, he had wanted to walk the first one or two miles of Bright Angel for old times' sake. I had been dreading this because I had read that the trail descended 1,000 vertical feet in its first mile and a half. Since I did not want to stay inside the Grand Canyon forever, I would have to ascend those same 1,000 feet in a mile-and-a-half to get back out.

Posted warnings about patches of ice on the Bright Angel trail at the visitor center that morning had been enough to deter Robert from doing this hike. I was relieved. Now that I could see the trail, I feared I was not in good enough shape to make it back up that small section. I knew with metaphysical certitude I could not have handled the 20-mile round-trip with 4,300 feet of elevation change each way to take Bright Angel to the bottom and back.

Instead of hiking Bright Angel, I had initially wanted to take one of the daily mule tours into the canyon offered on this iconic trail, but alas, the tour group had informed me I was too fat to ride a mule. The weight limit for a person taking a mule tour is 200 pounds, so achieving mule-tour weight would require me to adopt a regimen of not just diet and exercise but amputation, as well.

Just past the village, we found a bench with a canyon view, sat down, and snacked on trail mix. A squirrel approached within inches of

Robert's feet, stood on its back legs, cocked its head, and held its paws out in apparent supplication. When Robert did not oblige him, the adorable rodent tried the same tactic on me.

We had seen many people feeding squirrels directly out of their hands all day despite the many signs in the park warning that park squirrels may carry disease (including the plague!) and might bite. This squirrel must have been the recipient of handfeeding to get so brazen. In retrospect, its begging was timid compared to the squirrels I much later saw climbing into tourist backpacks left open on the ground at Zion National Park.

Park visitors should never feed wildlife because animals fed by humans lose their fear of humans. That is a relatively minor problem with squirrels, but feeding predators like bears or alligators creates hazardous situations that may force park rangers to kill an animal. Robert and I did not feed the squirrel but could not resist shooting photos. Robert managed pictures so great you would think the squirrel was a paid model, but my cheap point-and-shoot and lack of photographic skill only produced fuzzy blurs.

After the squirrel sighting, the rest of our visit was a fuzzy blur, too. We walked to many more viewpoints. The thrill of seeing the canyon was not wearing off for me, but the various views were not sufficiently different that I recall individual details. At least at some of those later viewpoints —like Hopi Point—the Colorado River and the slot it had cut through those basement rocks were visible. At the earlier views, I could only see the river through binoculars.

I was still entranced with the canyon, but at a spot called The Abyss, Robert announced he was done walking for the day. We found the nearest bus stop and took a shuttle back to the parking lot. We started driving out of the park on Arizona highway 64. East of Mather Point, you can drive to some canyon viewpoints, so we briefly stopped at a few, including a stunning spot called Desert View.

The day after that Grand Canyon visit, Robert and I had another hodgepodge sightseeing day that ended at Four Corners. On this spot, the borders of the four states we were visiting on this trip—Arizona, Utah, Colorado, and New Mexico—meet at a single point inside a Navajo Reservation. The actual corners were marked on a metal disc in the ground. Accessing it required a five-dollar-per-person entry fee.

Robert and I each posed for pictures standing on the metal disc with some portion of our anatomy in each of the four states simultaneously. While standing there grinning while Robert took my picture, I felt silly because, at that moment, I suddenly realized I had not come to Four Corners to experience standing in four states at once. I had only come here so I could later tell people I had stood in four states at once.

Standing in four states at once felt the same as standing anywhere else. Standing on a corner in Winslow, Arizona had not felt different than standing on any other Arizona street corner. I only went there to collect a whimsical brag. I realized so many places I stopped on past trips had been similarly motivated, like the time I visited a giant Minnesota ball of twine mentioned in a "Weird Al" Yankovic song or the time I had my sister photograph me walking across the London crosswalk that is on the cover of the Beatles' *Abbey Road* album.

It is no coincidence that I became acutely cognizant of such frivolity in my past travels the day after hiking on the rim of the Grand Canyon. That canyon had given me chills and moved me intellectually, aesthetically, and emotionally. I departed the park filled with wonder at its beauty, better educated about nature, and viscerally reminded that human life is so brief compared to the vastness of geological time.

FOUR
MESA VERDE NATIONAL PARK
MAY 12, 2011

"DON'T BE A WIMP. You can do that," Robert Wright insisted.

Robert and I were at the counter in a Mesa Verde National Park visitor center where tickets are sold for the guided tours required to access two of the park's best-preserved ruins of Native American cliff dwellings. We agreed while driving here only to take the Cliff Palace tour because I made it clear I would not go on the Balcony House tour under any circumstances. Robert had wanted to go to Balcony House, so he reopened this debate in the visitor center, presumably thinking he could shame me into changing my mind.

I had a big—well, more accurately—a small problem with the Balcony House tour. The NPS website said its route required crawling through a tunnel only 18 inches wide. I saw no way my giant carcass could fit through an aperture so diminutive.

"Robert," I said in a firm tone, "If I enter an eighteen-inch-diameter pipe, I'm never coming out of it."

"The Balcony House tour requires passing through an 18-inch wide, 12-foot-long rectangular tunnel, but I would not call it a pipe if that helps," the ranger behind the desk told us. "We have a demo tunnel here in the visitor center you can try," she offered helpfully, no doubt hoping to convince us to argue elsewhere.

"Why don't you try the demo tunnel?" Robert asked.

"I don't need to get stuck here to know I cannot crawl through an eighteen-inch pipe," I seethed.

"It's a tunnel, not a pipe," the now smirking ranger gently corrected.

"Look, you can do Balcony House if you want. I'll be happy just to chill out or do another hike while I wait, but I cannot do that," I said definitively as I could, hoping to end the argument.

Robert sighed, turned to the ranger, and said, "Just two tickets for Cliff Palace since he is a wuss."

This was the third instance in twenty-four hours of Robert saying I was a wuss and while probably true, I was getting irritated. The other two instances occurred the previous day at our two stops before we went to the Four Corners.

We had first traveled to Monument Valley, a Navajo Reservation Tribal Park made famous by John Ford westerns. It was essentially a geological formation, but I had used its film history to convince Robert it was an Old West attraction back when we were haggling over what to do on the trip. It is a rust-colored desert plain near the Arizona-Utah border from which 1,000-foot-tall, dark brown sandstone monoliths stick up like sore thumbs. The two most famous formations here are called The Mittens because these gargantuan rock formations have thin spires positioned so that, from certain angles, they look like giant mittens with upright thumbs. We saw Monument Valley in low-impact fashion, cruising on the valley's scenic dirt road.

The other two previous times I had been said to be showing wussiness happened later that day during our visit to Utah's Natural Bridges National Monument, named for three enormous stone arches over a canyon. While I found these natural formations resembling manufactured bridges delightful, the trail to one of them was not fun. While classified as moderate, it was the most strenuous hike I had yet done.

All trails I had previously tackled were smoothed paths, either paved or hard-packed and covered in fine gravel. Our first hike in Natural Bridges was my first "natural surface" trail, and I soon learned that the surface could make all the difference. Here the trail was not a manufactured path but a set of written directions to follow while walking over the natural slope of a rocky canyon wall. I labored both on our way to the arch and away from the arch because I was being careful with my foot placement, fearing I might twist an ankle on the uneven surfaces. Robert, by contrast, bounded in both directions and teased me that I was slowing him down.

When we left Natural Bridges, Robert took the wheel of the Mustang, announcing he had discovered how to defeat the electronic speed limit he had inadvertently given the car earlier in the trip. I assumed he meant he had learned how to re-program the key, but I was wrong. During this drive, the road descended 1,500 feet via steep slopes and serpentine switchbacks, often right next to a cliff. Robert built up speed on one flat stretch. When the asphalt started sloping down, he did not brake, allowing gravity to accelerate the car beyond eighty. Impressed by Rob's ingenuity, I congratulated him for defeating the speed limit with physics.

Robert then said I should get a picture of how close our car was to the cliff edge to our right, so I made the mistake of looking over said cliff edge and the sight of the drop we would take if the car went over that edge caused my heart to pound and my brain to repeatedly play the stock footage of a car tumbling down a mountain side that they used to use in those old *SNL* Toonces the Driving Cat sketches. I asked Robert to slow down before I had a heart attack.

When our third disagreement concluded, at which my nervousness was at root, we drove from the visitor center into the heart of Mesa Verde. This land in arid southwestern Colorado was topologically interesting, with mesas and plateaus topping out at 7,000 feet above sea level, but not so interesting that it would likely have become a National Park without its archaeological sites. It is a National Park because it contains many buildings constructed around 1,000 C.E. by ancestors of the Pueblo Native American tribe.

The most famous Native American buildings here are the cliff dwellings constructed inside concave voids in the cliff faces around the area's mesas. Voids form in cliffs when hard rock layers atop a mesa erode more slowly than softer rock layers below. Native Americans erected buildings in these natural cliff alcoves throughout the Southwest, but Mesa Verde has the biggest surviving complex of them, with over 600 individual cliff dwelling sites ranging from one-room buildings to small villages hundreds of feet long.

The archaeological record suggests that the first Mesa Verde residents lived atop the mesas in wooden pit houses and, later, in stone pueblos. They moved into the cliffs near the end of their time here. No one knows for sure why they relocated. Building multi-story structures inside a cliff would have been a difficult construction feat and posed ongoing daily challenges, too. Climbing ladders or ropes to the top of the mesa would have been necessary every time they needed to access farming sites or gather supplies. Just as mysteriously, these dwellings were abandoned around 1200 AD. Tree ring data shows a long drought happened simultaneously; most experts believe that caused the residents to leave.

Cliff Palace, the biggest complex in Mesa Verde, has 150 rooms, once housed two hundred people, and includes a four-story building. During our tour of Cliff Palace, a ranger guided our group to it via a trail that was only half a mile long, but it dropped 100 feet in that short distance via switchbacks and wooden ladders. Once we arrived in Cliff Palace, proximity to these 1,000-year-old buildings sent tingles up my spine.

So many archaeological sites I have visited are strictly ruins—invaluable for archaeologists but not much help for a casual tourist like me trying to visualize the place's past. In Cliff Palace, little imagination is needed. The buildings are intact and superficially still look habitable, as if the residents are on vacation and due back any minute. This is due to several factors, including the durability of the original construction, the relative environmental protections afforded by the dry climate and placement inside a cliff, and the preservation efforts of the National Park Service.

Before coming here, I assumed these buildings were made of adobe—or mud bricks—like many old structures in the Southwest, but I was wrong. These were built from stone blocks held together by mortars. Inside the buildings, wooden beams created the floors of upper stories. Cliff Palace also featured many kivas, underground meeting rooms believed to have been used for religious ceremonies. Kivas in Mesa Verde have round floor plans and, although now open to the elements, would have once had stone roofs with a hole in the middle supporting the ladder used to enter them. Most kivas had stone benches ringing the outside wall.

Robert and I looked at several other sites from above that tourists cannot enter before hiking into Spruce Tree House, the park's third-largest cliff dwelling. It is accessible by a straightforward trail—no ladders or tunnels—and does not require a guided tour. Smaller than Cliff Palace and lacking a single building as impressive as the four-story tower in Cliff Palace, Spruce Tree House still impressed me with its 130 rooms and eight kivas.

We also visited the park's excellent museum near the Spruce Tree House trailhead and leisurely perused its displays of locally unearthed artifacts, like tools, pottery, and animal bones. It also had a series of charming old-school dioramas depicting life around the cliffs. One case had a piece of plaster broken from a Mesa Verde building with the fingerprint of an Ancestral Puebloan on it, which I found quite affecting.

At our last stop, Far View Sites, we walked around the ruins of mesa-top pueblos, examples of how Ancestral Puebloans lived before they moved into the cliffs. The basic floor plans were clear. Portions of the stone walls were standing, but these were indeed ruins, not intact buildings. Most memorable was a large round structure that, according to a sign, was thought to have held water for irrigation. A plaque indicated this was a Civil Engineering Landmark because it was part of an early American irrigation system. In an excellent example of how science is constantly learning more about this place, I read a news story in 2015 saying some scientists had newly proven this was not an irrigation reservoir but most likely another kiva-like ceremonial structure. I wondered if civil engineers had rescinded that plaque.

When we left the park, we drove to Durango, Colorado, a college town of 15,000 people, because the next day, we would board a scenic train trip that began there that Robert had insisted on taking when we planned the trip. We spent that night in a Residence Inn. Robert and I had been staying in standard double hotel rooms with two beds a few feet apart during each night of this trip. I used Marriott points at this hotel to upgrade to a suite with two separate bedrooms because I wanted to avoid Robert's snoring for a night.

Robert occasionally snored in our college dorm room, but we had not slept in the same room since those days, so I did not know his snoring had become constant and impossible to ignore. I sometimes snore, but I toss and turn early in the night. Robert was a pass-out-when-his-head-hit-the-pillow type, so I was asymmetrically suffering.

After a week on the road together, I had become so familiar with Rob's nocturnal nasal intonations that I had classified them into five varietals: the "buzzsaw," the "jackhammer," the "guard dog warning growl," the "hard-starting lawn mower," and my favorite, a combination low growl and moan I called the "plaintive Wookiee call." In my private bedroom, I enjoyed a blissful snore-free night of sleep. That was good because the train trip the next day sometimes made me cranky, even when fully rested.

Durango was at an elevation of 6,500 feet. The short railroad we were to ride was built in the late 1800s to connect Durango to Silverton, a town of 600 in the San Juan Mountains just fifty miles to the north, but at an elevation of 9,300 feet. Silverton was a boomtown when the railroad was built due to a gold and silver mining frenzy. This railroad spur line brought the precious metals mined in Silverton to a pre-existing rail line through Durango. The tracks were built on narrow "shelves" in the mountains between the two towns, necessitating the line using a smaller than standard space between the rails or a "narrow gauge."

Since a highway now connects Silverton to Durango and the mining boom is long over, steam trains only travel on the narrow-gauge railroad as a tourist attraction. While this sounded interesting, the train ride took four hours each way. There was also a two-hour break between rides, so the combo killed a whole day. I thought that time would be better spent in a National Park, but Robert wanted to do this, and I had relented.

Robert had taken this train trip in his teens while his family killed time in Durango because their Volkswagen van had broken down near there during a summer vacation and needed to get fixed. Robert was excited to repeat it, but I at least talked him into streamlining the excursion slightly. The tour company offered buyers the option to take a bus ride to Silverton in the morning, then take the afternoon train to Durango. The bus ride was only an hour, so even though it left an hour later than the train, it still arrived in Silverton two hours earlier. I was most excited by the later departure, but Robert was sold on having more time to explore Silverton. He said it had many exciting attractions, like museums and Old West kitsch such as simulated gunfights. I would love it, he assured me.

That next morning, we joined a small group on the bus to Silverton, which traversed a serpentine mountain road that offered breathtaking views of snow-covered 14,000-foot peaks. Upon arrival in Silverton, I found the town charmingly picturesque with its late 1800s buildings at the base of those mighty mountains.

The charm soon wore off because we found nothing much to do. The Old West attractions Robert recalled were either closed for good or not due to be open until Memorial Day weekend. Some souvenir shops and restaurants were open, so we browsed some of the former and ate a leisurely lunch in one of the latter. Fortunately, we were already seated in the restaurant when the morning train arrived. A crush of train riders soon emerged for their noon meal. When not shopping or dining, we shuffled aimlessly around Silverton's largely empty streets. I have had far worse days, but the thought that I could have bagged a National Park this day instead of ambling in a mountain town was chief among my thoughts as we boarded the train.

The first half of the train ride to Durango was admittedly excellent and briefly made me forget the National Park opportunity cost it represented. The line descended from Silverton on a narrow ledge in a steep, snow- and-conifer-covered slope hundreds of feet above the roiling Animas River. The scenery was stunning and the engine's chuffing, the black smoke from the stack, and the time the train stopped to take on the water allowed us to experience the senses of a bygone era of transportation.

Midway through, however, my opinion of the train trip shifted from excellent to tedium. Once clear of that thrilling initial steep section, the train cruised through unspectacular terrain and made stops to drop off passengers at lodges north of Durango. The last ninety minutes felt like nine hours. Robert showed no signs of my mounting frustration during that final stretch. As we returned to our car in Durango, he asked—clearly fishing for praise at his suggestion—what I thought of the train ride. I held nothing back, so we were both cranky as we ate dinner in a Durango barbecue joint.

Somewhere during the return trip, it dawned on me that I had once heard this train trip described in a song. You may be familiar with C.W. McCall's 1970s number-one-hit song "Convoy," which depicts truckers utilizing CB radio to organize 18-wheelers into a sufficiently long caravan to evade law enforcement interference while they break speed limits. Most of McCall's oeuvre also involved trucking, but he got out of his comfort zone for "The Silverton," which described the train trip we had just completed.

From an audio production standpoint, if you have heard "Convoy," you have heard "The Silverton." It has similar sonic irritants but not the somewhat redeeming humor. In a baritone drawl, McCall intones descriptions of the railroad in spoken-word verses, between which female singers belt the cloying chorus, "Here comes the Silverton up from Durango. Here comes the Silverton shoveling coal."

Over dinner, I downloaded "The Silverton" to my iPhone. While Robert drove us to our hotel for the evening in Farmington, New Mexico, I said I had found a musical tribute to his beloved train and then played the song on repeat. I thought forcing Robert to listen to this song was an appropriate penance for him having made me spend a whole day on this trip. During the third spin, Robert announced, "If you play that again, no judge will hold me responsible if I slammed the car into a mesa passenger-side first."

I decided Robert had atoned sufficiently.

Our hotel in Farmington, New Mexico that night had no two-bedroom suites available, so when Robert nodded off in a chair and started snoring just minutes after we checked in, I drove to a nearby store and bought the thickest earplugs they had.

The next day, we drove back to Albuquerque, where we would return the rental car and fly to our respective homes the next morning. We had some fun visits left on our itinerary inside Albuquerque, but during the long drive there, I began pondering the many things I had to do when I returned to the office on Monday. Robert must have been doing the same because thirty minutes passed without either of us speaking.

Finally, I broke the silence and asked, "What do married couples talk about all the time?"

"I'm single like you, so hell if I know," Robert replied. "Why do you ask?"

"Well," I said, "We are old friends who only see each other a couple of times a year. It only took us eight days to run out of things to say to each other."

Robert laughed. I then told him that despite my earlier churlishness about the train ride, I was glad he had joined me for this trip. I did not further elaborate then, but his presence had eased my apprehensions about hiking in National Parks. He gave me tips on how to get the most out of time in National Parks that I used on most future trips. Also, despite our late trip friction, it was nice to have had some company. I suspected I might be making all the rest of these trips alone.

To meet my ambitious four-year goal with limited vacation time, I could only compromise my schedule a little. I asked many friends about joining me in National Parks. I thought they would jump at the chance since I offered to pay for everything but their food and flights, but most had no interest. A few were interested in the most famous parks but had no interest in less famous ones and wanted to mix the trip with other, in my view, time-wasting activities. For example, one friend wanted to go with me to Yosemite and Sequoia in California but spend the rest of the trip in San Francisco or drinking wine in Napa Valley.

Only three parks in, I was confronting the fact that traveling alone would often be my only option unless I wanted to compromise my plan to visit 46 parks in only four years drastically. I decided I would rather travel alone than do that. The last sentence was probably why I did not know what married people talked about, but that was too heavy a thought for the waning hours of a vacation.

FIVE
SAGUARO NATIONAL PARK
OCTOBER 30, 2011

AS MURKY WATER flowed upward into the toilet and bathtub of the upstairs bathroom in the house I had just purchased three weeks ago, I realized there was no landlord to call. I would have to deal with this.

Renting had been so much simpler. I then worked in Barrington, a Chicago suburb with high home prices. Unwilling to make long commutes from a more affordable suburb, I had always rented cheap places in Barrington that left much to be desired but came with the luxury of calling a landlord when home infrastructure issues arose.

Early in 2011, I decided to move when my lease ended because I was unhappy with the house I had been renting. Plan A was to find a new place to rent, but since home prices had cratered after the 2008 financial crash and I had decent savings, I felt I should at least consider buying, but only do so if I found a place that met all my criteria, which were legion. I would only consider a detached home that I could buy for cash that was move-in ready. Also, I wanted to keep walking to work, so it had to be within 1.5 miles of the office.

With such narrow criteria, I started a home search assuming it would be fruitless and punctuated by signing a lease on a different rental house. To my immense surprise, I found several options. I loved one of them so much that I placed an offer on it in April. The seller accepted. A mid-May closing date was set, but the deal would be repeatedly delayed a few weeks at a time until August because it was a "short sale"—meaning the seller was letting it go for less than they owed—and the seller's bank took three months to approve that.

On the morning of the closing, a storm hit Chicagoland with such extreme winds that a section of the wooden privacy fence around the backyard of the house I had been renting separated from its posts and flew across the lawn like a sheet of paper. Downed tree limbs littered my neighborhood, and power outages were ubiquitous in the suburbs. Nonetheless, the closing still happened. I emerged as a first-time homeowner.

Wanting to brag about this milestone, I called my mother from the car. After I described the closing, our conversation shifted to more typical topics like the weather, so I mentioned the nasty morning storm.

My mother asked, "Before the closing, did you check to ensure the storm didn't damage your new house?"

I had not done that, so I made a panic-fueled drive to my new house. I breathlessly inspected the home I had just bought for a six-figure sum then I relaxed after finding no damage. This moment is burned in my brain as it was my introduction to the stress included free of charge with a home purchase. Problems with rental places meant only inconvenience; problems with a house I owned might cause changes in my net worth.

Even though I hired a home inspector to evaluate the house before buying it, I soon found minor problems to fix after moving that the inspector had not. The dishwasher leaked, one toilet leaked, and the other would only occasionally flush. I repaired these but doing so swallowed hours. Many needed repairs identified by the home inspector, like the furnace past its recommended service life and a crumbled asphalt driveway, cost much to fix.

My move-in stress peaked on the very rainy Saturday after my third week in the house when the brown water flowed into the toilet and bathtub. I tried to bail out the two fixtures by using a large plastic bowl to scoop out water and toss it out an open window, but the rate of upward water flow exceeded my scoop rate. In time, I realized I should stop reacting like a panicked new homeowner, think like a degreed chemical engineer, and find and fix the problem's root cause.

If water flowed upward, I realized after taking a breath, a pump must be pushing it. Chicagoland's water table is high enough that sump pumps are needed to keep water from seeping into basements. Rainwater was streaming into my sump and being pumped away as designed, but I found that my main sewer pipe was blocked, so the pumped water was instead heading into the toilet and tub in the upstairs bathroom.

Shutting off the sump pump stopped the rise of water into the bathroom but repairing an underground sewer pipe blockage was beyond my capabilities. The plumber I called needed two hours with a snake to restore some measure of drain function, then he showed me via a camera that a large section of pipe buried in my backyard had collapsed and needed to be replaced. Five thousand dollars and five days later, the sewer was repaired. I had a muddy mound in the middle of my backyard where the excavation had occurred.

Fearing more money-sucking maintenance might emerge made me delay a trip to six California National Parks I had once planned for September. Instead, that summer, I hiked in places near Chicago that friends recommended. In Starved Rock State Park, I walked beneath lovely waterfalls plunging down 80-foot stone cliffs that seemed miraculous in pancake-flat northern Illinois. In Indiana Dunes National Lakeshore, just east of Gary, Indiana, I climbed 150-foot-tall sand dunes to the Lake Michigan shoreline. I also hiked many miles in Chicagoland forest preserves. Once in the new house, my daily round-trip walk to work went from half a mile to 2.5 miles, and round trips to the grocery store were two miles. By the end of the year, all this walking had added up to 500 miles, and I had reduced my weight by eighteen pounds.

By October, no new disasters had struck, so my financial panic subsided sufficiently for me to book a three-day weekend trip to the area around

Tucson, Arizona that I dubbed my "Gadsden Getaway" as it was within the strip of land the US purchased from Mexico in 1853 called the Gadsden Purchase. I toured a Titan missile base, saw an old Spanish mission, and caught a re-enactment of the gunfight at the OK Corral in Tombstone.

My main objective was a day in Saguaro National Park, which protects a large and dense cactus forest. I learned here that a cactus forest differs from the eastern forests, where many tall trees form a canopy of branches and leaves shading the ground below. This cactus forest looked more like a garden because most trees were stubby here, and the lack of desert rainfall meant most plants needed significant space around them to collect enough moisture.

Cacti were familiar to me since I had taken many business trips to Phoenix, where they are planted in median strips, but I needed to learn more about the various species, and I had not seen them in a natural setting. My ignorance was reduced by hiking the Desert Discovery Trail, which had signs describing the cacti species.

Prickly pear cacti only stood two feet off the ground and had several flat, circular green pads studded with bumps from which spikes protruded. Without spikes, I thought, each pad resembled the rubber disks people use to help open jars. The barrel cacti seemed misnamed as they were not barrels but squat, needle-laden spheres. The organ pipe cacti had thin, vertical arms rising three feet or more into the air from the central root. The pencil cholla cacti had myriad spindly arms, most with multiple sharply angled bends, making each tree resemble a pipe cleaner sculpture created by a hyperactive elementary school art student.

My favorite was the "teddy bear" cholla, a three-foot tall cactus with a trunk and branches covered in thousands of needles, making them, from a distance, appear as fuzzy as a teddy bear. This was the first time I felt a literal urge to hug a tree, but doing so would have sent those needles into my skin, so I resisted.

All were dwarfed, however, by the world's largest cactus and the park's namesake, the saguaro. Most people probably think about this tree when they hear "cactus." Mature saguaros could have cylindrical trunks two-feet wide and twenty-feet high from which thick "arms" branched. Most arms bent upward, meaning many mature saguaros were shaped like a trident. Young saguaros did not yet have arms and were, thus, just spiky green cylinders. Of course, "young" here is relative. Since water is scarce here, the trees grow slowly. An interpretive sign said many saguaros do not develop their first arms until they are fifty years old.

The saguaro's natural range is limited to the Sonoran Desert, which covers a big chunk of Mexico, but in the US, it only covers southern Arizona and some of southeastern California. Nonetheless, the saguaro is so iconic that it is frequently used to symbolize the entire American southwest. The Mexican food brand Old El Paso uses saguaros in its logo even though El Paso, Texas is a four-hour drive from the saguaro's range.

Cacti, along with yucca, agave, and most other plants here, are succulents, meaning they have fleshy parts that can expand to store rainwater for later use, enabling them to thrive in arid regions. I had always thought that, apart from the needles, cacti were soft and fleshy throughout, but upon inspecting the remains of a dead saguaro near the trail, on which the fleshy green exterior had withered and dried, I saw the tree had a woody interior support system that looked like a bundle of sticks one might use to start a fire.

Apart from length, the online descriptions of all the park's other trails seemed essentially the same as the first trail I walked. All passed by cacti and had mountains looming in the background. Thus, my pre-trip itinerary was composed of six arbitrarily selected hikes with names like the Valley View Trail, the Cactus Wren Trail, and the Wild Dog Trail. Saguaro did not have a world-famous wonder like the Grand Canyon or paleontological wonders like Petrified Forest. It just had a web of trails to different areas of the forest.

Why was I throwing that diminishing "just" into the previous sentence? This was a novel landscape to me, even if it was not spectacular. Each trail was an invitation to explore it. A National Park need not be a cabinet of curiosities; it can just be a protected piece of nature. Once I stopped grousing about a lack of grandeur and observed what was around me, I noticed subtle bits of nature that enchanted me, like birds' nests tucked in holes in saguaros, individual yellow and pink petals remaining from otherwise long-gone cactus flowers, and a saguaro with a downward-bent arm that formed a partial arch over one trail.

The most vital takeaway from my time in Saguaro was not a nature experience. As a new homeowner walking and driving in this park, I realized for the first time that infrastructure in National Parks—the roads, trails, and buildings all helping me access them—must be expensive to maintain. If it cost $2,500 to repave my little driveway, what must it have cost to pave all these roads?

Ken Burns' National Park documentary emphasized that National Parks were not owned by the federal government because the American people owned the parks. As I watched the series, I found whimsy in the notion that I was a co-owner of National Parks, so I was a boss of these places. More accurately, I was a boss of these places along with more than 300 million other bosses. Still, that made me a park co-owner.

As a new homeowner, I was aware ownership made me the boss of my house, but that carried obligations. I could remodel my home in ways I could not have done as a renter, but I had to pay to get pipes fixed. When National Parks need fixing, funding comes from taxpayer money. Some National Park co-owners care a lot about National Parks, some do not care about them at all, government revenue is not limitless, and the government runs many things besides National Parks. For these and other reasons, at the time of writing, over ten billion dollars of needed infrastructure maintenance in National Parks currently needs to be funded.

The official National Park charity partner, the National Park Foundation, has tried to address some parts of that massive shortfall. Upon learning that, I started making annual donations to it. Sure, I paid taxes, but as a newly frequent National Park visitor, I should kick in extra to be a responsible owner. After buying my house, I knew writing an annual charity check was different from owning land. I will not, for instance, need to call plumbers if water flows upward into the toilets at Saguaro National Park.

SIX
BIG BEND NATIONAL PARK
JANUARY 14, 2012

DONALD TRUMP once promised to build a wall along the border between the U.S. and Mexico and make Mexico pay for it. If he had been to Big Bend National Park, he would know there were already some walls between the U.S. and Mexico that geology paid for.

To put my National Park project back on track after the previous year's home purchase hiatus, I used the Martin Luther King, Jr. holiday weekend to fly to El Paso and then drive a rental car to the two National Parks in Texas and the one in New Mexico. Up first was Big Bend National Park, which is at the southern tip of the extreme western section of Texas, which on a map, looks like an arrowhead lodged in Mexico. That figurative arrowhead's tip is formed by the park's namesake, the Big Bend, a roughly 90-degree turn in the course of the Rio Grande, the river used as the border between Texas and Mexico.

After driving 230 miles from El Paso's airport to Alpine, Texas, I spent the night in a hotel, woke before dawn, and drove one hundred more miles to the park's northernmost entrance station, Persimmon Gap. Western Texas is part of the Chihuahuan Desert. It is a stark, arid countryside with only widely spaced scrubby vegetation on the lowland plains and seemingly barren brown mountains looming in the background.

Long stretches of road had no adjacent signs of human habitation besides power lines and ranch fences.

Big Bend is such an enormous park that even after entering it, my first planned hike was still fifty miles ahead to the southeast. After seeing so little life outside the park, I was surprised to see so much wildlife in it. Pig-like javelinas rooted in dirt, coyotes hovering above roadside carrion eyed me warily, and black-and-white, long-tailed birds called roadrunners scurried along the shoulder. At one point, I spied a roadrunner ahead to the right and a coyote just a few feet away from it to the left of the road. I stopped to view the pair before nervously hitting the gas, realizing an Acme anvil could fall from the sky at any moment.

Once at the trailhead, I made the short hike into Boquillas Canyon, a gorge around the Rio Grande. After walking down a hill, I reached the riverbank in a wide plain just outside the canyon entrance, where the river entered a narrow slot between one-hundred-foot-tall stone walls. A Latino man stood there wearing a cowboy hat, sporting a bushy gray mustache, and belting out a song in Spanish. He had a donkey by his side, and a blanket at his feet covered with souvenirs for sale, like painted walking sticks and a scorpion doll made of beads. He said he was Singing Mexican Jesus from the nearby Mexican village of Boquillas, tried to sell me his wares, and offered to sing a song by request, an act that is to date the only busking I have ever encountered in a National Park.

I have read that in days past, the border here was open and residents of Boquillas and National Park visitors crossed at will, with the latter often buying souvenirs and refreshments south of the border. Crossing here that way is no longer legal, but Singing Mexican Jesus had done so on this day. He must have been doing so often, as he was listed as a park attraction on Trip Advisor. His presence was surprising as I had seen several Border Patrol agents on the road, including one who appeared to be operating a drone. I already had to stop at two Border Patrol checkpoints while driving to the park, even though I had not crossed the border.

As I continued walking along the river until I was well inside Boquillas Canyon, the canyon's craggy beige and gray walls made little impression on me. They did not have the striking beauty or scale of the Grand Canyon. To be fair, I did not ponder this canyon's geology or aesthetics too deeply because I felt an irrationally giddy, almost transgressive thrill to be standing alone on the Mexican border, a line of demarcation so frequently in the news. The river flowed gently and appeared shallow on this day, so as far as I could tell, only my aversion to wet boots prevented me from breaking the plane into Mexico.

Later that morning, I walked to a natural hot spring on the banks of the Rio Grande that had once been the site of a long-ago closed early 20th Century spa. Since I had not yet seen ten people in the park, I was startled to find a church youth group at the spring cavorting in a brick pool, which I learned from an interpretive sign was the now water-filled foundations of the old spa's long-since demolished bathhouse. Several boys in the group showed off by jumping directly from the steamy hot spring water into the chilly river, but most were soaking and talking loudly. I considered asking the rowdy crew if they could make enough room for me to soak my feet in the naturally hot waters, but then I remembered I had not brought a towel, I had many more miles to walk, and, as already established, I had an aversion to wet boots.

In the late morning, I drove a road that climbed into a mountain range called the Chisos, which ended at a high plain offering fabulous views of the rugged peaks. My afternoon was spent driving through the western side of the park on Ross Maxell Scenic Drive, a road designed by a geologist to lead tourists to scientific points of interest. Along it, I stopped to admire twin mammoth rock spires called the Mule Ears; walked a short trail to a white slot canyon with walls made of volcanic ash; and hiked two miles round-trip to The Chimneys, weird vertical formations of igneous rock formed by lava spit by a long-ago volcanic eruption.

The scenic road saved the best for last: Santa Elena Canyon. Like Boquillas Canyon, Santa Elena was a Rio Grande gorge with steep rock walls, but it was far more beautiful than Boquillas and the one absolute "can't miss" feature I saw in Big Bend. Hiking to the inside of this canyon from the parking lot at the end of the scenic road required a 1.75-mile round trip walk on a trail that crossed a small creek, climbed 100 vertical feet up a rocky hill, and then descended to river level on stairs cut into the canyon's northern wall.

Santa Elena Canyon was stunning. Sheer vertical cliffs were on each side of the river, sporting rock layers not as colorful as those in the Grand Canyon but just as easily distinguishable and slanted downward relative to the horizontal so that they looked like sketched-in perspective lines. Enormous gray boulders projected above the river. By hopping on a series of them, I could view the canyon from a third of the way across the water without suffering wet boots. While standing on that boulder, I stretched out my arms and wondered if my left hand had just visited Mexico.

After twenty minutes in the canyon, another group arrived, so I decided to pass on the gift of solitude I had enjoyed and started my walk back to the parking lot. On the level ground outside the canyon, I saw three boisterous teens laughing on the riverbank. They became as quiet as church mice as I approached, so I quipped, "No worries. I'm not a cop, but you sound like you might be having more fun than is legal."

"We're skipping rocks into Mexico," one told me after we exchanged pleasantries.

"That is awesome!" I exclaimed and attempted the feat myself. After several failed tries, I got the range and successfully skipped a rock into Mexico, an accomplishment that caused a goofy smile on my face that did not crack for my entire two-hour drive back to Alpine.

Border security is an important topic meriting serious debate. I do not have enough knowledge to have an informed opinion about whether a border wall would curb smuggling or illegal immigration. At least in Big Bend National Park, I fervently hope any walls erected are non-literal because I am sure a manufactured border wall would be deleterious to the stark yet still stunning desert vistas. The river is a water source for the park's animals, and many species freely migrate across it. Biologists say a literal border wall would significantly harm the park's wildlife, for whom national borders are purely arbitrary.

The concept of a border seemed arbitrary to me during those giddy moments I spent skipping rocks across a lazy river into a Mexican desert that looked no different than the Texas desert on which I stood.

SEVEN
GUADALUPE MOUNTAINS NATIONAL PARK
JANUARY 15, 2012

HEARING local radio DJs call western Texas "the Permian Basin" while I drove to Guadalupe Mountains National Park surprised me. The Permian was a geological period that ended 250 million years ago. It felt odd for a place to market itself with a name based on something so esoteric as a geological period, especially in Bible Belt Texas, where many residents do not acknowledge that time stretches back more than 6,000 years. The surrounding area was rife with rigs pumping oil and gas that had been deposited in the Permian, so geology may get a pass here since it left such a lucrative legacy.

The Permian was also when the rock began to form that makes up the white peaks of the mountain range near the Texas-New Mexico border for which this National Park is named. Two of those mountains, one with a bare limestone cliff called El Capitan and another called Guadalupe Peak, the tallest mountain in Texas, towered over the visitor center where I started my visit to the park.

I first walked a nature trail that described local scrubby vegetation, which included lots of yucca and cacti, though only short ones. No mighty saguaro grew here. Another trail led to the broken stone walls of a long-defunct station for the Butterfield Overland Mail. From 1857 to 1861,

Butterfield coaches carried loads of mail from St. Louis to San Francisco in only 25 days, which sounds slow in the era of Amazon Prime, but it was much faster than the months-long sea voyage that was then the only other option. The station was built near a natural spring that provided a water source in this brutal desert.

The Butterfield is little remembered now even though it carried far more mail than another Missouri-to-California overland mail service of the same era, the Pony Express, which is a household name to this day. I idly wondered if this was because men on horseback seem more romantic than stagecoaches or if it was a matter of branding since Pony Express has a great ring to it and Butterfield Overland Mail is a drab mouthful.

More history was on display a short drive away at the park's Frijole Ranch Museum, an abandoned nineteenth-century ranch now actively farmed by the NPS to demonstrate how pioneer agriculture worked in this arid environment. This ranch site had been chosen by its original owners because it was near two natural springs. A two-mile hiking loop led from the ranch to both springs and back. While walking it, I saw one of the springs was a water source for wildlife as mud surrounding it exhibited myriad tracks, including, rather unnervingly, cougar tracks.

A chocolate brown conical mound named Nipple Hill stood behind the other spring. During subsequent visits to western National Parks, I encountered many other natural features with mammary-inspired nomenclature, so I assume it was lonely to men in the Old West. Although I was alone on this trip, Nipple Hill looked more like a Hershey's Kiss than a nipple to me, which might go a long way toward explaining my weight issues.

My biggest challenge in visiting National Parks alone had been getting pictures of me in the parks' notable spots. In 2012, I had not yet heard the word "selfie" and was still toting an iPhone without a screen-side camera. Thus, when I found a place where I wanted to photograph myself, I sought a fortuitously placed bench, interpretive sign, or tree branch, sat my cheap point-and-shoot camera on it, started the camera's ten-second timer, and scrambled into the shot before the photo was snapped. When other hikers found me preparing one of these proto-selfies, they always offered to take my picture. I always accepted, but regretfully since I had developed a perverse pride in my photographic self-reliance.

Nipple Hill seemed as good a spot as any for a picture of me in this park because the hill was striking, and I had a juvenile sense of humor. There was an interpretive sign near the spring, so I set my camera on it. I pointed it toward Nipple Hill, set the timer, and hustled into the shot. Just as the ten-second timer ended, a sudden burst of wind sent my camera careening through the air and ultimately crashing into the rocky soil. My camera never worked right after that, so I later replaced it and begrudgingly invested in a tripod.

After this morning's hodgepodge of short walks, I spent the early afternoon on a four-mile hike into a canyon called Devil's Hall. Initially, the trail led into a gradually narrowing gap between two mountains on a hard-packed earthen path, but then the traditional trail ended, and the hike continued on a stream bed that was dry but was where water would flow during rare desert rains. The NPS trail guide called this feature the Hiker Staircase since traveling on it required climbing on the sloped stream bed's loose piles of water-worn stones. Finally, I arrived in the Devil's Hall, a narrow canyon with short, sheer rock walls.

On the trip back down, those shifting stones in the "staircase" proved more treacherous. After a near tumble, I decided one section would be best traversed by scooting down on my ass. Since scooting would be easier without a backpack, I took it off and tossed it well ahead of me, aiming for the edge of the creek bed, so it was out of the way in case any hikers approached in the other direction.

Past this tough section, I stood, retrieved my backpack, and promptly yowled in pain. Panic at the thought that some poisonous desert creature had bitten me subsided when I found a cactus needle jammed into the fleshy part of my palm. The best guess I can hazard is that a cactus needle stuck into one of my backpack straps while the pack sat on the ground, and I had managed to transfer the needle into my palm when I retrieved the bag. I carefully removed the cactus needle and finished the hike, but I gradually became paranoid that the little spike might have carried poison. At the visitor center, a ranger assured me there was no danger beyond the standard infection risk of anything non-sterile penetrating the skin.

I was spending the night after finishing in Guadalupe at a hotel in Carlsbad, New Mexico. Thus, before this three-park trip, I had asked a co-worker who knew this area well if there were any great restaurants in that town. He did not offer much in food sales. Instead, he raved about Carlsbad's Living Desert Zoo and Gardens State Park, a combination zoo and botanical garden focused on life in the Chihuahuan Desert. At 3 PM, I considered my National Park obligations met for the day, and I hauled ass to Carlsbad to see the zoo and gardens. Since it was only open for 75 more minutes when I arrived, my visit was a whirlwind. The botanical garden was delightful, with examples of all the plant species I had traipsed past in the Guadalupe neatly arranged and labeled in beds, allowing me to put names to the leaves—or needles in the case of the cacti.

Surprisingly, the zoo was less interesting than the gardens since most animals were asleep. There was, however, some action at the two big cat enclosures, my last stops before leaving. In the bobcat enclosure, I was surprised to see a hard hat on the patch of ground on which the three twenty-five-pound cats were pacing. Had these bobcats eaten a construction worker or gone into construction?

The second enclosure housed two cougars, the powerful 100-pound feline killing machines also known as mountain lions. While I had no reason to think the zoo's designers had done faulty work, being this close to a pair of alpha predators was unnerving, even though these cougars were doing nothing remotely threatening. The pair were both awake but in repose and facing away from me. One yawned, revealing large, pointy teeth that prompted me to silently give thanks that I had only seen cougar footprints in the National Park.

After taking a photo of the cougars with my scratched and now sickly-sounding camera, I made a series of loud noises in hopes that one or both cats would look directly at me so I could get an even better photo. My catcalls caused neither cougar to look my way.

Then I realized the problem. I had recently turned 37, far too old to attract the attention of a cougar.

EIGHT
CARLSBAD CAVERNS NATIONAL PARK

JANUARY 16, 2012

"THERE ARE NO FLIES IN HERE," a ranger said to me while I gazed awestruck at a sixty-foot-tall stalagmite in The Big Room of Carlsbad Caverns National Park.

"What?" I asked. I had heard her, but "what" reflexively came out of my mouth because I did not understand why she had provided this unprompted entomological factoid.

With a wry glint in her eye, she replied, "I said, 'there are no flies in here,' so you'd know it's safe to stare with your mouth open."

Above the surface, Carlsbad Caverns National Park looked a lot like Guadalupe Mountains National Park, just with slightly shorter mountains, which makes perfect sense as that other park is only thirty miles away. The reasons this place is a National Park, however, are subterranean. Dozens of caves are found in this park, but most are off-limits to all but the most serious cavers. For average tourists like me, the park's draw is the namesake cave filled with towering, intricate rock formations.

My native Missouri calls itself The Cave State because it has 7,000 caves. Many are privately owned show caves offering guided tours for a fee. My family visited several of these while I was a geology-obsessed kid, and those are among my favorite childhood memories. Fantastic Caverns is so wide that visitors ride into the cave on trailers towed by Jeeps. Meramec Caverns was once allegedly used as a hideout by Jesse James. Indian Burial Cave featured Native American remains. Bridal Cave conducts weddings before a beautiful rock formation vaguely resembling an organ. Those had all been amazing enough to see, but now I was visiting a cave so impressive that they had made it a National Park. I could not have been more excited.

Since I had spent the previous night in nearby Carlsbad, New Mexico, I slept in late a bit by my standards and still arrived early enough to be second in line when cave tickets went on sale in the visitor center at 8:30 AM. At most caves, you can only enter the cave as part of a tour group led by a guide, but here you can opt to enter the cave on your own and see it at your own pace, which is what I did.

The most famous section of Carlsbad Caverns, called The Big Room, is 750 feet below the surface. Most visitors get there by riding an elevator down from the visitor center, but I opted for the more strenuous option of hiking down to The Big Room via a steep, 1.25-mile trail starting at the cave's natural entrance. My desire for a more strenuous experience only went so far; I had every intention of riding an elevator back up.

Just outside the cave's natural entrance was a large, manufactured amphitheater. Most National Parks have a small amphitheater or set of bleachers near the visitor center for rangers to use when giving talks to tour groups, but this was by far the biggest I had yet seen. I asked the ranger checking visitor tickets about it. She indicated it was seating for visitors to use while watching bats fly out of the cave. Carlsbad's bats are migratory and had long since flown south to Mexico for the winter, so none were around to watch during my visit, but in the summer, hundreds of thousands of bats poured out of this opening nightly.

The trail into the cave wound through a seemingly unending series of switchbacks and was steep and ankle-straining for long stretches. During my descent, I hoped to see something astonishing that I could brag about having seen to any of the comparatively lazy people who rode the elevator down. Alas, this section was much less spectacular than what I later saw in The Big Room. There were a few pretty rock formations along this trail, but the only thing that made a lasting impression on me was a boulder of eye-popping enormity that an interpretive sign said had fallen from the roof of the cave thousands of years ago and weighed 200,000 tons. The sign did not indicate who had weighed the boulder or how they had done so, but even more importantly to me, it did not indicate how we knew no other boulders would join this one on the floor while I was inside the cave.

There are many types of caves, but Carlsbad and those I had seen in Missouri were all examples of solution caves, which form when acidic rainwater seeps into the ground and dissolves away underground rock bit by bit until a cave forms. Most caves are dissolved out of layers of two similar calcium-containing sedimentary rocks called limestone and dolostone.

A related process may eventually "decorate" the cave with "speleothems," the scientific term for rock formations inside a cave. If acidic rainwater dissolves calcium carbonate out of limestone above the cave, it can re-deposit the mineral inside the cave one drip at a time, slowly building stalagmites, rock formations that stick up from the cave floor, stalactites, which hang from the ceiling, or other formations.

When the steep trail down from the natural entrance ended and I entered The Big Room, I was giddily expecting a view of its famed enormous stalagmites and stalactites, but instead, I found a restaurant. Known as the "lunchroom," this little in-cave cafe sells drinks, food items, and souvenirs. It also features a mailbox from which you can mail a postcard while 750 feet underground.

Since visitors can access the cave via an elevator ride from the visitor center, which features a full-service restaurant, this in-cave lunchroom is far from necessary. The National Park Service, in the name of environmental protection, tried to eliminate it in 1994, citing issues like food smells drawing animals that would not usually be in the cave, the potential for cleaning chemicals to alter the growth of cave formations, and lights in the lunchroom restricting bat flight. However, the lunchroom generates two million dollars of revenue annually for the company that runs it, so it has lobbied Congress repeatedly to keep it open. Congress has responded by annually passing a law preventing the NPS from closing it.

The budding National Park obsessive in me did not think a restaurant belonged inside a precious natural wonder. Why I had trouble with that and not the electric lights that had long ago been installed and enabled me to walk around a cave that would otherwise be pitch dark, I cannot say. By contrast, the part of me that asked a friend to photograph me standing on a corner in Winslow, Arizona thought it would be fun to eat a meal 750 feet underground. Luckily, it was mid-morning, and I was not yet hungry, so I could defer this inner conflict to a later time.

Minutes later, I found that the Big Room had everything I had dreamed of seeing. It was an eight-acre subterranean wonderland covered in a dazzling variety of speleothems. Thousands of small, cylindrical stalactites called soda straws, no bigger in diameter than a pencil, hung from every square inch of one section of the cave roof. Spindly, milky white stalactites hung in similar densities from another section, making it look like the cave was ice cream melting on my head. In another passage, tightly grouped stalactites formed structures looking like drapes. Another area was covered in golf-ball-sized deposits called cave popcorn.

The Big Room's most memorable spot, the Hall of Giants, had the most immense stalagmites I had ever seen, rising 60 feet above the floor. To think those had grown a few millimeters a year, drip by drip over millennia is one of many thoughts I have had in a National Park that put the brevity of a human lifetime in sobering perspective. That thought was still not sobering enough to keep me from sporting a goofy grin throughout The Big Room.

I walked the 1.5-mile path a second time because I did not want to leave this cave so soon. My second lap was at a more leisurely pace since curiosity about what wonder lay around each corner was no longer propelling me to rush. Subtler features I missed while admiring the 60-foot giants during my first go-round caught my attention on this second trip, like a pair of almost identical conical dripstones with a small cylinder protruding up from their peak. Since these somewhat resembled breasts and nipples, I wondered if the guy who had named Nipple Hill in Guadalupe National Park had ever made it inside this cave. He probably could not have handled the excitement.

When I finished my second Big Room lap, I was hungry and about to leave the cave, so my internal conflict could not be deferred. Purely by culinary standards, I knew a better lunch could be had in the restaurant in the visitor center or a host of restaurants thirty minutes away in Carlsbad. That goofy allure of eating lunch 750 feet underground won out. I was soon seated at a table inside a cave, eating a wrap and a cookie with a side of guilt. I felt ashamed to patronize an eatery the NPS deemed an environmental issue.

Even if no sandwiches were eaten here, my presence in the cave posed contamination risks. For example, many eastern caves are struggling with white-nose syndrome, a disease devastating to bat populations caused by a fungus that people could spread to western caves. Before I entered the cave, I had been asked if any items of clothing or anything else I planned to take into the cave had ever been in a cave in the eastern United States. I had been to a Missouri cave a couple of years before, but I was sure everything I was wearing had been purchased since then except my shoes. I admitted I could not remember if my shoes had been in a cave, so the woman who asked gave them a precautionary cleaning with soap to kill the fungus.

Visitors are also told not to touch speleothems because skin oils can stop mineral deposits from sticking and prevent the speleothem from growing. I did not see anyone else violating the no-touching rule, but I am sufficiently cynical to suspect that some of the 300,000-plus visitors each year will not be so scrupulous. Plus, there were tight spots where someone could accidentally bump into a formation.

Even if everyone keeps their oily mitts off the cave, human visitors inadvertently deposit another substance that hinders speleothem growth, a menace I learned about from a woman I saw in the Big Room delicately stroking the bristles of a tiny brush across the surface of a stalagmite.

Puzzled, I jokingly asked her, "Are you giving it a fresh coat of paint?"

She laughed in a clipped manner, suggesting she had heard this line before, then told me she was removing lint because visitors' clothes scatter lint in the cave that collects on speleothems, which stops or alters their growth. She said volunteers in Carlsbad annually remove 150 pounds of it.

"Thank you for removing it," I said sincerely. I did not doubt the operation was necessary, but I could not see lint on the formations here, so it must be widely distributed. I pondered the hundreds, if not thousands, of hours of work it must take to brush 150 pounds of widely scattered lint off the surface of this enormous cave.

I should have left the conversation at that, but I could not resist adding, "It makes some sense there would be lint in here since a cave is like the earth's belly button."

NINE
JOSHUA TREE NATIONAL PARK
FEBRUARY 4TH, 2012

AT CAP ROCK, a boulder pile in Joshua Tree National Park topped with an enormous flat rock jutting past the rest like the bill of a baseball cap, I was irritated that some of the stones here had been defaced with graffiti meant to commemorate that this was the site of rock music's best known DIY cremation.

As a passionate music nerd with over 2,000 CDs and LPs, my primary association with the two-word term "Joshua Tree" was not the giant yucca plants for which this National Park is named but U2's mega-hit 1987 album *The Joshua Tree*. While planning this trip, I wondered if that record's iconic cover photo was shot in the park, but Internet research revealed that the picture had been taken in a different National Park altogether: Death Valley. I still packed my CD copy of *The Joshua Tree* to play while driving to the park.

The subject of the attempted rock star cremation was a less well-known musical artist named Gram Parsons, a singer, songwriter, guitarist, and member of both The Byrds and The Flying Burrito Brothers who had just made two excellent country rock solo albums when he died from a drug overdose in 1973 at age 26.

MY NATIONAL PARK DIET

Parsons frequented Joshua Tree, and after he died, his roadie, Phil Kaufman, insisted Parsons wanted to be cremated and have his ashes spread at Cap Rock. Parsons' family ignored this and made plans to bury him at a family plot in Louisiana. Kaufman then stole Parsons' coffin from LAX, drove it to Cap Rock, drenched it in gasoline, and set it ablaze, producing a fireball that attracted law enforcement. Kaufman fled the scene leaving a gruesome, flaming mess. Although later arrested for his necro-larceny, Kaufman was ultimately only fined for stealing the coffin because California then had no law against stealing unburied corpses.

While I had seen a movie about that incident called *Grand Theft Parsons*, I had forgotten it occurred in this National Park until seeing all the graffiti and trinkets that Parsons fans had left at Cap Rock. Park rangers likely have better things to do than remove litter left here in tribute or remove all the messages carved on the rocks like "Fallen Angel." This vandalism angered me but also prompted me to pay my respects to Parsons and his music here in a non-destructive manner.

When walking outdoors near home, I always listened to music. In National Parks, though, I had made it a rule to hike in silence to focus my mind on the novel environs better. Just this once, I felt an exception was justified and donned my earbuds to listen to some of Parsons' music on my cell phone while walking the trail around Cap Rock. Scrolling through his song titles, it was immediately apparent the most apropos choice for this location was his lovely duet with Emmylou Harris entitled "We'll Sweep Out the Ashes in the Morning."

This Cap Rock walk was near the midpoint of my day in Joshua Tree National Park, which I entered around sunrise from I-10 on the park's south side and planned to exit around sunset in Twentynine Palms, California on the park's north side. The park's website recommended a list of twelve short trails that would give visitors sort of a Whitman's Sampler of the park's various environments. Two of those were well off my north-to-south route through the park, so I skipped those. I made the others a ten-point plan for my day here.

The first three walks were on the extremely arid south side of the park, where few plants grew on dusty plains. Two of the trails were unmemorable, but the third passed a stand of the teddy bear cholla cactus I had found so delightful in Saguaro National Park. The scenery changed radically for the better after the road passed through a mountain range. I emerged north of the peaks in an otherworldly scene.

Past the mountains were broad plains dotted with numerous fifty-foot-high piles of smoothly rounded khaki boulders, often seemingly precariously stacked by an insane landscape architect. Boulder piles are expected at the bottom of a rocky cliff, but these were strewn about an otherwise featureless expanse as if they fell from space. One of the park's namesakes grew from most spots not buried in boulders. Although called Joshua Trees, interpretive signs insisted these were not technically trees, just tall yucca plants. Since they grew up to twenty feet tall and towered over anything growing here, they seemed like trees to me.

Then again, they looked like no tree I had ever seen. Mature Joshua trees had numerous curvy branches. From the end of each, scores of individual sword-shaped leaves jutted in every direction so that the entire cluster looked like a green sphere from afar. The trunks and branches had a peeling bark that gave them a shaggy appearance. A Joshua tree looked like a hirsute octopus cheerleader waving green pom poms. Young Joshua Trees that had not yet developed branches just had a straight vertical trunk ending in one of those leaf puffs, so they looked like those trees for which the Lorax spoke.

Since they had not seen cheerleaders or read Seuss, 19th-century Mormon settlers named these plants after the Biblical Joshua because they thought yuccas resembled that patriarch holding his arms in the air to keep the sun from setting at the Battle of Gibeon. Maybe Joshua had more than two arms in the Book of Mormon.

My first three walks on this side of the park all passed numerous Joshua trees en route to odd-looking rocks: Cap Rock; a natural arch imaginatively named Arch Rock; and Skull Rock, a boulder that genuinely resembled a skull with three depressions in its surface arranged like a cranium's eye and nose holes. I am usually all about geology in a National Park, but strangely shaped individual rocks could not compete with the overwhelming strangeness of the Joshua Trees or the overall landscape. No wonder Parsons came to Joshua Tree to get high. I was stone-cold sober, but you could have convinced me I was hallucinating this place.

The seventh of my ten planned walks led to an old dam and the reservoir behind it that ranchers had built long before this place became a park. The shimmering deep blue of the small lake ringed by boulder piles in this otherwise bone-dry place was yet another odd sight in a park replete with them. At the trailhead for that walk, I learned of a trail that led to a long-abandoned farm called the Wonderland Ranch and a defunct mine called the Wall Street Mill. This sounded intriguing, so I hiked it even though it was outside my ten-point plan. While I walked past a windmill, dilapidated buildings, a mine tipple, and rusty trucks, I felt like an archaeologist discovering an area depopulated by a 1940s apocalypse.

Resuming my ten-trail plan, I hiked into Hidden Valley, a dusty plain completely enclosed by another ring of the park's ubiquitous khaki boulder piles. Although once used as a hideout by rustlers, this Hidden Valley was not, I was disappointed to learn, the source of the salad dressing. Walking up the boulder piles going into and out of the valley made this trail more fun than the flat walks I had done this day. I then reflected that I had come a long way as a hiker if I now found any elevation gain fun and not a cause for distress.

Keys View, the penultimate stop on my ten-point plan, was a scenic overlook in the mountains reached by driving a twisty road up to a ridge at over 5,000 feet in elevation. From it, I saw a magnificent view of 10,000-foot peaks, the San Andreas Fault, and the Salton Sea, a vast salt lake east of San Diego. My tenth and final planned walk was a short one at the one park's visitor center near the town of Twentynine Palms to a desert oasis where a lush stand of palm trees, for which that town was named, ringed and shaded a desert spring.

The Joshua Tree was still in my CD player, so Bono wailed that he still had not found what he was looking for while I drove into Twentynine Palms at twilight.

"Bono should visit more National Parks," I mused to no one.

TEN
ZION AND BRYCE CANYON NATIONAL PARKS
FEBRUARY 17-18, 2012

SPONTANEITY WAS NEVER MY THING. I did not jump to that conclusion; I thought long and hard about it. Of course, jumping to conclusions requires spontaneity, so you probably guessed that.

My references to itineraries and pre-trip research in past chapters were not exaggerated. Before each trip, I crafted a detailed itinerary weeks before boarding my flight. Each was assembled after spending many evenings on the Internet determining optimum driving routes and choosing the hiking trails I wanted to walk. For each day I spent in a National Park, I spent at least three hours pre-planning that trip and usually more.

Zion and Bryce Canyon were the only National Parks I ever visited without my usual meticulous planning because eHarmony had made me self-conscious about my lack of spontaneity.

In my mid-thirties, meeting a woman interested in dating me was difficult. Meeting women interested in dating me had always been difficult, but meeting women even theoretically interested was increasingly more challenging for me as I was becoming less socially active, and most women my age had already paired up.

Internet dating sites seemed a possible solution, but I had long avoided them as the concept seemed cold and impersonal, like shopping for love on Amazon. Several friends, however, enthusiastically recommended eHarmony to me, including one who met his wife on that site. He gave a heartfelt toast of thanks to that site's founder, Dr. Neil Clark Warren, at their rehearsal dinner even though Warren was not present.

So late in 2011, I took the plunge and joined eHarmony. Upon starting an eHarmony account, I had to answer a slew of multiple-choice questions, write a lengthy profile, and post pictures. The process took about two hours. Compared to newer dating apps I later tried, like Tinder and Bumble, where users swipe left or right at photos, my eHarmony experience now seems as quaint as chaperoned courting.

Once the pre-work was complete, the site matched me with five or six potential partners per day. All were said to be compatible with me based on a scientific algorithm. Since I had told eHarmony I was a straight male, but men and lesbians still appeared as possible matches more than once on the site, I had doubts about how scientific their algorithm was. Still, most matches were in the realm of possibility.

A head-scratching trend among my early matches was that a handful of women had profile pictures where they were posed with a tiger. The women in these pictures were not standing outside a zoo enclosure with a tiger pacing behind sturdy glass. These women were all lying on the grass with an arm casually draped over a reclining tiger. Each looked like the photo of a bestiality enthusiast with an extremely high-risk tolerance.

When I mentioned this phenomenon in a conversation with my friend and former Grand Canyon travel companion, Robert Wright, I asked, "How on earth are they getting these tiger pictures? Why do they think they are relevant on a dating profile?"

While I meant this question rhetorically, Robert pondered it and responded, "That sounds highly relevant to me. A woman posting a picture with her arm around a tiger is either telling you, 'I own a tiger' or 'I am an idiot.' Either is something you want to know."

If I was interested in an eHarmony match after reading her profile, I sent a request to enter a three-phase "Guided Communication" process with her. If she accepted, we asked each other five multiple-choice questions in the first phase. In the second phase, we exchanged ten-item bullet-point lists of "must-haves" and "can't stands," i.e., "I must have someone who wants kids" or "I can't stand someone who smokes." In the third phase, we both answered three questions our match had selected, which each required a longer text answer. I called this the "essay section." After all of this, if both parties agreed that the results of the three phases had been acceptable, you could freely message each other or arrange a meeting.

The most common question women sent me in the "essay section" was, "Describe the most spontaneous thing you have ever done." The first few times I received such queries, I replied with a flippant "I don't understand the question" and elaborated with a paragraph about how deeply I prized careful planning. That never ended well. Several matches quickly stated they only valued a spontaneous man and blocked me.

Their emphasis on spontaneity befuddled me. To me, spontaneity means doing things with no plan, off the cuff, at the spur of the moment, and by the seat of your pants. I am not sure why all spontaneity idioms involve something one wears, but living without a plan was no way to live as far as I was concerned. Sure, some things are too trivial to require planning. Sometimes life throws your careful plan a curveball, and you must deal with it as best you can with a spontaneous reaction. Still, spontaneity was not something I had ever viewed as an essential virtue to cultivate in myself or to seek in a romantic partner.

Doing new things can be exciting, so I understand a desire for novelty, variety, and surprise in life or a relationship, but you can still plan a surprise or plan to do new things. Did women want men who did not plan at all? Did they want a man who randomly chose their anniversary gift at Walgreens on the way home from work instead of carefully selecting one a month ahead after weeks of careful thought? For a vacation, did they want their guy to start driving randomly somewhere instead of carefully planning a trip?

Once I realized spontaneity was so prized, I started obsessing on seeming spontaneous to broaden my romantic appeal even though being a 330-pound nerd with no sense of style was likely more limiting to my romantic attraction than my spontaneity shortcomings. Blaming an abstract quality was more palatable psychologically somehow.

Before an unplanned trip to Zion and Bryce Canyon, I had spent four days in Phoenix working at a Gatorade plant. I had expected the trip to last only two days, but it grew longer because my manager had asked me to handle something else at the plant after I arrived. I was about to re-schedule my return flight for Friday morning when it occurred to me that it was ludicrously cold in Chicago, it was delightfully warm in Phoenix, and the coming Monday was the President's Day holiday. A spontaneous man, I decided, would take Friday off, re-schedule his flight for Monday night, and spend a four-day weekend in sunny Phoenix.

Spontaneity needed corporate approval, in this case, so I called my manager and explained that I wanted to stay the weekend, would not charge PepsiCo for any weekend expenses, and had already checked and documented that it cost no more to fly back Monday night than it would cost for me to fly on Friday morning. My manager saw no issue with any of this and gave his approval.

Even after having to ask permission, making this abrupt decision to stay the weekend gave me an illicit tingle, like biting forbidden fruit, but minutes later, I stressed out, wondering what to do with my time in Phoenix. Before leaving the plant, I asked a group of its employees with whom I had been working what they would do with a four-day weekend in their city. The entire group said, in near-perfect unison, "Vegas!"

It did not speak well for Phoenix that the universal recommendation of these residents was to leave town immediately. As I am both too cheap and cautious to enjoy gambling, Vegas never held obvious appeal for me.

I was trying to be spontaneous, so maybe I should try something out of my comfort zone.

My co-workers made Vegas sound like a short jaunt from Phoenix, but Google Maps said it was a five-hour drive away. Still, that was doable in a four-day weekend. I next noticed two large green blobs, each about two hours from Vegas. Upon closer inspection, I saw they were Zion and Death Valley National Parks.

Forget Vegas and leaving comfort zones. This was now a spontaneous National Park trip.

Soon I had a rough plan to drive north Friday, spend Saturday in Zion, Sunday in Death Valley, and return to Phoenix on Monday to catch my flight. Initially, I resolved to reserve only a rental car and make the rest of the trip up as I went along. Five minutes later, I panicked at the possibility, however remote, of driving so far and finding no hotel rooms were available. I thus reserved a room near Zion for Friday night and one in Vegas for the next two nights. Spontaneity would have to come in baby steps.

I drove to the Phoenix airport Friday morning to return my work-paid rental car. I next picked up a personally paid rental car. At the counter, the agent asked what I was doing for the weekend. I told her I had planned a spontaneous trip to Zion and Death Valley.

"That sounds so awesome," she cooed flirtatiously while typing whatever car rental agents typed into their computers. Her reaction made me think this spontaneous stuff was indeed the key to impressing the ladies until, seconds later, she asked in the same tone, "Since you are taking such an awesome trip, wouldn't you like to upgrade to a sporty Dodge Challenger for only an extra $8.95 per day?"

The Challenger was a sports car with styling meant to evoke the 1960s Dodge Challenger muscle car. It looked utterly badass, so I was sorely tempted, but ever the cheapskate, every fiber in my being screamed that I should not pay more to rent a sports car when it would be less comfortable than the sedan I had reserved, less fuel efficient, and utterly unnecessary. Had I not been frustrated with Robert when he rented the same type of thing in Albuquerque last year?

After telling her this upgrade was of no interest to me, a little voice in my head said, "a spontaneous man would choose the Challenger." I then told her I had changed my mind and accepted the upgrade.

When I saw the Challenger in the rental car lot, I felt another forbidden fruit tingle. That thrill diminished after I contorted myself into its cramped interior and disappeared altogether when I learned this specific Challenger model had a V6 no more powerful than the one in my Ford Five Hundred at home.

The drive to Zion was long, but at least dynamically scenic, since the landscapes out my windshield transitioned from the cacti-filled desert of Phoenix to the evergreen-covered mountains around Flagstaff to the stark red rock buttes of southern Utah. During the drive, I discovered the Challenger did have one entertaining feature: a built-in zero-to-sixty timer. In Utah, I found several flat and deserted stretches of highway where I could come to a complete stop without impeding traffic, cue up the timer, and mash the accelerator to the floor. The V6 could not muster impressive times, but I had fun trying.

In mid-afternoon, I entered Zion at the east entrance station on Utah highway 9 and then drove west past red, white, and tan banded mountains and mesas. Even though the temperature here was in the mid-fifties, higher elevations on these features were colder and covered in snow. Just before the road entered a tunnel through Mount Carmel, there was a parking area. A sign there indicated that this was the trailhead for the one-mile Canyon Overlook Trail. I parked there and read the trailhead sign. It said this trail was an easy walk leading to a great view of the canyon for which the park was named. After five hours cramped in the Challenger, a spontaneous two-mile round-trip hike sounded like what I needed.

After a short series of stairs, the trail was mostly a level path on a wide, level ledge in a cliff wall. Despite comfortably walking in a light jacket, I was surprised to find some patches of ice on shady sections of the trail. I saw all of those coming and avoided them, but the presence of ice was unnerving, as slipping off this trail could lead to a long fall. The narrowest, most potentially dangerous sections of the trail had safety railings, but I still walked warily until I reached the end of the trail at a ledge from which I peered down into Zion Canyon, which was framed by parallel two-thousand-foot-tall reddish cliffs of bare rock, some topped with white peaks. This was a view worth a long spontaneous trip.

After returning to my car, I drove into the mountain tunnel, which was enormously long and had large windows cut into the side offering canyon views. After the tunnel exit, the road dropped to the canyon floor via switchbacks. It was nearly sundown when I reached the bottom, so I made no further attempts to explore the park that day and drove to my hotel in Springdale, a small town outside the park entrance.

While checking in, I asked the desk clerk about park conditions and good trails to hike the next day because I wanted to get started hiking before the NPS Visitor Center opened and thus would not be able to ask a ranger for advice before starting. The clerk was very knowledgeable and warned me that even though high temperatures were now in the fifties, evening temperatures were below freezing, so trails above the canyon floor, like the famous Angels Landing trail, were closed due to ice forming on the trail. He recommended two short trails inside the canyon that I could do safely.

During the peak tourist season, the only road in Zion Canyon is closed to most vehicles except shuttle buses, but on this sparsely visited winter day, the road was open. In the morning, I drove into the canyon lit by the first rays of morning sunlight. Now I was looking upward at those massive stone cliffs that wowed me from below the previous afternoon. Considering this was a desert in winter, the canyon was surprisingly lush with gobs of green conifers on level surfaces. Green plants even grew in crannies in the canyon walls making the place look like a hanging garden. Between those towering cliffs flowed the greenish Virgin River.

A hike called The Three Emerald Pools was the first recommended by the man at the hotel. The trail started near a lodge inside the canyon, crossed the river on a bridge, then climbed 200 feet up slopes in the canyon wall in two miles, passing a series of three pools of water. Each pool was higher than the last one and fed a small waterfall. At the trailhead, a sign warned that there was ice on the trail between the middle and upper pools, so hiking there was not recommended. I made it to the lower pool without issue, which on this day, was just a puddle at the base of the cliff and nothing much to look at, but the waterfall flowing into it was impressive as the water was freely falling nearly seventy feet.

Just past that first pool, I hit the trail equivalent of black ice, slipped, and landed hard on my rear. With aching glutes, a wet pants seat, and wounded pride, I bailed on the rest of the trail and slinked back to the trailhead. Since I had not expected to be hiking on my business trip to Phoenix, I had not packed proper hiking boots. Too cheap to buy a pair when I had perfect boots at home, I decided to hike in the steel-toed safety shoes I wore in Gatorade plants, which purportedly had non-slip soles even though I had just managed to slip with them. At least I would be protected if a rock fell off the canyon and hit only my toes.

Stopping occasionally to gawk at the towering canyon walls and the peaks looming above it, I drove deeper into the canyon until the road abruptly ended at the trailhead for the second hike recommended by the guy at the hotel, The Riverside Walk. This easy, mile-long trail straddled the Virgin River up to the entrance, or I supposed, more technically, the exit of an area of the canyon called The Narrows. Here, the canyon's walls are so close that the waters of the Virgin River fill its "floor."

The Riverside Walk ended at the last bit of a dry riverbank. I lingered there, marveling at the scene. In warmer months, I read that one of the most popular hikes in the park is wading up into the Narrows. That looked fun, but not on a 50-degree day. As if they timed their arrival to demonstrate my wussiness, six people clad in wetsuits and carrying wooden walking sticks brushed past me just then and strode into the river one by one. I asked, "What are you doing?" They said they were hiking up The Narrows.

They had rented the wetsuits and the walking sticks at an adventure outfitters store in Springdale. The last one to enter the river, presumably unknowingly, said my current trigger word when he teased, "I'm sure they have more you can rent if you're feeling spontaneous."

Spontaneity be damned, I thought, after plunging my finger into the chilly river and then withdrawing it with haste. No date seemed worth wading for miles in fifty-degree water, even when wearing a wetsuit.

Before noon, I had already done both hikes the man at the hotel recommended and driven the canyon road's entire length. Out of ideas for what else to do, I went to the Visitor Center outside the canyon, which sat below a striking peak called The Watchman that resembled a red shark tooth.

The ranger at the center's information desk asked how he could help me. I unleashed a torrent of verbal diarrhea on this public servant in which I described my National Park goal, my current spontaneous trip, and my lack of my usual hiking gear. After recapping my experience in Zion to this point, I told him I had the remaining daylight hours to spend here before I needed to drive to Vegas.

"What would you recommend I do with the rest of my day in the park?" I asked in conclusion.

The ranger chuckled and said, "I'm not sure I caught all of that, and I am not sure what else you can do in Zion, considering the conditions. If you're trying to see all the parks, why don't you go to Bryce Canyon National Park for the afternoon? It's just two hours away." He handed me a map and gave me directions.

Going to Bryce Canyon would mean I was violating my workday standard in two parks since I had only spent about six hours in Zion between stints in two days. When I reached Bryce Canyon, I would only have three hours to hike there. Also, it would add two more hours to my evening drive to Vegas. Nonetheless, adding another National Park to my tally proved irresistible.

Two hours later, after a drive that gained 4,000 feet of elevation, I arrived at my second National Park of the day. Of course, having come here sans plan, I had little idea what I would see and no idea what I would do. From a brief segment in the Ken Burns documentary, I remembered Bryce Canyon was a giant hole in the ground filled with eroded pillars of picturesque rock. That was all I knew.

While the Visitor Center and primary scenic road in Zion are at the canyon bottom, Bryce Canyon's visitor center and scenic road are on the upper rim, like the Grand Canyon. After talking to a ranger at the Visitor Center, I learned that just like the Grand Canyon, Bryce had a Rim Trail leading to various named viewpoints. Many other trails led down into the canyon, but the ranger warned that many of these were icy in winter, so I should stay on the Rim Trail unless I had crampons. You could rent those in the Visitor Center, but I had only three hours until sundown, so it did not seem worth the trouble or cost. In any event, I had so loved the Rim Trail at the Grand Canyon that this seemed like the way to go for me.

Minutes later, I parked near Sunrise Point, strolled to a spot on the rim, and peered into a bowl-shaped orange-and-white-rimmed hole in the ground studded with clusters of oddly shaped rock pillars that geologists call "hoodoos." Hundreds were visible. The hoodoos were never just smooth cylinders. They had widely varying shapes. Many had sturdy bases but then tapered to thin spire-like church steeples. Others had a craggy, bulky top above a narrow central spindle. Some seemed to have a stylized face on top, like a chess piece. Each hoodoo in isolation was an interesting rock column but not necessarily beautiful. Grouped in such big numbers, though, they were gorgeous and overwhelming.

NPS interpretive materials emphasized that Bryce Canyon was not technically a canyon because a river or creek carved canyons at their base. Bryce has instead been hollowed out from above by precipitation and wind, a process still happening, as evidenced by the sign in the visitor center indicating one popular trail was closed due to recent large rock falls dropping off one specific hoodoo.

Instead of a "canyon," the NPS says Bryce is a "natural amphitheater." I think I know what they are getting at with its bowl shape. However, that term would never work as a literal natural amphitheater, like Red Rocks in Colorado, because hoodoos would obstruct almost every view. Then I chuckled, thinking maybe it was an amphitheater for concerts, but hoodoos were the audience.

From Sunrise Point, I walked the Rim Trail to Sunset Point, where I found another awe-inspiring view, and then I tried to continue walking to Inspiration Point, but this segment of the Rim Trail was covered in snow that had not been shoveled. Where the snow was soft, this was not a big problem, but much of the snow on the trail had developed an icy rind because tourists had melted the surface of the snow with their steps by day, and then it re-froze into a slick sheet overnight. On one of these ice-covered snow patches, I slipped and landed on my ass for the second time in one day. I decided I was done hiking for the day.

Of course, I was not done hiking as I had to walk back to my car. I managed to do that without injury or further embarrassment. From then on, I just drove the park road to more named viewpoints, all of which were outstanding. The snow that made walking treacherous made the views more stunning as the patches of white stuff that had lingered on some of the hoodoos glistened in the afternoon sun. My visit ended at Sunset Point, watching the glorious namesake event over the hoodoos.

My day continued with a dull, four-hour drive in the darkness to my Las Vegas hotel, which was two miles from the city's famous strip. After spending a day in two quiet National Parks, the hustle, bustle, and bright lights as I arrived in Sin City shocked my system. Now I should invoke "what happens in Vegas, stays in Vegas" and imply I spent my evening engaged in a bacchanal, but in all honesty, I read about Death Valley online in my hotel room, made a detailed plan for the next day, and then slept.

While I would not describe most developed areas of the National Parks as highly dangerous, there are always potential hazards. One should only visit the sites when prepared to handle those risks. My day slipping and sliding in Zion and Bryce Canyon was a prime example. I had not brought the correct equipment and did not arrive at them with the proper knowledge to enjoy either park fully or safely.

That night in Vegas, I decided National Park spontaneity would not work for me. I further decided spontaneity was not going to work for me in general. I should not even consider dating any eHarmony matches who were so adamant about finding a spontaneous man. I must be true to who I am.

When I violated that resolution two weeks later, I answered an eHarmony match's spontaneity query in the eHarmony "essay section" by citing this trip as the most spontaneous thing I had ever done.

ELEVEN
DEATH VALLEY NATIONAL PARK
FEBRUARY 19, 2012

CROSSING DEATH VALLEY on foot is far from the most challenging hike I have ever made in a National Park, but it was the most badass-sounding hike I have made. To clarify, I only crossed Death Valley, not all of Death Valley National Park, which includes an enormous 3.3 million acres of the Mojave Desert in southeastern California.

Death Valley is a long, narrow plain between the Panamint and Amaracosa mountain ranges best known for extreme heat and justifiably so. The hottest air temperature ever recorded, 134°F, was measured here. Since the sun can heat surfaces well beyond air temperature, sidewalks here can hit 190°F in summer. Out of whimsy, the NPS once posted an online video showing someone cooking an egg in a skillet on a park sidewalk. The clip went viral, which backfired when tourists started imitating the video sans skillet and leaving messes for park staff to clean. As the high temperature would only be 65 on this February day, I had to settle for scrambled eggs from a hotel continental breakfast before leaving Las Vegas.

Much of Death Valley is below sea level. Its lowest spot is the lowest above-ground point in the United States at 280 feet below sea level. A prehistoric salt lake once filled the valley. Its water evaporated long ago, leaving the salt behind as a crust. The valley is surrounded by mountains and cannot drain. On the rare occasions that rain falls here, the salt-covered lowest part can briefly become a salt lake again, but any water that collects here is not potable because of the salt, so the place is called Badwater Basin.

Since I had never seen a salt flat and loved the idea of being able to say I had been to the lowest place in America, Badwater Basin was my priority Death Valley stop. I drove there immediately after entering the park. A short boardwalk led from the parking lot to the salt's edge. Past the boardwalk, visitors could go anywhere they liked because the basin had no defined trail. Roughly two dozen fellow tourists stood on the edge of the salt crust, which was white apart from the plentiful places it had been punctured with footprints, through which I could see the lumpy dry brown dirt underneath.

The park map showed the salt flat spanned five miles. Because no vegetation grew here, I could see where it stopped abruptly at a barricade of barren mountains to the west. Although the salt felt grainy to the touch, from a distance, it seemed to be a smooth, glistening alabaster slab except for the spider-web of uneven, roughly half-inch-tall ridges jutting above the rest of the surface that subdivided it into hexagons and pentagons, making it look like this place had been formed by flattening a salt-encrusted soccer ball.

Nothing here fit my standard conception of natural beauty, yet the place mesmerized me. I needed to explore it further. Knowing how little most Americans walk, I strode west, assuming I would only need to do so a short time before finding untrammeled salt. Besides, after the "Stay on the Trail" signs I had seen in other parks, permission to move freely on a natural wonder was too thrilling to forgo.

The lack of trail, novel terrain, and absence of life ahead made walking west on Badwater Basin feel like exploring a new planet. Exhilarated, I kept walking long after finding footprint-free salt, but the lack of trail was unnerving. I repeatedly glanced backward to ensure I still had my bearings. Since there was no trail with a posted path or distance, I started a walking distance app on my phone when I stepped onto the salt to track how far I walked on it. When I pulled my phone from my pocket to take a picture, I noticed I had been out here an hour—even though it seemed like much less—and had already hoofed three miles. Not only the parking lot but my rental car was still visible three miles from where I had left it.

It occurred to me en route that after terminating my dalliance with spontaneity the day before, I was now doing something quite spontaneous. I was sixty percent across, so why not keep going? How cool would I sound when I told people I crossed Death Valley on foot? I had been excited to say I had been to the lowest place in the US, but saying I hiked across "Death Valley" would make it sound like I completed a tremendous feat of endurance. I would only admit it was under seventy degrees outside at that time if cornered. This thought proved irresistible. I reached the western edge of the salt in forty minutes.

Soon after beginning the return trip to my car, I felt parched like I never had before. Despite the cool temperature, low humidity plucked every water molecule from my person not tethered by potent chemical bonds. Since I had only intended to stroll at Badwater briefly, I had not brought my usual backpack with me. I was carrying only a one-liter water bottle. I had opened and drained that bottle minutes into the return trek. Late in the walk, my eyes frequently darted back to the bottle, hoping to find a hitherto unnoticed moisture reservoir. When I returned to the east edge of the boardwalk, all I could think about was water.

An even larger group of tourists were now milling about just off the boardwalk. The male half of one middle-aged couple there called out to me, "We were looking out across there and you emerged like that scene from *Lawrence of Arabia*. We couldn't believe anyone was out there." Several others asked in almost reverential tones what it was like out there. I admitted it always looked the same across the basin before taking leave of my admirers to chug another one-liter water bottle I had stashed in the car.

MY NATIONAL PARK DIET

From Badwater Basin, I drove towards the Furnace Creek Visitor Center, stopping to see more points of interest like a natural stone arch; the Devil's Golf Course, an area of rough terrain strewn with coarser salt crystals; and Artist's Palette, a spot where otherwise drab chocolate brown mountains were streaked with yellow, orange, pink and green. I walked a short distance into Golden Canyon on a smooth trail between two towering walls of crumbly dirt. Like at Badwater, there were no plants or animals to be seen.

At the Visitor Center, I reviewed exhibits on the valley and learned that some animals and plants do eke out a living here. Most shockingly, when significant rain falls in the valley—an event that happens only roughly once per decade—the ground can suddenly teem with wildflowers in a "Super Bloom." That this seemingly lifeless place could be awash in bright-colored flowers was hard to fathom.

After reading about Death Valley's unlikely industrial past in the visitor center, I drove to see what was left of some of it at Harmony Borax Works, the ruins of an 1880s mining operation near one of the park roads. Death Valley holds significant deposits of borax, a mineral with many industrial uses that was also once a popular household cleanser. Harmony built this processing plant inside Death Valley to convert borax ore into pure borax for shipment east. Interpretive signs on a short trail through what was left of the plant explained how borax was dissolved from the ore and crystallized here, which was easy to visualize since a surprising amount of the equipment was still intact. I spent a long time here as I knew this was likely the only time my chemical engineering degree would be of direct use to understanding something in a National Park.

Scalding Death Valley was a strange place to build a factory, especially since it could not be run in the summer because it was too hot outside for the separation process to work. There was no railroad to Death Valley then, so borax was hauled out in wagon trains pulled by teams of twenty mules. The park displays a period ore wagon with seven-foot-diameter wheels that would have held thousands of pounds of borax and a period wheeled water tank that would have held the 1,200 gallons of drinking water needed to get the twenty mules and the men that drove them out of the desert alive.

One borax household cleanser brand named itself Twenty Mule Team Borax in tribute to this era of Death Valley borax production. It used images of mules traversing Death Valley on its packaging and ads long after more modern transportation methods had replaced mules. That brand name was created in the 1890s by an executive named Stephen Mather, who later started his own borax company.

At the visitor center, I had seen a plaque honoring that same Stephen Mather. I had seen or would later see a plaque honoring Stephen Mather at all the other National Parks I visited. None of these plaques was meant to honor his work in borax. The Mather plaques commemorated his second career, which started in 1915 when he volunteered to run the National Parks for the Interior Department and helped push legislation through Congress that created the National Park Service in 1916. Mather became the service's first director and passionately promoted National Parks to politicians and the public for thirteen years.

Mather's myriad accomplishments are beyond the focus of this book, but his story is particularly fascinating because he accomplished them while suffering from a mental illness that caused several nervous breakdowns. He developed his passion for the National Parks when he found time in nature helped him recover. Mather's principal focus as NPS director was making National Parks more accessible so more could experience their benefits as he had. He initiated projects that built many new roads, trails, and lodges.

Although the story of how National Park infrastructure was built is much less celebrated than the political actions that first made the places parks, as I drove to my last planned stop in the park, Zabriskie Point, and walked the short trail to the overlook there, I realized infrastructure work like the projects Mather initiated were the only reason I could travel to a place so remote and forbidding that it is called Death Valley.

The bare hills surrounding Zabriskie Point that erosion has carved into sinuous shapes are, like Badwater Basin, not conventionally pretty but fascinating because I had never seen anything like them. The place still seemed familiar as it was pictured on U2's album *The Joshua Tree* and my favorite antique store find. I enjoy browsing antique shops. To give me something cheap there to collect related to National Parks, I often bought pre-World-War-Two postcards depicting places in them. Most had no writing on the back, so they presumably were kept as souvenirs. A postcard picturing Zabriskie Point became my favorite buy because a Civilian Conservation Corps worker mailed it from Death Valley to his family in St. Louis.

The CCC was one of many New Deal programs FDR initiated to get money flowing during the Depression. It hired jobless young men and sent them to public parks to work on construction and conservation projects. They lived in military-like camps and were paid a dollar per day by the federal government. While it was tragic that so many young men could not find jobs during the Depression, there is the slightest sliver of a silver lining in the many amazing things these hard-working CCC employees built for the National Park system and other public lands. The CCC had constructed many of the facilities I used in National Parks.

The postcard sender's signature is unfortunately illegible to me, but he wrote that he was a member of "two companies, comprising 450 men" who were to "make a National Park of Death Valley for winter tourists." He mailed the card in November of 1933 but comments, "It's still quite warm," with what I assume was a comedic understatement. In those rare instances that National Park infrastructure is celebrated, visionary leaders like Mather are more likely to get accolades than workers like the man who mailed that postcard. Zabriskie Point was a good place for me to take a moment and thank the young man who sent that postcard and anyone else who swung a hammer, turned a shovel, or did any of the other hard work that made National Parks easier to visit.

The National Park Service's mission has always seemed a paradox because it is charged with conserving the environments it administers for future generations and making parks more accessible to visitors. Striking the right balance between building infrastructure to promote visitation and leaving the parks' undeveloped places of pure nature to promote conservation is an ongoing debate in National Park history. Based solely on my day here, I thought Death Valley had it right. A road took me to Badwater Basin, but I walked across it.

TWELVE
SHENANDOAH NATIONAL PARK
MAY 20, 2012

SKYLINE DRIVE TRIED MY PATIENCE, but once I resigned to its languid pace, this scenic road through Shenandoah National Park charmed me with its manicured overlooks offering gorgeous mountain vistas.

While I enjoy driving, I had never considered it a National Park activity. When I drove on a road in a National Park, that was just how I moved from one hike to the next. Shenandoah, however, had been designed from the beginning for "auto touring." A 1920s committee chose this location as part of a plan to promote Virginia tourism with a new National Park featuring a scenic road through an Appalachian range called the Blue Ridge Mountains.

Shenandoah's Skyline Drive is that road. I planned to drive its entire length and stop for hikes along the way. I always obeyed speed limits in National Parks as I did not want to be permanently kicked out of parks or hit wildlife in one. Thus, I was first expecting to spend three hours driving on Skyline because it is 108 miles long and has a 35-mile-per-hour speed limit. It soon became evident that even a pokey 35 was too optimistic as an average pace.

The first problem slowing my drive was heavy traffic. It was a gloriously sunny spring day, so locals likely were enjoying Sunday drives here along with out-of-state tourists like me. The second problem was that many RVs on the road were driving slower as they could not navigate its twisty sections at 35. There were few places it was safe or legal to pass them. The third and most confounding problem was that many drivers stopped, seemingly paralyzed by indecision, every time this road approached a scenic overlook.

The latter factor was a big issue because Skyline Drive has 75 scenic overlooks, averaging one roughly every 1.5 miles. Each was a small parking area on a mountain ridge landscaped with lovely stone walls meant to give drivers a place to pause and enjoy the surrounding landscapes. Once I realized there was nothing I could do to go faster, I accepted I was making a five-hour trip, not a three-hour one, and resolved to enjoy the languorous cruise. From then on, I stopped at every single overlook, each of which had a name indicated on a sign. I was tickled to see one called "Jeremy's Run," which I interpreted as a personal tribute, although the word choice was puzzling as I only walked. I had not run anywhere in at least a decade.

In the direction I traveled that day, the scenic overlooks to my left were scenic gems because they looked out on the lushly forested Blue Ridge Mountains. I knew academically that the foliage on those trees was green in the late spring, yet somehow the mountains looked blue from this vantage point, so the many rounded peaks suggested waves on an ocean. Overlooks to the right were less exciting as they mostly offered views of the towns in the Shenandoah River valley west of the park.

The hikes I made in Shenandoah were all memorable and fun. The Stony Man trail passed a bare rock cliff that resembled a person's face if you squinted at it. A short trail to the summit of Blackrock Mountain ended in a panoramic view more impressive than the Skyline Drive overlooks. A steep trail descended to a pretty waterfall called Dark Hollow Falls. The Limberlost Trail was a leisurely stroll through a forest flush with wildflowers, trees, and mosses. My noisy lumbering on it often sent startled squirrels, deer, and songbirds scurrying. None of the animals or plants I saw seemed exotic, but a National Park so obviously teeming with familiar wildlife was a welcome change after eleven desert parks.

Despite the high traffic on Skyline Drive, most trails were lightly hiked except Dark Hollow Falls, which was all but choked with humans and dogs. The presence of the latter irritated me, not because I am anti-dog, but because posted signs at the trailhead said dogs were not allowed there. I was not sure why dogs were not allowed, but I was sure the National Park Service had a good reason for the rule. Thus, each leashed Lab lunging toward my crotch or spaniel yipping at my ankles contributed to my steadily mounting feeling of self-righteous indignation towards the tourists so wantonly disobeying National Park rules.

At the base of the most spectacular part of the waterfall, I removed my backpack and rested by sitting on a rock. When ready to resume my hike, I leaned forward to retrieve my pack. The key card for my hotel room dropped from my shirt pocket, plopped in the creek, and was whisked downstream. I sheepishly backed away, hoping no one had seen that. I then mused that perhaps I could cut people over-stepping the posted pooch prohibition some slack as I had just polluted a mountain stream with non-biodegradable plastic.

My final Shenandoah hike went to the top of Bearfence Mountain via a ridge studded with upward-pointing wedge-shaped boulders that made it look like the back of a stegosaurus. Passing this rocky ridge required hands-and-knees rock scrambling that I would not want to do for an entire day, but on one short hike, it was a fun change of pace.

Returning from Bearfence Mountain, I congratulated myself on having come a long way as a hiker. On this day, I completed all the hikes on my itinerary and, in the process, logged eight miles, several of which were relatively tough. I still felt fresh as a daisy somehow.

Soon after Bearfence, I approached a Skyline Drive intersection in my rental car called Swift Run Gap. There were only two places to exit Skyline Drive between its two ends. Swift Run Gap was the second in my direction of travel and, thus, my last chance to exit before the road's southern terminus. Thanks to the traffic and stopping at overlooks, it was late in the afternoon. I needed to exit now and drive towards the airport to stay on schedule.

Despite completing all my hiking goals in Shenandoah with ease, driving the complete length of Skyline Drive had proved beyond my capabilities.

THIRTEEN
CUYAHOGA VALLEY NATIONAL PARK

JUNE 9, 2012

"HOW IS THIS A NATIONAL PARK?" Chris Taylor asked incredulously while driving in Cuyahoga Valley National Park thirty miles south of Cleveland, Ohio, a city not typically associated with natural beauty. His confusion was prompted by the fact that we had just passed a sign welcoming us into the National Park and minutes later passed houses and a strip mall without seeing any sign indicating that we had left the park.

"I warned you this was America's lamest National Park," I reminded him.

Chris and I became friends while studying chemical engineering at the University of Missouri-Rolla in the 1990s. Although originally from the Chicago suburbs, he now lived and worked near Toledo. I convinced him to join me in exploring Ohio's only National Park this weekend, so after work on Friday afternoon, I made the four-hour drive to Chris' house. We woke early on Saturday morning and made the two-hour drive to the National Park, which Chris was already finding underwhelming.

"You said it was lame," Chris conceded, "but this is more like a Cook County Forest Preserve than Yellowstone."

Since Chris and I were Midwesterners, a Midwestern National Park could never strike us as exotic as geysers in the Rockies. This place was also anomalous among National Parks. It is not remote wilderness but surrounded by suburbia. It is not a giant block of land like Yellowstone but has an almost serpentine shape since it is mainly composed of narrow land parcels near the Cuyahoga River.

The Cuyahoga flows through this stretch of northern Ohio before emptying into Lake Erie in downtown Cleveland. It is best known for once having been so extravagantly polluted that chemical slicks on its surface caught fire in Cleveland multiple times. One such fire in 1969 garnered national media coverage. Since water is usually fire retardant, images of a river engulfed in flames captured the nation's imagination.

That Cuyahoga fire became a flashpoint—all puns intended—for the burgeoning environmental protection movement. Earth Day, the creation of the EPA, and the Clean Water Act were all spurred by it to some extent. Various municipal, state, and federal projects were initiated to clean up the river. Some of the federally owned lands that were part of that remediation effort later became this National Park.

Chris was familiar with the river's history, so I told him the purpose of this National Park was not about protecting awe-inspiring natural wonders but leaving some Cuyahoga River watershed undeveloped to help the river recover. Then I told him it was initially not a National Park but a National Recreation Area. That is the designation Congress usually gives places run by the National Park Service that have been heavily altered by human habitation or construction, like the reservoir behind Hoover Dam.

"I'm not sure why," I told Chris while concluding my park history lesson, "but in 2000, Congress changed Cuyahoga Valley's designation from National Recreation Area to National Park. The thought was that 'National Park' would sound more impressive and help the place attract more tourists. After all, garden variety weirdos like me want to go to all the National Parks, but only the weirdest of the weird collect all National

Recreation Areas. In fact, in all honesty, that name change is the only reason I am here."

"You're only here because someone from Ohio bribed Congress into changing the name of this place so they could fool suckers like you into visiting it?" Chris asked.

"Absolutely! I'm still happy to be here!" I crowed, refusing to allow the logic of his skepticism about the place to dampen my National Park enthusiasm.

This conversation ended when we reached the parking lot near Brandywine Falls, the waterfall I had selected as our first stop in the park because my pre-trip research suggested it was the one legit natural wonder here. From a viewing platform just steps from the parking lot, we saw Brandywine Creek plunge down a wide bare rock cliff before splashing into a rocky stream bed 75 feet below. Sure, the bridge over the top of the falls and the tire laying at the base marred the scene a bit, but Chris and I agreed that this was a stunningly pretty waterfall and a National Park-worthy view.

We differed, however, in that Chris was ready to return to the car after this first look, while I wanted to walk the two-mile loop trail leading to the bottom of the falls. Although Chris was in better physical shape than I was and an experienced hiker, he had broken his kneecap when he had tripped while jogging a few months before. Thus, he was still wary of taxing it even though doctors had deemed his recently reformed patella sufficiently healed for walking. Before the trip, I had assured Chris I only wanted to do short walks in the park, not long hikes. We had divergent views of what "long" meant on this day. I thought two miles was a short walk. In a knee-protecting frame of mind, Chris deemed two miles too extreme. Things do change. I would have considered two miles a very long hike just two years before this day.

Chris succumbed to my nagging and gave it a go. He completed it without issue, but I apologized for goading him into it once we finished. I had thought from an online trail description that this hike would lead us to a clear view of the falls at its base, but when the trail finally reached the level of the bottom of the falls, it was at a spot well downstream of the cliff. We could not even see the falls from there.

While Brandywine Falls was spectacular, the two-mile trail around it was just a stroll through the woods: nice but hardly spectacular. Those last four words would suffice as my review of the entire park. We strolled to several more points of interest, including Blue Hen Falls, a much shorter waterfall; an old wooden covered bridge; and The Ledges, a series of fifty-foot-tall bare sandstone cliffs. I enjoyed each site, but I would have happily foregone any of them for another five minutes at the Grand Canyon.

Chris was feeling more confident about his knee at this point, so I talked him into a four-mile round trip stroll on the old towpath of the Ohio and Erie Canal, which had been constructed in the 1820s to provide a shipping link from the Ohio River to Lake Erie. The towpath was originally the route the mules would walk when pulling barges up the canal. Since the canal was long since out of use, the section of the towpath near the Cuyahoga River had been converted into an 85-mile-long hiking and biking trail. As engineers, we could not resist inspecting the old canal and one of its locks along the towpath.

We parked at a picnic area near Ira Road and strolled north. We soon arrived at Beaver Marsh, a wetland in the park created by the work of the namesake proverbially busy aquatic rodents. The NPS had constructed a boardwalk that protruded into the marsh. From it, we spied sunbathing turtles, darting fish, floating mallards, geese, and flying great blue herons. Seeing any wildlife here was a testament to the success of the river cleanup process since pollution left this river almost entirely devoid of fish in the 1960s.

The trail was more popular with bikers than walkers. Constant vigilance proved necessary to avoid being smacked by someone swooshing by on a Schwinn, but I still reached my goal: a place where the towpath was directly next to the Cuyahoga itself. I was glad to finally stand on the banks of the park's namesake river. We stood quietly while watching the lazy blue river flow past forested hills. It was a lovely scene, but the power lines paralleling the river disrupted the natural vibe.

"In desert parks," I said to Chris, "they have signs saying 'Fire Danger: high or low or whatever depending on how dry it is. How do they not have such a sign at the Cuyahoga? It used to burst into flames all the time."

"Shouldn't Smoky the Bear be out here warning people not to flick cigarettes into it?" Chris added.

"Smokey does not work for the National Park Service," I replied. "He works for the National Forest Service."

"Only you would know that fact," Chris retorted.

"Only you can prevent forest fires," I countered.

Chris groaned and announced he was hungry, so it was time to leave for lunch. I was a few hours from my "workday standard," but Chris had been a good sport, and this National Park underwhelmed me.

Thus, we left and ate lunch in Akron before driving to Canton, Ohio, the site of our next planned stop. That was the site of The Pro Football Hall of Fame. We spent the rest of the afternoon reading exhibits on the history of football, admiring bronze busts of NFL legends, posing for pictures with the Lombardi Trophy, and taking turns comparing our comparatively tiny fingers to a replica of former Chicago Bears player Refrigerator Perry's size 25 Super Bowl ring.

"The Hall of Fame was way better than the National Park," Chris taunted as we exited the Hall.

I did not attempt to argue.

FOURTEEN
PINNACLES NATIONAL PARK
JUNE 30, 2012

A MAN with a German accent yelled at me in a campground restroom during my first moments at Pinnacles National Park. Well, technically, Pinnacles was still a National Monument while that happened.

The previous day, I had flown to San Francisco to initiate a nine-day trip through California and Oregon, with which I planned to visit six National Parks. After spending Friday night at a hotel in San Jose, I woke early on Saturday to complete the 90-minute drive south to Pinnacles before 7 AM so I could finish my longest-planned hike there long before the day reached its predicted high temperature in the mid-90s.

This trip was the one I had planned to do the previous year before panic about my new house derailed my plans. It included some spectacular parks I had dreamed of seeing since childhood. As such, finally starting this trip had me giddy. Wilderness writer John Muir's oft-repeated quote, "The mountains are calling, and I must go," reflected my mood as I started the drive. As I neared Pinnacles, I needed to go in another sense. I was feeling a more urgent call of nature—call #2, if you catch my drift. There was a campground near the park entrance, so I parked near its restrooms and hastened into the lone stall on the men's side.

While washing my hands after finishing, the German-sounding man walked into the restroom, entered the stall I had vacated, turned around, approached me, pointed at my chest, and barked, "Is not clean in there!"

This restroom seemed clean, especially considering it was in a National Park campground on a weekend during the summer tourist season. In any event, I was not the janitor, so I looked at him quizzically, trying to figure out why he was filing his complaint with me.

"Is not clean in there!" he repeated with increased agitation.

"I don't work here. What do you want me to do?'" I asked.

"Is not clean in there!" he shrieked, pointing at my chest with one arm and waving the other wildly in the direction of the stall. He then moved to the stall door and pointed at it while stomping his right foot.

The last time a German spoke with gestures so emphatic, a world war started. Thus, I had better do something. Sighing, I walked into the stall and wondered how he came to have this phrase—but only this phrase—in his English vocabulary. Nothing seemed amiss at first, but then I noticed the tiniest turdlet, no more than a quarter inch in diameter, floating in the otherwise empty bowl.

I flushed the toilet, announced, "Is clean now," and departed the restroom before he could resume shrieking.

While walking back to my rental car, I noticed something large and black flying in the empty blue sky above the mountains to the west. I looked up, assuming it was a low-flying small plane, but upon closer inspection, it was one of the most famous residents of Pinnacles: a California condor.

The California condor is the largest native bird in North America, a vulture with a ten-foot wingspan. It nearly went extinct in the 1970s due to habitat loss and poisoning from DDT and lead. Conservationists took the drastic step of capturing all live California condors and breeding them in captivity until the 1990s, when they began releasing them back into the wild. Today, there are over 400 California condors in the wild.

Pinnacles National Park is one of the best places to see them. Twenty-seven condors were living there during my visit. I never encountered a condor on the ground, but I caught several glimpses of one soaring far overhead. At a distance, condors can be confused with the smaller but still sizable turkey vulture, but I had read how to distinguish between the two using differences in the white pattern on their otherwise dark wings.

As I mentioned before, Pinnacles was still a National Monument at the time of my visit, not a National Park. The classifications given to the various places run by the National Park Service are varied and confusing. For example, historic battlefields in the care of the NPS are called different things, like "National Battlefield," "National Battlefield Park," or "National Military Park." There is no significant distinction between those labels that I can find. "National Monument" is the most confusing classification of all. That term sounds like it should apply to something like Mount Rushmore, which is run by the National Park Service but is designated a National Memorial.

When used to classify public lands, "National Monument" refers not to the type of place being protected but the political method by which it became protected. It is a classification created by a controversial 1906 law that helped rapidly expand the National Park system.

In the late 1800s, there were various ways ordinary citizens could file property or use claims on unoccupied federal lands, including homestead claims or mining claims. There were several incidents in which people filed a claim on a parcel of federal land that had recently discovered Native American artifacts. The claimants then used their land access not to mine or start a farm but to take control of the archaeological site and carry off artifacts found there. This happened at Mesa Verde, which prompted outrage that ultimately led to Mesa Verde being made a National Park by Congress, but the legislative process to make it a park took so long that a significant number of artifacts were already removed.

To protect future archaeological finds, Congress passed a law in 1906, now known as the Antiquities Act, that allowed the president, by executive order, to declare a parcel of federally owned land a National Monument if it contained items of historic or scientific interest. Declaring a piece of federal land a National Monument restricted claims that could be filed on it and gave it most of the protections that National Parks have. While protecting archaeological sites led to this law, it did not limit what historic or scientific interest meant.

Since conservation-conscious Theodore Roosevelt was president when the law passed, he soon used his new power under this law to create National Monuments that were not archaeological sites but natural wonders that Congress had not yet made National Parks, most notably the Grand Canyon. Pinnacles was among the first rush of Roosevelt National Monuments in 1908.

Virtually every president since 1906 used the Antiquities Act to create National Monuments; there are now over 100 of them. During my trip to the two Texas National Parks and Carlsbad Caverns in New Mexico, I made a brief three-hour stop at the lovely White Sands National Monument on the day I drove back to the El Paso airport and caught a flight back to O'Hare. I found the white gypsum sand fascinating as it was soft and less scratchy than the far more common sand made of quartz. Unfortunately, at the El Paso airport, I found lots of sand on my pants, socks, and shoes. All that sand had landed there during my brief time hiking at White Sands. Still, I had enjoyed seeing the place enough that I thought I should consider visiting any nearby National Monuments if I had time on my upcoming National Park trips.

Some National Monuments were later renamed National Parks by Congress, but most have stayed National Monuments. Some on the political right are generally hostile to public lands and National Monuments especially. They want to stop the creation of more and open some existing ones to oil exploration and mining. There have been Republican-led unsuccessful attempts to repeal the Antiquities Act, and at time of writing, the Trump administration rescinded National Monument status from some areas of Utah.

The National Park Service administers most of the National Monuments, so there are few tangible differences between visiting an NPS-run

National Monument and a National Park. In fact, per a law passed in the 1970s, the classification of a National Park Service unit, i.e., National Park, National Lakeshore, etc., does not affect its funding or management. Still, just as Ohio worked to reclassify Cuyahoga Valley, some Californians knew "National Park" carried greater prestige than "National Monument." In 2012, they were actively attempting to re-label Pinnacles as a National Park. One article mentioned that legislators expected more foreign tourists to visit Pinnacles once it was renamed a "National Park."

Aware that Pinnacles might soon become a National Park, I had preemptively added it to my itinerary for this trip. When the bill to make Pinnacles a National Park passed later that year and was signed into law by President Obama in January 2013, I retroactively declared this a National Park visit.

My main objective in Pinnacles was a 5.5-mile hike called the Balconies Loop, a recommended day hike on the NPS website because it gave a good sampling of the terrain and went through a talus cave. The hike started at a spot called Old Pinnacles Trailhead and began with an easy walk on a trail parallel to a creek bed that was virtually dry during my visit. It was a gorgeous day aesthetically, with no clouds in a stunning cornflower blue sky, but the day did not feel beautiful as it was already hot in the early morning.

Soon into the hike, I passed several spiky volcanic rock formations that looked like someone had shot an arrowhead from below the earth's surface, and the tips had poked out into the sky. The trail was surrounded by parched grass and a mix of short shrubby trees, some evergreen and some deciduous. This type of vegetation is called chaparral and is common in western California. In one spot, I saw a half-dozen wild turkeys scratching at the earth and making so much noise.

Two miles into the trail, I came to the talus cave. "Talus" is a geology term for piles of rocky debris at the bottom of a hill or mountain. In this case, the base of the cliffs often had piles of pinkish-gray granite boulders, some ten-plus-feet wide. Since these boulders are irregularly shaped and do not pack together tightly, this leads to voids forming in the boulder piles that are wide enough for people to crawl through. These voids are called "talus caves."

When I first entered it, I thought this was more of a talus tunnel than a cave. Yes, there was a pile of disconcertingly large boulders forming a "roof" above me, but the "floor" was a flat bed of gravel-sized rock, so it almost looked like someone had built a road through the pile. There were enough gaps in the boulder pile that it was still well-lit, so it was not dark like a cave.

This talus cave was initially less than four feet tall, so I had to walk hunched over with my back parallel to the ground. My backpack kept dragging against boulders here and halting my progress, so I eventually wised up and made my backpack a front pack. Later, it became more cave-like as the gap narrowed enough that I had to crawl, and it became dark enough that I needed to use a headlamp. Here, the bottom was not a level gravel "floor," but I had to crawl through the center of an uneven boulder jumble that I had to navigate carefully. Even though I knew tourists had been clambering through this cave for more than a century, it was unnerving crawling through massive boulders that were not fully fixed. They were just randomly resting on each other. I hoped this day was not when they decided to rearrange themselves and land on top of me. They did not move, and I decided that place had proved giddy fun when I exited the talus cave.

My hike continued for a couple of miles past sheer, brown cliffs of bare stone called the Balconies, which gave this trail its name. Park signs indicated the rock here was volcanic and originated from a 23-million-year-old volcano. During this section, I soon found the trail blocked by a ranger-led tour group of about twenty people. The group hike had stopped here. They were listening to the ranger talk about plants in the area. I waited for her to finish speaking and planned to ask permission then to pass them. Her speech ended by saying that part of a specific plant she was describing followed the Fibonacci sequence.

A woman in the group asked the ranger what the Fibonacci sequence was and why it was called that. The ranger floundered a bit, so hoping to speed things along, I announced from behind the group in a booming voice that the Fibonacci sequence was a series of numbers that shows up in many natural processes. Each number of the series after the first two, I then said, was the sum of the two previous numbers. "So it goes 1, 1, 2, 3, 5, 8, 13, etc. That's because 1 plus 1 equals 2, 1 plus 2 equals 3, and so on," I finished.

"Why is it called the Fibonacci sequence?" a man asked. The whole tour group pivoted towards me.

"Fibonacci was the name of an Italian mathematician in the 1200s," I answered. "He wrote a book called *Liber Abaci*, which sounds like a flamboyant piano player, but I think that means Book of Calculations. It introduced Europe to Arabic numerals, his sequence, and a bunch of other math stuff he stole from the Arabs or maybe the Indians. Forgive me, it's been a while."

"How do you know this?" asked the woman who had asked the ranger about Fibonacci. "Are you a mathematician?"

"No, I am just a working engineer and a retired trivia player," I replied. "If you would kindly let me pass now, I have to hike ahead and share my useless knowledge with many other strangers."

To my surprise, that worked. The group moved to one side of the trail and let me pass. Once I returned to my rental car, I drove to a part of the park called the Bear Gulch Day Use Area, where several more trails started, including one leading to a larger talus cave than the one I saw in the morning. Unfortunately, that cave was closed during my visit. It has large bat populations and is closed when bats nurse their young.

Since another cave was not an option, I hiked the Condor Gulch Trail, which led to overlooks for more volcanic rock formations. After two miles, I made a U-turn on this longer trail and returned to my car as the temperatures were now well into the nineties, and the sun was beating down on my head like an anvil. I had had enough of this heat, so I spent the rest of my time in the park perusing exhibits in two visitor centers.

Between my morning and afternoon hikes, I ate the lunch I had packed at the picnic area by the Bear Gulch parking lot. My lunch was small by my standards: a turkey sandwich, a bag of baby carrots, and an apple. I realized at that moment the irony inherent in my eating light in a National Park where I was spending the day climbing trails and clambering through a cave. I realized I would have eaten something more substantial during my lunch hour in the office, where I usually sat all day.

While on these hiking and driving trips, I tended to eat the minimum amount of food needed to keep me vertical so that I would not feel bloated or need to squat in the bushes near a trail. This must mean, I realized, that my regular diet must at least sometimes be more than I needed to meet my energy needs.

This epiphany was interrupted when a deep blue bird called a Steller's jay alighted on the picnic table and tried to nab the half of my sandwich that I was not holding in my hands. I covered my lunch with my arms and ate guardedly while the jay stalked it in an arc on the table, always staying about six inches from my arms and looking for any opportunity to strike at any unguarded victuals.

Although irritated by the jay, I at least gave thanks that I was not protecting my food from a 10-foot-wide condor or a bear.

FIFTEEN
SEQUOIA AND KINGS CANYON NATIONAL PARKS
JULY 1, 2012

FLAMES FLICKERED on dry needles littering the earth beneath a giant sequoia as I walked through Round Meadow in Sequoia National Park. Since these massive trees were the most magnificent living things I had ever seen and the news so frequently features footage of California forests engulfed in flames, I freaked out and began forming a plan to prevent this small fire from becoming an inferno.

What was the phrase? Stop, drop, and roll? No, wait…that was if I was on fire, not to extinguish a fire. Maybe I should sprint to the nearby museum and call for help. Whom was I kidding? I was not going to sprint anywhere, and since the museum did not open for an hour, I had no idea if anyone was in there. I had two bottles of water in my backpack; maybe I should toss their contents on the flames.

While still deciding both the best fire suppression approach and how I would display the medal the National Park Service would no doubt give me for saving these sequoias, I noticed for the first time a large sign indicating visitors should not worry because this was a controlled burn started intentionally by the NPS.

Giant sequoias are one of only three redwood species still growing on earth and the biggest tree species. These conifers grow only in California in small groves on the western slope of the Sierra Nevada. They live for thousands of years, often have trunks more than twenty feet wide, and many achieve heights more than 200 feet tall.

Cheating my "workday standard," I visited both Sequoia and Kings Canyon National Parks in one day, which I deemed justifiable since they are run like one big park by the National Park Service with common management, brochures, and a website. Congress created both in 1890 after conservationists lobbied to protect two different stands of Giant Sequoias from logging. The southern grove was named Sequoia National Park. The northern grove was named General Grant National Park because the biggest tree there had been named in honor of the Civil War general and president. Although still technically two parks, both have been expanded until they are contiguous. One road called the Generals Highway loops through both.

Combined, Sequoia and Kings Canyon National Parks contain 800,000 acres with a wide array of landscapes and natural wonders: Sierra Nevada peaks, a canyon with towering walls capped by enormous bare granite domes, waterfalls, and caves. The sequoias are still the main attraction, so I made a beeline for their most famous grouping, the Giant Forest, after entering the park near Three Rivers, California. During the twenty-mile drive there from the park entrance, the Generals Highway, the park's main road, gained 5,000 feet of elevation via a series of nearly dizzying switchbacks.

Catching my first glimpse of a giant Sequoia gob-stopped me like few things I have ever seen. At my time of writing, three US states did not even have a building as tall as many of these trees, and there were dozens of them here. While driving to the Giant Forest, I had been cruising in bright sunshine and listening to satellite radio, but the Sequoias now blocked much of the sunlight and all the satellite radio signals.

Of all the wondrous things I saw in 47 National Parks, only the Grand Canyon delivered such an immediate, visceral gut punch of grandeur as I felt upon first seeing Giant Sequoias. The Grand Canyon's large size, stunning beauty, and novelty astonished me. The sequoias, by contrast, astonished me because they were something so familiar, an evergreen tree, but blown up to a ridiculous size. To make a transportation analogy, seeing the Grand Canyon was like encountering a gigantic alien spacecraft; seeing the sequoias was like walking out to my driveway and finding my car was suddenly 200 feet long.

I only remember a little detail of the many trails I walked in the Giant Forest because I was always too busy staring at trees. The first walks were quiet and peaceful as I arrived before 7 AM, but by 9 AM, the quiet was gone. Over a million people visit Sequoia National Park every year. You could have convinced me they were all here on this day. Still, I was so enthralled by the trees that I scarcely noticed the throngs.

When I went to the Giant Forest Museum to see its exhibits, I asked a ranger about the controlled burn I had seen earlier. He said setting small fires controls the build-up of dried material on the forest floor that can lead to larger forest fires. Also, fire is part of the lifecycle of a sequoia because the cones do not release their seeds until a fire heats the cone. This is presumably an evolutionary adaptation that ensures seeds only sprout after a fire has cleared enough space for them to get some sun.

The museum displayed the seed cones of sequoias and several other native trees. I was surprised to see that the sequoia cones were quite small. I had seen some nine-inch-long cones on the ground, which I had assumed must have been produced by sequoias, but now I learned the sugar pine produced these. The sequoias instead made cones barely an inch long. Each tiny cone held many far tinier seeds. It was amazing to think trees so massive could start life as such a diminutive speck.

From the museum, I took a shuttle bus up Crescent Meadow Road, which is closed to cars during the busy summer months and leads to two popular attractions: Moro Rock and Tunnel Log. Moro Rock is a bare granite, dome-shaped rock topping out three hundred feet above the road and 6,700 feet above sea level. Visitors climb a 400-step stairway cut into it by the Civilian Conservation Corps. I was gasping for breath at the top, but the exertion was worth it because, atop Moro Rock, I could both look down on those massive trees and see some of the still snow-capped high Sierra Nevada peaks to the west.

Tunnel Log was less interesting. It was a dead sequoia trunk that had fallen over a park road in the 1930s, so the Civilian Conservation Corps cut this eight-foot-tall tunnel through it so that cars could pass through. A bypass road was built later, which is what the shuttle bus used, but bus passengers could disembark to inspect the tunnel log closer. I did so, but since I could not drive my car through it or watch someone else drive their car through it, there was not too much excitement to be had there.

After returning to the Giant Forest Museum via bus, I drove to see the Giant Forest's biggest star: General Sherman, said to be the largest tree on earth based on its volume of wood. Its unrivaled bigness was not due to its 275-foot height, which was not so anomalous in the Giant Forest but instead driven by its enormous 36-foot-wide trunk that tapers less than most other sequoia trunks do on the way up. There is a small parking lot right next to General Sherman that those with disabilities can use, but most visitors descend to the tree's base via a 0.8-mile paved trail, from which you can see sections of the tree's trunk on the way down. I loved this. Walking even part of the tree's height was a great way to dimensionalize its immensity.

At the bottom was a little sign engraved with General Sherman's name and a queue of people waiting to take their picture with the tree. While I certainly trusted the NPS that it was bigger than the other trees in the grove and the rest of the world, honestly, these sequoias were all so immense that it would not have been evident to me that this was the grand champion without having been told so. Still, I was here and wanted my picture with it like everyone else. I knew better than to attempt one of my tripod selfies. I asked someone behind me to take my picture when it was my turn. She stood far back with no zoom and took a vertically oriented photo. The resulting snapshot looked good but did not even reach its canopy branches.

A fence had been erected around the base of the tree to protect it from vandalism or even the excess of benign trampling and handling it would experience from the many tourists visiting it. They might stay well back on their own if they knew that in 2006, a 140-foot-long, four-foot diameter branch fell off General Sherman, smashed that fence, and put a sizable crater in the paved walkway around it.

It struck me as odd that this tree had been named in the 1800s for William Tecumseh Sherman, the Civil War general who torched a swath of Georgia from Atlanta to Savannah in 1864. Naming a tree for someone most famous for setting fire to a vast swath of countryside seemed out of kilter. Since this was the biggest tree in the world, Sherman had a bigger tree named for him than his Civil War boss, Ulysses S. Grant.

General Sherman is over 2,000 years old. Standing beneath this giant and thinking of the human history that transpired while this tree has stood here alive puts the brevity of human life in perspective. General Sherman has stood here growing and photosynthesizing while many of history's famous generals, like Caesar, Genghis Khan, Washington, Napoleon, Pershing, Patton, and Zod, have come and gone.

The main attraction I planned to visit in Kings Canyon was more gigantic trees, so I wanted one non-sequoia hike in between as a palate cleanse. I had chosen a trail to a 1,200-foot-tall waterfall called Tokopah Falls. The trailhead was said to be in the Lodgepole Campground, but passing through the campground parking lot, I could not find the trailhead. I drove to the nearby Visitor Center to ask a ranger how to find it.

The Lodgepole Visitor Center was a hive of activity. A line four deep was at the information desk, so I took my place and waited my turn. Moments later, a portly middle-aged man walked in, strode past the queue, pounded his fist on the front desk, and demanded, "Where do I drive through the tree?"

The ranger told him where Tunnel Log was and that the road through it was closed. The line-cutting man cut the ranger off and said, "No, I saw a picture of a live tree that you can drive through. Where the hell is it?"

Because it was mentioned in the Ken Burns documentary, I suspected he was thinking of the Wawona Tree. In the early 1900s, a hole had been cut through a living, standing sequoia by that name so tourists could drive through it. It died and fell in the 1960s, and even if it was still standing, the man was at the wrong park because it had been located 100 miles north in Yosemite National Park, which also has sequoias. The attraction was never recreated because NPS policy today is to minimize park visitors' impact on nature. No longer cutting tunnels sawed through botanic wonders for shits and giggles is part of that policy.

Instead, the ranger told him there were privately-owned places where one could pay to drive a car through a Coastal Redwood, the other enormous redwood tree species of California, which primarily grows near the Pacific Coast. He gave the man their locations but cautioned that they were hundreds of miles to the north.

After the line cutter sputtered in protest and left and groups ahead of me were assisted, the ranger showed me how to find the Tokopah Falls trailhead. I soon started the 3.5-mile round-trip walk, which passed a forest of very sizable evergreens that seemed tiny after a morning in the Giant Forest. The waterfall was underwhelming, too. I had thought "1,200-foot-tall waterfall" meant the Kaweah River plunged down a tall sheer cliff, but the river had little free fall here. It gently cascaded down a rounded outcrop of bare granite.

In time, I learned that the overall height of waterfalls, the metric cited on park websites, is different than what best predicted whether I would find them spectacular. The quoted height usually included both steep drops where water plunged and gentle slopes where water smoothly cascaded. My favorite parts were free falls and steep descents, so I eventually learned to look for more detailed online guides that cited if the waterfall had free-fall height. Even if less exciting than I imagined, I reminded myself while nitpicking the 1,200-foot-tall cascade of water in front of me that this was not something I could see in Barrington, Illinois.

Generals Highway next took me into Kings Canyon National Park. I parked at the lot for General Grant Grove, the stand of sequoias that was the genesis of the original General Grant National Park. Sequoias here were similar to those in the Giant Forest, but the thrill of walking among them had not diminished. General Grant, this park's original namesake tree, was the third-largest tree in the world. It was the star at 267 feet tall and 28 feet wide at the base.

Weirdly, I was more wowed by seeing The Fallen Monarch, a dead sequoia already on the ground when the first white settlers arrived in General Grant Grove in the early 1800s. Although the dead trunk still had a strong ring of outer wood, it was hollow in the center over its whole length. Sequoias are highly resistant to rot and, given their size, prove quite a substantial meal for the microorganisms that rot them. Parts of their trunks can last for centuries after their death and nourish or shelter various other plants or creatures.

Tourists can walk into the Fallen Monarch where the roots would have started and through the tree's trunk to where the branches would have started. Even more so than standing beneath their bases, reading facts and figures on interpretive signs, or walking a trail down to the bottom of one, the enormity of these trees was made the most tangible to me by walking through a long-dead one. The void in this dead tree was so big that I never once needed to duck or shimmy, even with my height and considerable girth.

Most of the living trees in General Grant Grove had been named for states. Paper maps were available listing the trees' names. While I proudly beheld the sturdy Missouri Tree, a young couple asked if I would take their picture with this sequoia in the background. I happily obliged and complimented them for their excellent taste in posing with the tree named for the state where I was born.

They had yet to notice that the trees were named for states, so I showed them the map. They were from Georgia and asked if their state had a tree.

I could not resist jokingly replying, "I don't know, but I saw the giant General Sherman earlier. If that tree is anything like its Civil War namesake, it probably burned the Georgia tree down."

SIXTEEN
YOSEMITE NATIONAL PARK
JULY 2, 2012

AS I STARED DUMBFOUNDED into the canyon known as Yosemite Valley from the outside at an overlook called Tunnel View, I was astonished at its beauty and could not wait to explore it on foot from within. Once I had done so, I decided I liked it better from the outside.

Tunnel View was a scenic turn-out along the Wawona Road after it exited a mountain tunnel. From there, I could see down into much of the length of the seven-mile-long, mile-wide canyon. A lush evergreen forest surrounding the Merced River was at the base of the canyon, which was framed on each side by 2,000-foot-tall, bare white granite cliffs sheared by long-ago melted glaciers. Those cliffs were topped with spiky peaks and curvy granite mounds. The beautiful Half-Dome was a mountain shaped like the top of a thumb since it had a dome-shaped backside and a black-streaked cliff facing the valley side so perfectly vertical and flat that it appeared to have been cut with a band saw. Multiple waterfalls hundreds of feet tall plunged down the cliffs, most notably the 2,400-foot-tall Yosemite Falls, the tallest waterfall in North America. All of this was on display in one mind-rending vista. I did not have to turn my head to see all these wonders at once.

Yosemite Valley only covers roughly one percent of Yosemite National Park's total area. The rest of the park contains wonders like Sierra Nevada peaks, alpine lakes, roaring rivers, remote forests teeming with wildlife, and groves of Sequoias like those I had seen the day before. I saw none of those other places on this day because I had decided to spend my entire day in this famous valley. The pictures of it that I had seen were astonishing. At Tunnel View, I was sure I had made the right decision.

Once I drove into Yosemite Valley, however, I could no longer see that overwhelming whole, just fragments of it through gaps in the trees. I was mired in stop-and-go traffic for twenty minutes until a baton-waving park ranger in an orange vest, at last, guided me to a parking spot. After exiting my car, I walked on a sidewalk swarmed with fellow tourists and felt more like I was leaving a stadium after a ballgame than starting a National Park visit. After only thirty minutes into the valley, I was less sure of my decision.

Since I love waterfalls, my first walk was to the base of Yosemite Falls, which looked less magnificent up close. The creek completes its 2,400-foot plunge to the valley from the top of those mammoth cliffs in three different sections: a vertical 1,400-foot free fall, a gently sloped middle cascade, and a final 320-foot plunge. From the base, I could only see the bottom portion. Water flow was surprisingly puny since trail guides had warned visitors to bring ponchos to avoid being drenched. I learned from a park sign that Yosemite Falls is seasonal and often disappears in late summer or fall. The Sierras had received so little snow the previous winter that the creek and the falls were already petering out on July 2nd. The throng of people gathered at the falls' base was so large that I was elbowed in the ribs twice while observing it.

The low water level impacted another place in the valley that I had been excited to see. Half Dome and its beautiful sheer cliff were said to be fully visible above and perfectly reflected in a small body of water called Mirror Lake. After I walked to it amidst more massive crowds, I found the lake was scarcely bigger than a mud puddle on this day and not big enough to produce a mirror image.

There were waterfalls in the valley less prone to dry out in summer, so I decided to hike to two of those, but parking in the valley was so fraught that I dared not drive to their trailheads. Free shuttle buses run in the valley. I took one to the start of both these hikes, but the experience could have been more pleasant as each bus was chock full like rush hour subways. Vernal and Bridalveil Falls, though shorter in total, looked more spectacular at their bases than Yosemite Falls had since they carried more water on this day, and more of their heights were visible from a low vantage point. However, I was always in a crowd on the trails to them.

On past National Park hikes, despite being hundreds of miles from home in an unfamiliar environment, I often felt more relaxed than in my everyday life. When I first noticed this, I attributed it to how simple life is on a trail. At work, I managed multiple engineering projects with myriad simultaneous workstreams and could not focus equally on all of them at any given moment. Hence, there were countless prioritization decisions to make. I went home every night with a vague dread that something critical was slipping. Even at home, there were non-stop decisions to make about what to accomplish in the house or even how to spend my leisure time.

Once I started a trail, there was nothing to decide; I just had to keep putting one foot in front of the other and observing my surroundings. It was wonderful. However, walking crowded trails in Yosemite Valley was the exact opposite of calming. By noon, I was so frazzled with the crowds that clarity of purpose could not be the only thing I had found relaxing about other parks' trails.

It could not be solitude I was craving. I lived alone. What did I need with solitude? No, being in a crowd, I realized as the day continued, to me means more decisions. I cannot tune other people out. I am constantly aware of them and constantly think about them. Not anything profound, mind you, just a constant stream of logistical questions as I walked the busy trail. Is there enough room to pass that slow person in front of me? Where is a good spot to get off the trail and let those fast people pass me? Is that enormous dog those people are walking going to jump on me?

Hoping to find a trail without crowds, I scrapped my itinerary after the two waterfall hikes and tried hiking a horse trail that pedestrians were also allowed to use. This trail hugged the base of one of the cliffs a little above the valley floor. It was less busy, but it was too close to the cliffs to be very scenic and proved stressful in another regard as constant vigilance was needed to avoid stepping in horse crap. On this walk, I passed impressive piles of talus at the base of the cliffs, including individual boulders dwarfing me in height that provided a tangible reminder that erosion was still working on the valley's towering walls.

Tired of dodging crowds and manure, I abandoned the trail and left the park. After taking a bus to the lot where I had parked, I started my car so the air conditioner could start doing its thing on this hot day and opened my trunk. I stowed my backpack and started changing out of my hiking boots so I could wear more comfortable shoes for the drive. The driver of a fully loaded SUV seeking a parking spot noticed I appeared ready to leave and pulled his car in about a foot behind me as I unlaced a boot. He rolled down his window and asked if I was leaving.

"Yes, but I'm going to be a few minutes," I called to him.

"That's okay. I'll wait," he said. He backed up just a bit, but after doing so, he stared at me so intensely while I went about my business behind the trunk that I could swear two holes were being bored into my skin. I started hurrying, so much so that I managed to screw up tying one of my shoes the first time. When finished, I shut the trunk, looked up, and noticed a perfectly framed view of Half Dome through a gap in the trees around the parking lot. Forgetting my hurry, I gazed languorously at this beautiful mountain with the black streaks on its flat face shimmering like tears in the afternoon sun. What a stunning…

HONK! HONK!

"I thought you were leaving!" yelled the driver waiting for my spot.

I wrenched my eyes from Half Dome, sat in my car, and backed out of my parking spot. For the first time, I felt relieved to be leaving a National Park.

SEVENTEEN
REDWOOD NATIONAL PARK
JULY 4, 2012

THREE-HUNDRED-FOOT-TALL TREES TOWERED ABOVE ME, casting shadows so deep it looked like twilight at 1 PM on a sunny day. After rounding a bend and finding a black bear mother and cub standing one hundred feet ahead, I came to an utterly startling stop. The bears peered at me briefly before scrambling into the woods.

This happened not as I was hiking a trail in Redwood National and State Parks but as I drove on a road there. If I had seen bears that close on foot, I would have probably shit myself to death and not lived to write this. I only felt remotely safe when I saw two bears because I was driving a rented Chrysler 300 that was still going strong even after I had driven it into a redwood tree the day before.

After my day in Yosemite, I had a full day on my itinerary to make the 375-mile drive from Fresno to Arcata, California, a town just south of Redwood National Park. My route passed through Santa Rosa, which had a museum dedicated to the late Charles Schulz, writer and artist of the comic strip, *Peanuts*. Although I associated Schultz with his native Minnesota, he lived in Santa Rosa for many of the years he drew the strip. Having been a big *Peanuts* fan as a kid, I decided to stop and see the museum's great exhibits, which included some original hand-drawn comic strips, a reconstruction of Schulz's office, a replica of Snoopy's doghouse wrapped in tarp by the artist Christo, and a mural Schultz had painted in the bedroom of one of his children.

After eating lunch capped with a Charlie Brownie at the café inside the ice arena Schultz had built in Santa Rosa, I spent the afternoon driving to Arcata on Highway 101, called the Redwood Highway because it passes old-growth stands of redwoods in two different state parks before it reaches Redwood National Park. Coastal redwood trees are not the biggest trees in total volume but are very tall. While sequoias only grow in a small area on the western slope of the Sierras, coastal redwoods once dominated the northern California coast from San Francisco up into Oregon. Redwoods are not exactly rare today—groves are preserved in several places—but they have been so heavily logged that only a tiny fraction of the original forest remains.

I enjoyed driving near redwoods in two state parks on my route but did not stop since I had a long drive to finish and planned to spend time near redwoods in a National Park the next day. However, I detoured when I saw a highway exit labeled "Drive Thru Tree Park." I realized it must be one of the places the ranger at Sequoia mentioned to the rude person who demanded to know where he could drive through a tree. After turning off the highway, I confirmed this was indeed a place where you could drive through a tree for a fee.

This one was called the Chandelier Tree and had a roughly trapezoidal hole cut through its base. I bought my ticket, drove to the back of the line of cars, and waited for my turn. This rented 300 was a big car, so when I was next in line, I feared I would scrape the sedan's doors on the way through. I folded in the rearview mirrors, and once inside, I saw the hole through the tree was not quite that tight. There was still not much room for error. I also belatedly wished I could have a picture of me driving through the tree, but once inside it, I could not have opened the car doors to get out and hand someone else my camera.

After an uneventful evening in Arcata, I drove inside the National Park early the next morning and found a spot where 101 ran next to an ocean beach. Impulsively, I parked and strolled on sand while watching gentle morning waves reflect dawn's early light. Looking south, I saw a series of cliffs and was delighted to find one that housed a stone arch with an opening big enough to stand inside. Since my mental image of Redwood National Park was dense forests, not sandy beaches and rock formations, this was a pleasant surprise.

I next drove to my first planned itinerary stop, an old-growth redwood forest called Lady Byrd Johnson Grove. After President Lyndon Johnson had signed the law creating this National Park, the park dedication ceremony was held in this spot. Nixon later named it for LBJ's first lady, a conservation advocate.

I hiked the easy, mostly level 1.5-mile trail through it, all while gazing at redwoods fifty feet taller than the sequoias had been. At the risk of sounding blasé, they did not wow me quite as the Giant Sequoias had since, more than anything, the sequoias' width most impressed me. The redwoods, while still broad trees at their base, were svelte compared to sequoias. Had there been sequoias and redwoods side-by-side, the redwoods' extra height might have impressed me, but since I only saw redwoods in this park and their tops were too far above my head for me to directly sense, the extra height did not pack much oomph.

The density of life was more impressive in these forests than those in Sequoia. Redwoods were packed close together—sometimes two or three grew with their trunks touching at the base. I later learned this was because they can reproduce without seeds by sprouting a growth called a burl. In Sequoia, little else grew directly under the big trees, but here there were giant ferns and small plants almost anywhere I looked.

Two redwoods adjacent to the trail had been partially burned in fires that left cavities burned into their sides large enough for me to stand inside. I know that because I stood in them. It was amazing that these trees were strong enough to stand and could still process the water and nutrients needed to support such an enormous life form while missing humongous chunks from their trunk.

I then drove to a nearby National Park visitor center just before it opened because I wanted a pass to do a specific hike called the Tall Trees Trail. A specific redwood along this trail had been declared the tallest tree in the world at 375 feet. The NPS limits access to the grove in which it stood for various reasons, so only fifty passes are given per day for vehicles to drive to its trailhead. I arrived at the center fifteen minutes before it opened, but the line was already twenty people deep. I nonetheless ultimately secured one of the fifty coveted day passes and then drove to park at the trailhead, which was at the end of a long and winding road.

The two-mile hiking trail wound down a steep hillside, passing between redwoods and, at one point, through a hole cut in a dead redwood that had fallen across it. During the walk, I gradually noticed the mature trees in the forest all topped out at the same altitude, so I assumed that they were all growing until they reached the same height as other trees and, thus, received unblocked sunlight. This meant that while the forest would appear of even height, the trees at the bottom of the hill had to grow taller to reach the forest canopy.

At the bottom of the hill, the trail became a loop through Tall Trees Grove, a plain along a creek sporting the tallest redwood trees here and a lush collection of ferns and other plants at their base. As I strolled the trail, the environment seemed familiar to me. Later I realized why…I was on Endor. Okay, I was on the forest moon of Endor. Okay, fine, I was not traipsing amongst Ewoks, but I love everything *Star Wars*. Scenes set on the moon of Endor in *Return of the Jedi* were shot in redwood forests near the National Park, so this place had that vibe. Suddenly I was on the look for giant trap nets or Imperial speeder bikes.

When I came to the interpretive sign indicating I was at the base of the tallest tree in the world, I felt disappointed. It was not noticeably different from other behemoths I had been ogling. As I strained my neck upward and peered at the distant canopy, I could not tell if that tree was taller than its neighbors since the canopy was so far above my head. Long after my visit, I read that lightning later hit this poor tree, reduced its height, and knocked it down several rungs on the tallest tree list. At least I saw it while it was still on top.

My next itinerary item was in a state park. Reaching it required driving through a redwood forest on a five-mile-long dirt road where I had the previously mentioned encounter with two bears. NPS signs and brochures call this area Redwood National and State Parks because the National Park is adjacent to three California State Parks also protecting redwood groves. While my National Park pass would typically not grant free access to a state park, I was pleasantly surprised to find I did not have to pay to enter the Gold Bluffs Beach area of Prairie Creek State Park since the state parks here and the NPS had a cooperative agreement.

The Gold Bluffs were 50-foot-tall vertical cliffs on the Pacific coast made of a yellowish rock that one might charitably call gold in the right light, but their name resulted from past unsuccessful prospecting attempts here. From the state park's entrance station, I turned right and drove a road at the base of the bluffs to the trailhead for my next hike. I thought I had made a wrong turn when I came to a spot where a creek was flowing across the road. Surely I was not supposed to drive through a creek. While I waivered, a car approached from behind, swerved around me, and sped through the creek. Tentatively, I followed, had no trouble fording the shallow stream, and soon reached the parking area for the trailhead.

The trail was only a half mile and led to a canyon cut through 50-foot-tall bluffs by a small creek. While this canyon was not grand in dimensions, it became a famous attraction because its walls are covered in ferns. Fern fronds swayed in the breeze from virtually every square inch of the canyon wall. The stone walls were hardly visible since moss covered anywhere not fern smothered. Tiny waterfalls trickled down the walls. A creek meandered lazily down the roughly ten-foot-wide canyon floor. The place felt like a hanging garden.

Because flowering plants had not evolved at the time of the dinosaurs, but ferns had, this canyon is a rare place where one only sees plants that existed in the Jurassic. Because of that, it has been used as a filming location for documentaries on dinosaurs and the Jurassic Park sequel, *The Lost World*. I read all that before coming here, so maybe it was just the power of suggestion, but I felt a primal vibe walking here.

There was no trail in the canyon, but the creek never filled the canyon floor, so there was always a gravel bank on one side on which to walk. Logs across the creek often enabled crossing the stream without getting wet in places where the gravel bank became too narrow to walk along on one side of the creek. While walking across one of these logs, I heard a woman standing upstream scream and reach toward the water in an unsuccessful attempt to grab a dropped item. Assuming such a reaction must have been prompted by losing something highly valuable, I gallantly jumped from the log into the water and intercepted the black object I saw coming downstream.

With soaking-wet shoes and socks, I emerged on the opposite bank with the item in hand: a camera lens cap. The woman appeared, snatched the cap from my hand, thanked me perfunctorily, and left. I felt less soaked in gratitude than my shoes had been soaked in water. After more now soggy-footed canyon exploring, I found a beach spot, sat barefoot by the ocean, and let the sun dry my shoes and socks.

My last planned walk was a short one in the National Park called the Yurok Loop Trail, which led through the coastal prairie to a sandy ocean beach covered in driftwood that offered a view of wave-lapped rock spires just past the shore. While I sat on the beach and watched waves come in, a family of four soon arrived on the beach. That quartet's father asked if I was enjoying Independence Day. I truthfully said I had never enjoyed Independence Day more. The man grimaced and said they were from Wisconsin, on vacation, and camping in the park. He said it felt weird to hike around big trees on July 4th instead of watching fireworks.

"America was the first country to create National Parks," I said, "and author Wallace Stegner wrote they were America's best idea. Thus, there's no better way to spend Independence Day than in a National Park."

"National Parks are great," the man agreed, "but America has better ideas. Since it is the Fourth, I'd say the Declaration of Independence was a better idea."

"Well, then," I said, "there is no more American place to pursue happiness than a National Park."

EIGHTEEN
CRATER LAKE NATIONAL PARK
JULY 5, 2012

IN MANY WAYS, Crater Lake and the Grand Canyon could not be more different. The Grand Canyon is in an arid desert; Crater Lake is in one of the snowiest places in the contiguous states. The Grand Canyon is made of billion-year-old sedimentary rock gradually exposed by millions of years of erosion; Crater Lake is the result of a cataclysmic volcanic eruption less than 10,000 years ago. The Grand Canyon is awash in warm colors; Crater Lake is all cool colors—a giant sapphire oval bordered with green forest.

However, the mechanics of my visit to these two places were a lot alike. At both, I walked to various viewpoints on a Rim Trail, staring in awe into a geologically fascinating and visually astonishing hole in the ground. The namesake lake covers less than ten percent of Crater Lake National Park, but I could not turn away from it long enough to explore anywhere else in the park once I caught sight of it.

During my drive from Redwood National Park to Crater Lake, I made a planned stop at Oregon Caves National Monument, which is run by the National Park Service and protects a cave in the Siskyou Mountains. It was just a few miles off my route between the two National Parks, and even though not a National Park per my project's criteria, I put it on my itinerary because I love caves, and this one was different from any I had yet seen because its walls were made of marble instead of limestone. Since limestone is the stuff of gravel roads and marble is the stuff of Greek temples and mansions, I thought this must be one classy cave.

Marble is a metamorphic rock that forms when limestone is subjected to high pressures, altering its crystal structure and making it more durable. The change in mechanical properties is substantial, but the visual changes are subtle unless you study the crystal structure under a microscope. As such, I slowly realized over the ninety-minute tour cave that if I had not known this rock surrounding me was marble, I would not have noticed it was not limestone. The cave had some nice speleothems, but it was drab compared to Carlsbad or the ones I had toured in Missouri. Thus, I left a bit disappointed.

Because of visiting the cave first, I did not arrive at the visitor center on Crater Lake's rim until noon. I was on the rim and not the shore because Crater Lake sits deep inside a crater ringed by steep mountainsides topped with a mix of rocky peaks and forested plateaus. Hundreds of feet below me, roughly halfway filling the 2,000-foot-deep hole, was the park's namesake lake, an oval of water five miles in width and six miles in length that exhibited the deepest blue color I had ever seen in nature. Upon first seeing this beautiful lake, I wished I had skipped the cave tour.

Western Oregon and Washington have reputations for epic rainfall. At 6,000 feet of elevation, Crater Lake stays at cooler temperatures than the coast and more often gets precipitation as snow. The slopes down to the water were chocolate brown except where they were dotted with conifers or giant piles of snow still lingering here even though it was July. The mesmerizing blue of the lake's surface was interrupted only by two islands. One was an almost perfectly shaped cone. The other was a collection of jagged, rocky pinnacles.

The place was astonishingly beautiful. While I gazed at it transfixed from an observation deck, I heard a ranger starting an interpretive talk on the lake's formation. I tore myself from the stunning vista to listen to the ranger explain how, 7,700 years ago, a volcanic eruption 40 times more potent than the 1980 eruption at Mount St. Helens. The eruption at this spot had caused an explosion so powerful that it shattered the top of an enormous mountain that geologists call Mount Mazama. That mountain lost a mile of height in the resulting tumult.

The deep hole was the caldera from that cataclysmic eruption. The rim and jagged peaks surrounding the hole were the remnants of that collapsed mountain. Over the last 77 centuries, the crater has slowly filled with water, becoming the lake I had just admired. Since the lake is surrounded by steep slopes and muddy streams that cannot run uphill, all the water in Crater Lake fell into it as precipitation, so it is remarkably clear. A metal disk dropped into the water can be seen 30 feet below the surface.

The ranger told us those islands in the lake resulted from volcanic activity that had occurred since the eruption that made the giant crater. Wizard Island, the almost purely cone-shaped one, sticks out 750 feet above the water and is a volcanic cinder cone. It looked exactly how I would have drawn a volcano as a child, except it was in the middle of the lake. The smaller island, called The Phantom Ship, resulted from lava flowing from a fissure. It is only 500 feet long but had 170 feet tall columns jutting from its surface.

My options for exploring the lake were limited. There is a rim road around the entire circumference of the crater, and I had planned to drive its length and stop at viewpoints, but I learned upon arrival that only a tiny amount of that road was then open for driving because plows had yet to remove deep snow drifts from over half of the road's length. There was a boat tour on the lake, which required descending into the crater on a trail to the boat dock, but by the time I learned of this, I was too late to catch the last ride of the day.

So I just walked the Rim Trail and gawked at this natural wonder from various angles for the next several hours. First, I walked clockwise from the rim's visitor center a little over two miles, and during this stroll, I noticed Wizard Island, which had appeared perfectly conical from my first vantage point, had a long strip of land behind the central cone as if it had a tail. From here, the island looked like a stingray on the surface of the water, albeit one with snow and pine trees on its back.

I returned to the visitor center and walked two miles counterclockwise from the visitor in the direction of the Phantom Ship. During this amble, I caught sight of the tour boat on the lake's surface, which looked like a toy from this distance, even though it was loaded with tourists and must be quite a substantial vessel. How did they get that big boat into the crater? Did they Fitzcaraldo that thing?

As I returned to the visitor center area for the last time, the sun was sinking in the sky, and one end of the lake now perfectly reflected the rim's jagged peaks. The other end had sunk into deep shadows that had morphed the lake's blue water into an inky black. After one long last gaze at the lake, I reluctantly started the two-hour drive to Klamath Falls, where I was spending the night.

Midway to my hotel, I stopped at a gas station, stepped out of my car, picked up a pump nozzle, and inserted it into the rental car. A man with the filling station logo on his shirt sprinted towards my car. He shouted, "What do you think you are doing?"

"I am just going to fill up my tank," I responded, befuddled.

"No, you're not," he barked. "Trained attendants must pump all gas—that's state law."

Confused, I relinquished control of the pump and apologized for my transgression, meekly assuring him my unlawful pumping was caused by my ignorance and not meant as an affront to the essentiality of Oregon's trained gas station attendants.

This day had been my first visit to the state of Oregon. While waiting for the attendant to finish filling my gas tank, I reflected that in one highly efficient day, I had experienced three amazing, distinctly Oregon wonders: a marble cave, a lake in a volcano, and "I wonder why Oregonians can't pump their own gas?"

NINETEEN
LASSEN VOLCANIC NATIONAL PARK
JULY 7, 2012

WHEN FRIENDS whose taste I trust tell me a movie is terrible, I will not watch that movie. When friends whose taste I trusted once told me *Manos: The Hands of Fate* was the worst movie ever made, I had to see that movie. I am often attracted to superlatives, even if the superlative is a negative one.

Thus, had Wenny Ng told me hiking to Cold Boiling Lake was boring, I would have skipped it. When she instead told me Cold Boiling Lake was the lamest thing to which she had hiked, I had to see that for myself.

Wenny was a new co-worker who had joined the packaging group in which I worked the previous fall. She was a fellow National Park enthusiast with a goal of visiting all the National Parks. She had already been to 24 when I met her, so I started asking her for trail recommendations before my trips. Wenny was most helpful for this California trip because she had once lived in California and had already been to all the parks I would visit on this trip.

Drawn by the extreme vitriol Wenny expressed towards it, halfway through my day in Lassen Volcanic, I trudged through a mile of forest to the shores of Cold Boiling Lake, a placid body of water so small that I would have labeled it a pond. The park website indicated Cold Boiling Lake was a cold lake that looked like it was boiling because air bubbles constantly pierced its surface, but this lake did not appear to be boiling or doing anything but being wet. While scanning the lake in vain for bubbles, I noticed a separate puddle well to the left of the main lake that did have bubbles piercing its surface, but the rate at which bubbles emerged was closer to that of a glass of 7-Up that had sat on the counter for a few hours than a boiling pot.

There was still snow on the ground here, even though it was July. I assumed that melting snow would swell this lake in a month or so, and the bubbling puddle would be part of the main lake. Even after making that mental adjustment, this stream of bubbles was feeble and not worth a two-mile round trip. Still, these visually unimpressive bubbles indicated impressive stirrings below the earth's surface because they were an example of geothermal activity caused by proximity to an active volcano.

Lassen Volcanic National Park is named for Lassen Peak, the southernmost active volcano in the Cascade Mountains. It became a National Park in 1916 after Lassen became nationally famous for erupting several times from 1914 through 1921, including a powerful explosion that created an avalanche of rock in 1915.

Some of the most dramatic photos of those eruptions were taken by Benjamin Loomis, who witnessed them firsthand because he owned a homestead on Manzanita Lake just north of the mountain. Loomis promoted making the area a National Park and ran a museum about the site in a building on his property, which he eventually donated to the National Park. Loomis' old museum is now a National Park visitor center and still displays many of his dramatic photos. As it was the nearest visitor center to the northwest side of the park, where I had entered it, I made this my first stop to get oriented.

Since I arrived half an hour before the museum opened and there was an easy 1.5-mile nature trail around the lake, I started walking it expecting no more from it than stretching my legs. Although primarily just a nondescript walk in the woods, in several places, trees parted to yield views of the lake with Mount Lassen above it that would have been pretty any day but were stunning this morning because there was no wind and the still water perfectly mirrored the mighty peak. From this spot, Lassen exhibited none of the crags and angularity of the Sierras I had seen earlier on this trip but appeared smoothly rounded on top.

After snapping multiple postcard-worthy shots of the mountain reflected in the lake, I strolled through the museum marveling at Loomis' black-and-white photos of steam and ash pouring from that same mountain and over that same lake and once forested areas devastated by blasts or avalanches of ash from eruptions. It was so hard to imagine such devastation had ever happened at this now bucolic spot.

For the rest of my day, I drove the park's main scenic road around Lassen Peak, eventually exiting the park on its southwest side. Along the way, I stopped to walk several different trails. Only my 2.5-mile hike to a roaring waterfall called Kings Creek Falls had not been dominated by features that highlighted the park's explosive volcanic past and quiet but ominous present.

A short nature trail called Devastated Area passed through a field strewn with boulders taller than me and trees shorter than me. The boulders were part of an avalanche of debris blasted off the mountain in 1915 and laid waste to the mature conifer forest that had once stood in this spot. The short trees were new growth since the eruption. From here, Lassen did not look smooth but slumped on top, with the low spot directly above the deep trough from which the avalanche of debris had originated.

While Devastated Area showed the aftermath of past destruction, it took some imagination and education to understand how the place got this way. The park's many geothermal areas provided more immediately tangible and visually engaging evidence of the area's volcanic activity. Magma, relatively near the earth's surface here, was responsible not only for its volcanic history but is currently heating underground water and sending it above the surface to do strange things. This created those puny bubbles at Cold Boiling Lake and the far more eye-catching roadside wonder Sulfur Works, a pit of gray water that churned and bubbled like a witch's cauldron.

The park's most significant concentration of visible geothermal activity is an area called Bumpass Hell. Even though it was July, the four-mile round-trip trail to Bumpass Hell had been closed due to snowpack just two weeks before my visit. It can stay closed even later in the year than that in some years, so I was glad to have a chance to walk there. While most of the trail was now clear, the shadiest spots were still covered by two- to three-feet piles of snow with surfaces that had melted and refroze under hikers' boots multiple times, making them uneven, slick and just generally treacherous.

The slipping, sliding, and slow going all seemed worth it when I reached the trail's end. I emerged into a scene like something from science fiction. Bumpass Hell overwhelmed my senses with phenomena I had never experienced.

The ground was devoid of plant life and covered in smooth, white mineral deposits that would have looked like the surface of fine china bowls and plates had it not been streaked with bright yellow or rust-orange stains. Pillars of steam shot into the sky from holes in the ground called fumaroles. Scalding hot turquoise water trickled across the smooth white surface into pools. Mud pits that looked like movie quicksand spurted glop at irregular intervals as bubbles pierced their surface. Iron pyrite could be seen precipitating on the surface of black water puddles.

The place is named for Kendall Bumpass, the miner who found this place in 1865 and promoted it as a potential tourist destination. The white mineral crust coating this ground is thin in areas, and the water beneath is hot enough to burn on contact and often highly acidic. Mr. Bumpass once fell through the crust while showing this place to a reporter, and his leg was so severely scalded that it had to be amputated.

Tourists today walk through Bumpass Hell on boardwalks to avoid its namesake's fate. Despite standing on wood planks, I never felt at arm's length from the place. I truly felt in and among it as the wind blew steam from those fumaroles into my face, my nostrils twitched from intermittent strong whiffs of sulfur, and flowing hot water indirectly warmed my feet as its heat wafted upward through gaps in the lumber.

My only disappointment in Bumpass Hell was learning from a ranger that the first word was correctly pronounced as "Bump-us." Before learning this, I—and everyone else to whom I had spoken—pronounced Bumpass as "Bump Ass" with exaggerated emphasis on the second syllable and a barely suppressed smirk. I had barely restrained myself from making inappropriate comments earlier in the day when two attractive college-aged women had asked me if I could show them the best way to Bumpass.

Knowing that its name was not so funnily pronounced only slightly diminished the thrill of seeing it. I lingered in Bumpass Hell for over an hour, marveling at the otherworldly scene, staying longest on a wooden viewing platform from which I had a magnificent view of a particularly striking, yellow-streaked, glistening, white hill that reeked like rotten eggs, constantly belched steam from three large holes, and had a seemingly unnaturally blue-colored pool at its base.

A couple about my age joined me on the viewing platform during my long reverie here. I asked them in a gushing tone, "Isn't this place amazing?"

Both looked at me with mild disdain. "You've never been to Yellowstone, have you?" asked the man condescendingly.

"Well, no," I admitted, "but it is on my list…quite literally."

"Yellowstone has twenty places like this, but bigger and better," the couple's female half added. "Once you have been to Yellowstone, this is kind of sad," she continued. They then both walked away.

"Well, thankfully, I came here first," I called toward their backs and resumed my reverie.

Spoiler alert: in a later chapter, I will describe going to Yellowstone. Yes, it is packed with far more geothermal wonders and far more impressive geothermal wonders. Still, I think Lassen Volcanic National Park is a special place that merits a visit, even if you have been to Yellowstone. If nothing else, there are very few places to see these phenomena hinting at the immense power and heat inside our planet. Each one should be treasured.

Would I have been so enthralled with Bumpass Hell had I gone to Yellowstone first? Short of developing amnesia, there is no way I can answer that. I still think I would have loved seeing Lassen. However, a danger of my attraction to superlatives is becoming jaded or de-sensitized to the not-quite-as-big or showy but still wonderful wonders of the world. Would I yawn at a 250-foot-tall tree now that I had seen a 370-foot-tall tree? After my brief conversation with those jaded tourists, I decided the lesson of Lassen was that I must always strive to appreciate ever seeing the world's second, third, or even fortieth grandest canyon even though I had already seen the Grand Canyon.

That thought applies exclusively to the good end of the spectrum. If Wenny tells me some trail was her third-least-favorite hike, I will skip it.

TWENTY
ACADIA NATIONAL PARK
SEPTEMBER 1, 2012

"MAINE? Don't you usually go to Antarctica or African safaris?" I teased my sister over the phone.

Jennifer replied sardonically, "Yes, but we could not find an infant-friendly North Pole expedition, so it's going to be Maine. Anyway, I thought you might be interested in joining us since we are staying near Acadia."

Jennifer, the older of my two younger sisters, is an advertising executive living in New York City. She and her husband, Bradley Baldwin, are gung-ho world travelers who had been to all seven continents by their mid-30s. Having just welcomed their first child into the world a few months before, they were eschewing their usual far-flung vacations and opting for a relaxing weeklong stay in a rented guest home in Steuben, Maine. Knowing I must be heading to Maine sooner or later for my Acadia National Park visit, she had called me to graciously offer for me to stay with them for some of that time. I accepted enthusiastically, of course.

Jennifer and Brad are avid hikers, but they said they did not want to hike with the baby, so they did not want to visit Acadia with me. Thus, I built my itinerary around that fact and a desire to avoid using a vacation day since all of those had already been earmarked for other National Park trips. I flew into Maine Friday night and spent the night in Bangor. Then I would hike in Acadia alone on Saturday and spend the rest of Labor Day weekend with Jennifer and her family.

Most of Acadia is on Mount Desert, an island east of mainland Maine, so tourism promoters claim it sees America's first rays of sunlight each day. While I doubted this was technically true, it was so charming an idea that Friday night in my hotel room, I set my alarm early enough for me to drive to the park in time to see America's first sunrise. However, while changing time zones helped me get early starts in western parks, the Eastern Time Zone meant my sleeping time was an hour behind clock time. Thus, I slept through my alarm and had to settle for seeing the first rays of sunlight striking the Bangor Fairfield Inn parking lot.

When I finally did arrive in Acadia at 7 AM, I parked near Sand Beach, the park's only stretch of smooth sandy beach. Little swimming happens here since even summer water temperatures average 55°F here. When I arrived, the few people at Sand Beach were fully clothed and strolling along the shore. My mental image of Maine's coast had been formed by Winslow Homer paintings hanging in art museums, where squalls send surges splashing against piles of stones strewn on shorelines. The sand, sunny skies, calm sea, and cloudless brilliant blue sky on this day were not what I expected.

The weather remained sunny, and the seas stayed calm for my Acadia visit. To the south of Sand Beach, I could see terrain more like I expected. The sand ended at a massive jumble of boulders. Just past those were hills with evergreen trees on top and bare stone cliffs of pink granite facing the sea. A popular trail called Ocean Path led from Sand Beach to the top of those hills. My plan for the morning was to walk that trail to the top of a place called Otter Cliffs. At times, Ocean Path was a shaded, crushed gravel path through trees, but for other less pleasant stretches, it was a paved sidewalk adjacent to Ocean Drive, the busy park road paralleling the shore. Even when shoehorned next to the busy road, the trail at least afforded fantastic views of the ocean and those dramatic cliffs.

The most popular spot on Ocean Path is Thunder Hole, a rectangular notch in the seaside cliffs that causes giant splashes and loud noises when big waves enter it. I have watched Internet videos in which Thunder Hole splashes send sprays twenty feet in the air, but the calm seas this day stole Thunder Hole's thunder. There was a stairway leading from the cliff top to the side of Thunder Hole. I walked the stairs to the bottom without feeling a drop of water or hearing anything but seagulls. Monument Cove was another popular Ocean Path stop where erosion had carved free-standing granite pillars from the main body of the cliffs. Those reminded me of the hoodoos in Bryce Canyon.

The literal high point of Ocean Path was the top of Otter Cliffs, a 110-foot tall, sheer cliff facing the ocean. After enjoying that view, I made a U-turn and repeated the path in the opposite direction. The shoreline road near the trail now had a constant backup of cars. The Ocean Path was nearly choked with hikers, too. I wondered if this was a typical summer day or if it was busier due to the holiday weekend.

Back at Sand Beach, I wanted to make another short shore stroll, but I could scarcely see sand as most of it was covered by blankets under the backsides of other tourists. I gave up on walking here, retreated to the parking lot, and relinquished my now in-demand parking space. I navigated park road traffic jams to a spot further inland called Jordan Pond, which I assumed would be quieter since it was away from the ocean. To my surprise, this parking lot was also full. It took several patient laps to snag a spot. I learned later that a famous restaurant serves high tea here. That establishment must have been the primary draw here because I saw few people when I hiked the trail around the pond.

Although "pond" implies a diminutive body of water, Jordan Pond is a 180-acre lake gouged into area rock by Ice Age glaciers with steeply sloped sides plunging to a depth of 150 feet. Its deep blue waters were strewn with enormous water-worn boulders similar to those on the ocean shore and surrounded by more forested hills. At the end of the pond, I saw comely twin 800-foot-tall round hills called The Bubbles. Nothing here was so spectacular as Yosemite Valley or the Grand Canyon, but this park was devastatingly pretty in a subtler way. I enjoyed the 3.3-mile trail around Jordan Pond shore so much that I made an uncharacteristic spontaneous decision to tack on a challenging side trip to the top of one of The Bubbles, adding a mile-and-half of distance, 800 feet of elevation gain, and a bit of rock scrambling.

Everyone I knew who had been to Acadia told me I should see its carriage roads, the stone-surfaced lanes in the park built in the early 1900s on funding from the Rockefellers. They were designed for use by horse-drawn carriages, but visitors can now use them for walking, biking, or horseback riding. I only walked a mile on one carriage road, so take my review with a grain of salt, but they were not my scene. The roads had lovely landscaping, but the vibe was more Central Park than National Park. I only saw cyclists using the one I walked, and after one too many whizzed by me at an uncomfortably close distance, I returned to my car.

High teas and carriage roads were carryovers from Acadia's origins as a summer playground for the rich. In the late 1800s, many Gilded Age millionaires had mansion-sized summer retreats here called "cottages" with no apparent sense of irony. As the area developed, some locals promoted making some of the lands here a National Park to preserve the remaining undisturbed forests and shoreline. Unlike the western parks, most of Acadia was originally in private hands. George Dorr led an effort to buy land for the park, and the Rockefellers donated 11,000 acres. The government accepted the land they acquired as a donation. It became Lafayette National Park in 1919 and was renamed Acadia in 1929.

My park visit ended atop 1,530-foot-tall Cadillac Mountain, the tallest point in Acadia. It was named for a French explorer, but I chuckled at the thought that it could have been named for a car brand favored by the rich people that once lived here. There is a long hiking trail to the top of Cadillac, but I took the easy route and drove up the mountain to the visitor center near the summit. From the top, I had a fantastic view of the ocean, the park, and the nearby town of Bar Harbor across an ocean inlet called Mt. Desert Narrows, which had four small green islands across it lined up in a neat row across like they were steppingstones for a giant.

After that literal high point, I left the park and drove to my sister's vacation rental in Steuben. The homes there formed a jarring mix of seemingly brand-new construction and well-weathered seaside homes that looked straight out of a Stephen King novel. When I arrived, Jennifer and Brad lounged in the living room while their son Clinton napped.

"What are the main things you have planned for your week in Maine?" I asked

"This. Just this," Jennifer said wearily before she and Brad recounted tales of how their life had changed after becoming parents.

We did a little more than "just this" in my time with them, but only a little. We drove along the coast. We streamed a movie. We ate some excellent lobster rolls at a food stand. We beachcombed through the colorful shells dotting the shore across from the house. We also went to Petit Manan National Wildlife Refuge, just a mile from their rental. Although they had earlier said they could not hike with the baby, they decided they were up for an easy three-mile trail that passed through a forest and along more of that stunning rocky coastline. During this hike, Jennifer had Clinton in a carrier she wore on her front.

Little Clinton slept through the hike, and Jennifer did not seem slowed by carrying him, so I told her I was impressed she could hike so well while wearing a baby.

"I carried him all day for nine months, Jeremy," she responded, "This is nothing."

While not trusted with him in motion, I spent some of that weekend holding my newest nephew around the vacation house. When I did, little Clinton always stared at me as if expecting me to perform a task he could not yet verbalize or just crying and wailing. I felt like I was failing the little guy somehow.

Although I now loved spending time with my other two nephews, my other sister's sons Quincy and Alex, I remembered having similar flustered feelings holding them as tiny babies. Being Quincy and Alex's uncle was more fun later when I could play games with them or chat about their interests.

As a side benefit, I can tell entertaining stories that sometimes result from spending time with them.

There was the time I accompanied my sister's family for a tour of Fantastic Caverns in southern Missouri. The tour guide, trying to be funny, asked then-six-year-old Alex if he had a girlfriend. Since a girl of Alex's age was also on this cave tour, I assume the guide's next move would have been whimsically suggesting the pair form a couple. Alex interrupted him in a booming voice and announced, "I am a boy, so I have a *boy* friend." The rest of the tour group laughed uproariously.

There was a time at a restaurant when then three-year-old Quincy was playing "the claw" game where you control a metal hook and try to extract a toy from a pile inside a glass box. After he snagged a toy but lost it, Quincy moaned in disgust, "I dropped the motherfucker."

Clinton was a couple of years from talking well enough to drop a public f-bomb, but he would undoubtedly produce some fun stories someday. Even if he did not, I was now experienced enough as an uncle to know that no matter how much he fussed while I held him on this day, we would likely have more fun together at some point in the future.

TWENTY-ONE
GREAT SAND DUNES NATIONAL PARK

SEPTEMBER 29, 2012

ALTHOUGH GREAT SAND Dunes National Park is only 125 miles southwest of Denver, as the crow flies, I could not find a strong-enough crow to carry me there. Thus, I traveled to that park via a drive in a rental car that took four hours because highways must wind indirectly around Colorado's mighty mountains. I had flown from O'Hare to Denver the day before to start a ten-day trip to seven more National Parks.

Great Sand Dunes is in the San Luis Valley, which contains the Rio Grande's headwaters and sits between sub-ranges of the Rockies called the San Juan and the Sangre de Cristo. The park has a wide variety of terrain, but its primary draw is a series of 700-foot-tall sand dunes, the tallest dunes in the United States. They are so tall that the Gateway Arch in Saint Louis or Seattle's Space Needle could theoretically be hidden under one of them and not poke out the top.

Striking as their size was, it was even more striking how out of place they seemed. There was no surface vegetation here; they were just giant piles of shifting, bare sand. One would expect to see dunes in a desert. At Death Valley, I had seen but did not attempt to hike on 100-foot-tall dunes. Sand dunes had seemed to belong in Death Valley. The Great

Sand Dunes, however, were wedged between some of Colorado's 10,000-foot-plus-high peaks covered with evergreens, yellow-leaved aspens, and white snow caps. If I cast my eyes up, it looked like a ski lodge; if I cast them down, it looked like Tatooine.

Although I later hiked a forested nature trail highlighting other parts of the park, my main goal in Great Sand Dunes was to climb High Dune, the 700-foot sandy behemoth near the main park road. When I approached the dunes from the parking lot, it felt like I was arriving at a beach. Some families were sitting on the flat sand between the parking lot and the dunes on beach towels and wearing bathing suits. Small children played in the sand with plastic buckets, shovels, and other toys. Kids slid down small dunes on purpose-built or improvised sleds, like a boy I saw giddily riding on a flattened pizza box. Changing rooms with showers were located by the lot, so departing visitors could wash away the sand.

Amidst this atmosphere, I felt so out of place in my standard National Park get-up: hiking boots, backpack, and floppy khaki hat. I was also nonplussed when I realized that I would need to choose my own route because there are no trails on the dune. There was no point in building a trail here since wind-driven shifts could bury it in the sand. The laissez-faire approach worked here because, from any point on High Dune or any of the foothills of sand to the east, one could still see the distant parking lot.

The dune's surface was dry this day, so no moisture packed grains together. As each step landed, my foot sunk inches into the sand. Starting my next step required extracting that foot. It felt like 75% of the energy I was expending on this hike extracted my feet from the dune, and only 25% moved me up the dune. The sand suck and thin air at high altitude had me huffing and puffing with a distressing intensity only a short distance into my walk.

Before starting, I stopped at the visitor center and asked a ranger for tips on hiking on dunes. She recommended walking on ridge lines, but this confused me since I assumed "ridge line" meant the top of the dune. She explained that there were undulations and ripples throughout the dune surface. The top of each ripple or undulation in a dune was a ridgeline. She said walking on these would be much easier.

At the start of my hike, I followed this advice, but these lower ridge lines were randomly oriented and did not present a straight path to the top, so staying on ridge lines required me to zig-zag the dune in a manner that, if mapped, would have looked like I was staggering home from a bender. This proved dispiriting as I often walked parallel or sometimes even away from the top of the dune. It was hard to perceive progress that way. The sand at the crest of these little ridges was a little more tightly packed and thus easier on which to walk. This phenomenon only applied at the tippy top of the ridge, so I had to walk tightrope-style, carefully placing each foot to gain any advantage.

After twenty minutes of this, I decided that ridgeline walking was of little utility. It would be easier to charge directly up a slope. This proved a miscalculation. I successfully rumbled up one slope between ridgelines, but I sank deep into the sand and occasionally slipped down the slope, so I arrived at the next little sub-ridge with my heart beating so hard that I had to throw myself down on the dune top to rest.

Once my heart resumed some semblance of normal rhythm, I stayed on ridgelines for the rest of the walk to the top. Even walking that way, climbing to the top of that dune was among the most taxing hikes I have ever done. To enjoy this hike, I realized I would need to take lots of breaks to relax and catch my breath. This proved hard to do because I usually stuff so many trail routes into my park itineraries that I feel driven to finish the hikes swiftly so I can see everything I have planned.

The top of the dune undulated, just like the little lumps and waves of sand below the top. Throughout my hike, I had been aiming for a spot I believed to be the highest point on the dune. Once I finally reached it, however, I looked around me and noticed this was not the highest point after all. To the south of me, I saw a couple also on the top ridge of the dune but at least ten feet higher than me. I sighed and decided this spot was high enough.

I thought I could dispense with ridgeline walking on the trip down and walk directly down bare slopes. Now that I was going down, it would take less energy to walk. This proved to be another miscalculation. I could not get a solid footing in the loose sand. With gravity accelerating me, I slipped once and almost took a tumble. I once again resigned to zigging and zagging on ridgelines and cursed myself for not having the forethought to pack a pizza box.

A better writer could spin metaphorical life lessons from my High Dune experience. The straight-line path is only sometimes the best. Heed advice from those more experienced. It is important to stop and relax once and a while. Choose your goals carefully.

Honestly, the only lesson on my mind as I drove away from Great Sand Dunes that day was that walking up a 700-foot dry pile of sand is a major ass-kicker.

TWENTY-TWO
BLACK CANYON OF THE GUNNISON NATIONAL PARK

SEPTEMBER 30, 2012

THE MORNING after my Great Sand Dunes visit, I woke up at a drive-in movie theater.

When planning my trip, I reserved a room in a Best Western in a small Colorado town called Monte Vista because it was one of the few hotels I found between Great Sand Dunes and Black Canyon. Upon check-in, I learned this Best Western called itself Movie Manor as it was co-located with a drive-in movie theater. The hotel rooms were along one edge of the parking lot in front of the giant movie screen, and each room had a picture window offering a screen view and a built-in speaker that could play the movie's sound. This seemed a delightful concept, but this year's drive-in season had already ended.

In the morning, I drove three hours to Black Canyon of the Gunnison National Park through roads that climbed over some of central Colorado's mighty mountains. Driving up those slopes at any speed often required putting the pedal to the floor, but a gravity boost rapidly accelerated the car as soon as I entered a downward slope. I had experienced a version of this phenomenon driving on hills before, but never to this magnitude. The swiftness of the downhill mountain acceleration took me by surprise several times.

MY NATIONAL PARK DIET

A few miles outside of Gunnison, Colorado, on state highway 114, a well-hidden state trooper, likely aware of this downhill dynamic, caught me at twelve miles per hour over the speed limit on a downslope. After pulling me over, he asked me if I knew how fast I was going and where I was going.

When I told him I was driving to Black Canyon of the Gunnison National Park, the officer's demeanor changed abruptly. He talked excitedly about the place at length and said he was glad I was coming from so far to visit it. He let me go with only a warning and an exhortation to enjoy the park. As such, I have told friends that I owe Black Canyon since it got me out of a speeding ticket. Now that I think about it, I only was pulled over for speeding because I was en route to visiting Black Canyon, so I think we are even.

The last hour of this drive was on a much flatter section of US Highway 50 and paralleled the Gunnison River, which had carved the canyon I was about to visit. The Gunnison had been dammed twice for flood control, creating a lake called the Blue Mesa Reservoir, now an NPS-administered unit called Cuercanti National Recreation Area. The reservoir's wide expanses of sparkling blue water amidst the rocky hills here were quite pretty, but I kept driving for the relatively pristine National Park ahead.

When I entered the National Park and peered into the Black Canyon for the first time, I initially thought it had astonishingly steep walls and an inaccurate name. My assessment of the steepness was spot on. The canyon ranges from 1,800 to 2,700 feet deep both here and on the north side of the canyon. The north side was on the opposite side of the river from which I stood and had an almost straight vertical cliff of bare stone.

My thoughts on the name could have been more apt. I assumed "Black Canyon" meant the canyon walls were made of black rock, but the almost vertical cliffs on the other side of the Gunnison River were mostly gray with occasional pink streaks. I later learned that the canyon was not named for its rock color but for how dark it can be at the canyon bottom, where steep walls prevent the deepest parts of the canyon from receiving sunlight for all but one hour a day.

I had to take the NPS at its word because I went nowhere near the bottom of the canyon. The north walls of the canyon looked so steep in places that I could not imagine anyone getting down it without rappelling. The south rim below me looked a little less imposing as junipers and other evergreen trees were clinging on the steep sides, so it must not be completely sheer. Out of curiosity, I asked a ranger in the Visitor Center if it was theoretically possible to hike to the bottom. She said it certainly was, but it required Class 3 climbing skills. When I asked what that meant, she said it never turned into full-on rock climbing, but you would spend some time on your hands and knees.

Hiking the Oak Flat Trail was strenuous enough for me and left me panting with my hands on my knees near the end. It was only a two-mile round-trip trail, but it descended 400 feet into the canyon from the rim via dispiritingly steep and circuitous switchbacks before regaining that 400 feet via more brutal twists and turns. Aside from the steepness, I remember being most impressed that the loud noise of the turbulent flow of the Gunnison River below was audible to me 2,000 feet above its rough waters.

This National Park is relatively small at 30,000 acres. The canyon is its only major attraction. All my other hikes on this day led to overlooks offering views of the canyon. My favorite was Pulpit Point, where the canyon walls bent, creating a spot where one could look in one direction, and you were standing roughly halfway between the two walls of the canyon upstream. The Painted Wall was the most visually striking part of the canyon, a section of the north wall 2,250 feet tall, making it the tallest cliff in Colorado. Its dark-gray schist wall was interrupted with some diagonal streaks of bright pink pegmatite.

The arid land here received just enough rain to support small deciduous trees on the canyon rim, and since it was fall, the area was awash in red, yellow, and orange leaves, albeit tiny ones. One common tree here was an oak species with leaves no more than an inch long and a half-an-inch wide, which I noted since I spent a considerable portion of my teen years raking six-inch-long oak leaves in my family's one-acre backyard. A park brochure said these small leaves are an adaption that these oaks had developed to deal with a low-precipitation environment since plants lose water through the leaf surface.

That night I slept in a normal hotel without a drive-in movie theater in Grand Junction, Colorado. The next day I made a morning hike in the nearby Colorado National Monument, which protects a canyon with several giant rock formations between its walls, before starting the long drive to Delta, Utah. That small town was where I would spend the night before my next National Park visit. The drive there took me across most of Utah from east to west, mostly on I-70. I was shocked at how sparsely populated the land around this major interstate was. One sign said, "Ranch Exit." The exit did appear to lead to a single ranch.

There were still many cars on the interstate, so I was surprised to pass through multiple 50-mile stretches with no "service," the typical interstate catch-all term for gas stations and restaurants. Eastern interstates have exits every few miles. Virtually all of them frequently have somewhere drivers can fill tanks and stomachs. After this drive on I-70 through Utah, I later chuckled every time I drove I-70 through my native Missouri and saw a sign between St. Louis and Columbia that sternly warned drivers they were about to enter a thirteen-mile section of the interstate without services.

Despite sparsely populated surroundings, I observed the speed limit while driving across Utah. Telling an officer that I had recently driven to Black Canyon of the Gunnison would not get me out of a ticket this time.

TWENTY-THREE
GREAT BASIN NATIONAL PARK
OCTOBER 2, 2012

"IS it okay if the margarita doesn't have alcohol in it?" asked the waitress working my table in the Mexican restaurant across the street from my hotel room for the night in Delta, Utah.

"No, that's not okay," I quickly replied. "Why wouldn't it have alcohol?"

The waitress explained that Utah has restrictive liquor laws. Thus, the restaurant could not serve hard liquor. She could bring me a beer, but one weaker than those sold elsewhere in the US because Utah only allows beer with 3.2% alcohol by weight. I am usually not a big drinker, but I knew I would feel compelled to watch that night's presidential debate between President Obama and Mitt Romney on TV. A stiff drink seemed prudent before listening to politicians. I made do with the weak beer.

Delta only had a population of 3,500 and was one hundred miles from my next park, Great Basin National Park, but I had stayed here because it was the last town I would pass on my drive there from Black Canyon. While I designed most of my trips as loops for maximum efficiency, this one was essentially a line segment. I was heading right back to Utah after I finished in Great Basin and was thus staying in this remote hamlet for two consecutive nights. While eating, I looked at the Yelp app on my phone, trying to find a good place to eat or something interesting to do the next evening after I returned from the park.

Shockingly, Yelp showed Delta had four places classified as Attractions, so I clicked the link. Three were small museums in Delta, but the last attraction on Yelp's list was a place intriguingly called U-Dig Fossils. Saying U-Dig Fossils was in Delta was a stretch since it was 50 miles away, roughly halfway between Delta and the National Park. It was a quarry where visitors could pay to hunt for fossils, most of which were impressions of 500-million-year-old trilobites. The same third-grade geology fascination that prompted my survey of rocks in the hill behind my childhood home also made me dream of hunting fossils. I was finding complete T. Rex skeletons in those fantasies, not marine arthropods, but U-Dig Fossils still sounded fun. I resolved to find some way to do that and the park in one day.

To that end, I left the hotel well before dawn the next morning and drove west on US-50 toward the National Park. Ten minutes past Delta, I saw a road sign that read, "Next Services: 85 Miles." After long stretches without services on I-70 the day before, that was not a surprise, but an hour into the drive, not only had I seen no gas stations, I had seen no signs of human life whatsoever besides a few fences, the road, and power lines. Some distant mountains bordered the seemingly lifeless plain, but otherwise, it was not the most visually stimulating drive.

Eighty-five miles past Delta, I reached the Nevada border and found the promised services: a gas station with an adjacent liquor store and a small casino. The latter two, I assume, owe their business to those seeking a temporary respite from Mormon-influenced Utah liquor and gambling laws. I bypassed the backwater casino and continued driving to Baker, Nevada, the site of the National Park visitor center. It would not be open for more than an hour, so I continued driving to the trailhead for my first planned hike.

Great Basin is the only National Park in Nevada. From informally discussing parks with friends, it is the least well-known of all the parks I visited. This is a shame because it is among my favorites. It contains the oldest trees in the world, the rugged Snake Mountains, a glacier, and a beautiful cave in such a compact area that all could be easily sampled in one day. I had long planned to do just that and now hoped to do so early enough to visit U Dig Fossils on my way back to Delta.

While Baker was on a dry plain at an elevation of 5,300 feet, the scenery changed rapidly once I turned onto Wheeler Peak Scenic Drive, which climbed 4,000 feet up the side of one of those distant mountains I had been seeing via twelve twisty miles. As the road climbed up the mountain, the sparseness of the plains gave way to thick stands of evergreen trees and aspens with their white trunks and yellow leaves.

The road ended at a parking area, the starting point for the Bristlecone Trail, which was named for a pine species common in high-altitude areas of western deserts. The ones in Great Basin National Park are notable because they are extremely long-lived. This fact was brought starkly to light in 1963 when a graduate student at the University of North Carolina named Donald Currey was permitted by the US Forest Service (the area was not yet a National Park) to cut down a tree for research purposes that was believed to be very old and had been nicknamed Prometheus. When the rings in that felled tree were counted, it was 4,862 years old, meaning it was the oldest known living thing on the planet, or it had been just before it met the axe. Since then, even older bristlecones have been found through non-destructive means.

This trail leads to bristlecone pines that were not quite that old but still well over 2,000 years old, meaning they sprouted before the oldest sequoias. I was quite excited to see them, but when I started shivering involuntarily upon stepping out of the car, I realized it was not from excitement but from the chill of high elevation and early morning air. The temperature must have been at least fifteen degrees colder here than when I stepped into the car in Delta. I quickly donned a sweatshirt, a jacket, a hat, and gloves.

The ancient trees were another 600 feet up the mountain. The trail gained that elevation in 1.5 miles of steadily climbing slopes that never felt too tough, but whether through exertion or warming morning temperatures, I soon worked up enough body heat that I stripped off the layers of clothing I had added at the trailhead just a mile into the walk. Here, an interpretive sign explained that some of the evergreen trees were the trail's namesake bristlecone pines but relatively young examples of them. Nothing seemed particularly notable about them—they were just ten- to fifteen-foot-tall skinny pine trees. Another pine species often grew by the bristlecone pines. They looked scarcely different at first. An interpretive sign explained how to tell bristlecones from the other pines along the trail. The easiest way mentioned for me to do that was that bristlecone bristles formed in groups that looked like the end of a bottle brush.

A side loop off the main trail led me into a grove filled with trees more than two thousand years old. These trees looked different than any I had ever seen before, but not because of size. They were significantly wider than the younger bristlecones I had just passed, but they were not much taller. Many were only twenty feet tall, not even big by Midwestern backyard standards.

They looked different because of their shape, form, and condition. Many had trunks utterly bereft of bark, so at first glance, they appeared white but for a few reddish-brown streaks and knots. A few of these trees, though still alive, only had needles on one branch—or even just one part of a branch—and most had at least one large dead branch still attached. All these trees were gnarled with improbable twists and bends as if they had bowed and strained in gale-force winds and froze that way. It looked like a collection of bonsai trees cultivated by sadists.

The two-thousand-year-old sequoias I had seen seemed old because they were huge, and my mind just assumed it must take a long time for something to grow so big. These bristlecones, by contrast, seemed old because of their appearance, as if they were bent and stooped from severe arthritis in their elder years. Of course, their shapes and condition were not necessarily evidence of venerability but an artifact of how they had grown in response to the brutal arid, windy, and cold conditions here on an exposed desert mountain slope. It was a tough life, no doubt, but the bristlecones dominated here because few other trees could handle the brutal climate at this altitude.

An interpretive sign next to one dead tree along the little loop trail indicated it died in the 1700s, but the only visual difference I found between its still-living neighbors was the lack of needles on its extremities. An interpretive sign explained that the tree ages listed on signs here had been determined with dendrochronology—the technical name for establishing tree ages by counting tree rings—that had been performed non-destructively by taking core samples of the tree. For still-living trees, establishing an age this way is relatively straightforward, as the year of the last ring formed is always the current year. I was curious how they established this age for a dead tree and later read that it requires more detective work. Their age can be determined by matching ring-width patterns to the patterns on still-living trees. Those ring width patterns exist due to varying weather conditions since more growth happens in wet years than in dry years.

While admiring these gnarled but hardy, not-so-big, yet immensely old trees, I wondered, how small must those rings be? My best visual estimate of the diameter of one tree, said to be 2,000 years old, was two feet. Since rings were circles, each ring would have to fit in a radius of 12 inches. Mentally dividing 12 inches by 2000, I realized this tree must have an average ring width of 6 thousandths of an inch, roughly the diameter of the thickest human hairs. Bristlecone dendrochronologists must need powerful magnifying glasses.

The Bristlecone Trail ended with the loop that had led to the ancient bristlecones. From there, hikers could continue on the same path, now named the Glacier Trail, for another mile—and another 500 vertical feet past the tree line and ultimately to, unsurprisingly, a glacier.

The maintained trail ended inside a flat area rimmed by a C-shaped ridge topped with jagged, bare stone peaks, dominated by 13,000-foot-tall Wheeler Peak. That floor of the flat area was littered with large chunks of rock, all debris that had fallen from that bare, rocky slope protruding

2,000 feet above or crushed by the glacier when it was larger. At first glance, I saw nothing that looked like a glacier.

There was a pile of snow and ice at the base of the ridge just below that tallest peak, but from this distance, it looked scarcely bigger to me than snow mounds that plows make after clearing Chicagoland parking lots following foot-plus snowstorms. Was that what they were calling a glacier? Walking down the long lane of rock debris toward the snow and ice pile, I gradually saw that it was much bigger than it first appeared. The glacier covered part of the mountain slope. I had not seen that from a distance because the ice held enough rock debris on the surface that its surface had not stood out from the mountain rock. Eyeballing closely, I realized the glacier looked larger than a football field. I later read that it covered almost two acres.

Still, I had envisioned something bigger. "Glacier" conjured images of icy behemoths in Alaska sloughing off icebergs into the ocean. As I stood there staring at this glacier, I realized that for all my previous interest in geology, I had never learned the technical definition of "glacier." I later learned via Wikipedia that a glacier is a mass of snow and ice that never entirely melts and has a sufficient mass that it constantly moves.

Without cell or data service at the base of Wheeler Peak, I had to trust at that moment that the National Park Service knew what they were talking about and that this was a glacier. Whatever it was, this was a beautiful place. I was glad I had come here. It also hit me that I had just completed a 2.5-mile walk with 1,100 feet of elevation gain to a spot nearly two miles above the elevation at my house without once straining for breath. My hiking ability had come a long way.

After an uneventful walk down the same trail, I ate an early lunch in a lovely picnic area next to the trailhead. Then I drove back down the mountain to get a tour of Lehman Caves.

Lehman Caves is a single cave, despite the plural name, and it became part of the National Park system long before the bristlecones and the glacier I had just seen. Discovered in the 1880s, the cave is densely covered in beautiful speleothems and became so popular with tourists that in 1922, President Harding took a brief break from banging his mistress in the White House coat closet to use the Antiquities Act to declare it a National Monument. When an act of Congress formed Great Basin National Park in 1986, Lehman Caves was rolled into the new park.

Tickets and guided tours are required to enter Lehman Caves. I had found the tour schedule online and could have pre-booked a ticket, but I figured I would not need to do so on a weekday out of the main tourist season, so I decided to take a risk to give myself maximum schedule flexibility. After completing my drive down the scenic mountain road, I made a beeline to the National Park visitor center in Baker and asked if tickets were still available for the next tour. I was irritated when the ranger told me Lehman Caves had a separate visitor center, an artifact of when it was its own separate National Monument, and cave tour tickets could only be purchased there.

There was still an hour until the next tour. The ranger assured me it was a light visitation day, so I had little to worry about. She asked what I had done in the park so far. After I mentioned my morning hike, she said this visitor center displayed a cross-section of Prometheus, the aforementioned 4,862-year-old tree that had been cut down in the 1960s. That was something I wanted to see.

The slab was under glass. Little markers had been placed on the wood surface, indicating which growth rings corresponded to various notable historical events. The rings were tiny, so much so that often I could only see them through the magnifying glass that the NPS had placed above one area of the wood. The shape of the tree trunk cross-section was, unsurprisingly, given the gnarled shapes of the live bristlecones I had just seen, not a circle but an elongated irregular oval with a bend in the middle and a couple of wedge-shaped protrusions. The overall shape was roughly that of the side of a fish.

At the Lehman Caves visitor center, I was pleased to learn there were still plenty of tickets available for the next cave tour. Over a 90-minute tour, I saw beautiful examples of the most common cave formations, like stalagmites, stalactites, popcorn, and another formation I could not remember ever seeing before called shields. These were flat, circular formations sticking out horizontally from the cave walls as if someone had thrown a stone Frisbee at the wall so hard that it stuck. Many of these shields had later-formed stalactites handing down from them, leading to a combination formation that looked like a jellyfish or a parachute.

My original trip itinerary for this park included some short hikes, including one along a ditch that had once been dug in the park by 19th Century gold miners. A ditch was not interesting enough for me to forgo fossil hunting, so after emerging from Lehman Caves, I left the park and drove US-50 back into Utah across the same desolate landscape. About halfway back to Delta, I turned left on the ominously named Death Canyon Road, then navigated twenty miles of rough gravel roads to the quarry.

I expected a tourist trap vibe from the website for U Dig Fossils, but upon arrival, I found an empty gravel parking lot, a quarry, a port-a-potty, a trailer, and no people. The trailer had a counter on one side, as a food truck might have. The counter displayed trilobite fossils in a case, a price sheet, a walkie-talkie, and a sign indicating I should call for assistance. I contacted someone with the walkie-talkie. Minutes later, a gruff man arrived on a quad bike. After paying the minimum 28-dollar fossil hunting fee, which bought me two hours in the quarry, I signed a waiver with which I pledged not to sue them if I hurt myself. The man handed me a rock hammer and a bucket and led me to the quarry, where he gave me a terse trilobite hunting demo.

The man then left. I went to work while the quad bike's engine noise faded into the distance. The fossils were in a thick deposit of shale, a sedimentary rock formed from successive mud deposits settling at the bottom of an ancient body of water. Each successive deposit became a distinct, thin layer of shale only loosely bonded to its neighboring shale layers like a noodle in a rock lasagna. Despite the "U-Dig" name, I would not have to do any literal digging here because a rock cut had already exposed the fossil-rich rock layer. Thus, I could easily knock shale chunks off the exposed rock with a rock hammer.

Next, I would split a chunk into two pieces with smooth, flat surfaces by aiming the thin end of the hammer at the interface between two layers. The trilobite fossils were thicker than the rock layers and were made of a harder material than shale, so every time I split a chunk, I found a complete or partial trilobite fossil sticking out of one newly exposed flat face and a negative impression of that trilobite in the other exposed flat face.

Trilobites were bullet-shaped marine arthropods with wide heads, pointy tales, and, most importantly for the hunt at hand, hard exoskeletons that were easily turned into fossils. There were thousands of trilobite species. They were one of the most common life forms on this planet from 500 to 250 million years ago when they died out at the end of the Permian period in a mass extinction. I only knew all of this because, during my geology-obsessed third-grade year, I had once found a fossil trilobite tail in a piece of gravel in the driveway and then read so much about them. Some of the information was still stuck in my brain.

The trilobite fossils that I found were an inch long and gray, so they did not contrast much with the black shale. Once I split a shale layer and found a fossil, I could leave it in the shale chunk with the trilobite sticking out, which is called leaving it in the "matrix." Another option was to pry the entire fossil cleanly out of the shale. I tried both ways. Leaving them in the matrix was the safer approach as I accidentally cleaved some fossils in two trying to free them from the surrounding rock. Then again, the fossils looked more interesting to me out of the matrix, and they would be easier to carry on my flight back to Chicago that way.

During my brief tutorial, the man at the quarry told me that if I wanted to sell my fossils, I should leave them in the matrix because collectors prefer them that way. I wanted to keep mine and had never even considered the possibility of collecting fossils to sell, but purely out of curiosity, I had asked him what money a good trilobite fossil could bring. He said most would only fetch five to ten bucks, but a large example of a rare trilobite species would bring much more. He said one fossil found here had sold for two grand.

After an hour of fossil hunting amidst the black rock of this shade-forsaken quarry, my shirt was soaked in sweat, and a salty puddle had formed under my backside of a sufficient size that I feared might rehydrate this shale quarry into primordial ooze. I had paid for another hour, but my bucket already had more fossils than I could ever pack home, so I quit hunting. I packed my best finds for eventual airline travel using a clean plastic sandwich bag and tissues that I had in my car.

As I finished packing, the same gruff man led a new customer into the quarry, gave him the same cursory lesson, and left. The new customer asked me if I had found anything, so I showed him my packed sandwich bag, then handed him my bucket that was still filled with many broken trilobite fossils that I had decided not to tote home. I told him he was welcome to anything in there that he wanted.

He looked over the bucket's contents, then said, "Those bugs are neat, but I'm just here for dinosaur bones."

"Sorry, no dinosaurs are here," I told him. "This rock is Permian. Dinosaurs evolved in the Triassic, so the first one wasn't a gleam in its predecessor species' eye when these trilobites shuffled off the mortal coil."

"Really?" the man sighed before adding with an indignant tone and no apparent irony, "If this place is going to charge 28 bucks to dig fossils, they should have to put some dinosaur bones in here, too."

TWENTY-FOUR
CAPITOL REEF NATIONAL PARK
OCTOBER 3, 2012

WHILE I PICKED an apple in a century-old fruit orchard in Capitol Reef National Park, a fly landed on my purported insect-repellent shirt. I watched this fly with interest because I was not sure how the shirt repelled insects. Would the fly be irritated and leave? Would it spontaneously combust?

This scene was sowed months before when Wenny Ng, my co-worker and fellow National Park enthusiast, told me she and a friend started selling insect-repellent shirts called Six Legged Tees. Since Wenny had a chemical engineering degree like I did, I initially envisioned her mixing some self-invented chemical concoction in her garage and soaking shirts in it. She assured me the shirts used the common commercial insect repellent permethrin, which was applied to the shirts by a company qualified to do that. Wenny and her friend designed and printed these shirts, sent them for permethrin treatment, and then marketed them.

Intrigued, I ordered one, wanting to support my co-worker's entrepreneurial venture and thinking a shirt that repelled insects could be handy on hikes. My Six-Legged Tee arrived just before this Colorado-Nevada-Utah trip began. I expected few insect issues in the dry desert parks I would be visiting, so I chose to deploy it in Capitol Reef because this park had fruit orchards that I assumed had flies buzzing around.

While watching 150 miles of scrubby vegetation out my windshield while driving from Delta, Utah to the park, I struggled to envision orchards anywhere near this parched place. Once inside the park boundary, the landscape seemed even less conducive to fruit trees because the road was surrounded by a rocky plain ending abruptly at a seemingly endless line of tall red rock cliffs. These were the edge of a monocline, the geological term for an abrupt, stair-like fold in the earth's crust. This 65-million-year-old earth wrinkle is known as Capitol Reef because "reef" was pioneer slang for an impassable ridge. Some white, rounded peaks jutted up above the cliffs here, one of which was thought to resemble the US Capitol building.

My first hour in the park was spent driving east on Utah 24, the park's main highway, and viewing the reef from spots like Panorama Point. The side of the reef often had steep, near-vertical sides with horizontal grooves in them, so they looked like they had been built layer by layer on an enormous, low-resolution 3-D printer. One photogenic section appeared to have columns and was called Cleopatra's Temple.

The park's fruit orchards were a remnant of Fruita, a village founded by early Mormon settlers along the local Fremont River, which facilitated irrigation necessary for a desert town to become a fruit-producing center. The village was eventually abandoned as transportation improved, bringing access to far-flung fruit.

After the area became a National Park, the NPS preserves the orchards and Fruita as a historic area. The old orchard's trees are actively tended, and visitors can pick any in-season fruit growing in the orchards to eat on-site. One of the old village farmhouses is a museum with interpretive exhibits about the domestic and agricultural activities of the Mormon settlers who once lived here. It also sells food and preserves made with local fruit, including some fruit pies that I had read online that were truly amazing.

On one hand, I was trying to lose weight. On the other hand, I love good pies, and how often would I be in Capitol Reef? The latter argument won in my brain. I decided I needed a pie. The websites that had alerted me to the pies indicated they oft sold out early in the day, so I made this my first Fruita stop.

Luckily for my waistline, the pies were only six inches in diameter. Many fruit fillings were available, but I had enough self-control only to eat one and selected an apple pie. While paying, I asked the woman behind the counter if any fruit was still in season for picking. She said everything was gone except some apple varieties and mentioned the most likely spots for picking them.

My mother bakes some truly great pies. I grew up eating hers often. As an adult, I learned to make some of her recipes with decent success. Also, I have a sweet tooth, so I have sampled more than my fair share of pies in restaurants and bakeries. In short, I am a tough judge of pie quality. With the risk of being disowned by my mother, this might have been the best pie I had ever eaten. It was incredible.

Next, I headed into the recommended orchard area seeking an apple to pick. Despite the dry surroundings, the irrigated orchards were lush and green. The area's dry red plains were now beneath thick carpets of grass. Were it not for rocky cliffs visible above the trees, someone could have teleported me here and fooled me into thinking I was at an orchard near Chicagoland offering apple picking for an entry fee every fall.

While seeking an apple to pick, a pesky fly executed several erratic orbits of my torso covered with the alleged insect-repellent Six-Legged Tee. I began to be seriously irritated that this insect-repellent shirt I had purchased was not sufficiently repellent to stop this fly from buzzing around me.

The shirt, however, only claimed to repel insects, not stop them from flying. It did not have an impenetrable force field. I then thought the insect repelling chemical must only keep insects from landing on the fabric, but I then wondered what good was that on a T-shirt? A chemical keeping an insect from nestling on fabric might be valuable on a tent or a sleeping bag in which I was completely ensconced, but this T-shirt covered less than half of my ample anatomy.

The fly then stopped circling and landed on my right sleeve. While I could have shooed it away with the slightest shoulder flick, I remained motionless, wondering if anything would happen to the fly due to it touching the shirt. Nothing happened. It sat there cocking its head and rubbing its front feet together, which I interpreted as its way of mocking the shirt's impotence at insect inhibition. The fly left after only two minutes, but it felt like an hour. I resumed my apple-picking mission, chose a ripe specimen, and stashed it for a later snack since I had just devoured some of its tasty brethren in a pie.

From the orchards, I drove to the parking area for Capitol Gorge, a canyon through the reef. It served as a mountain pass—or reef pass, I guess—and was the route many early settlers used to get to Fruita or other nearby towns. In the 1930s, local communities started trying to attract tourists to see the rocky scenery by calling it "Wayne Wonderland." During that time, they cleared the natural accumulation of boulders and erosion-produced debris in the gorge so it could be used as a scenic road.

The NPS no longer allows driving in the gorge, so I hiked into it. The gorge was not a beauty spot as the walls were not dramatically shaped, just slightly tapered. It was mostly composed of white or tan sandstone that gave it a beige color that was disappointing after the pretty red rock reef. The walls did have human-made decorations of historical interest, including Native American petroglyphs and a section of rock the NPS calls the "Pioneer Register" because Orval Mott, C.F. Brown, and other early Mormon pioneers had scratched their names and the date of their journey into it.

A spur trail inside the gorge led to the top of its walls and waterpockets, depressions in the rock surface deep enough to retain a water pool. Those are common enough here that geologists call this the Waterpocket Fold. It helps a depression retain water in this arid desert if the spot spends part of the day in the shade. The first one I saw was nestled against a rock ledge, shady, and the area housed some small trees. To enjoy the shade on this warm, sunny day, I sat on a rock near the waterpocket to look at it. These pools are used as watering holes by wildlife in this desert, but the water here looked murky and unappetizing. Maybe that is why I had seen no animals in the park besides other tourists and that one Six-Legged Tee defying fly.

TWENTY-FIVE
ARCHES NATIONAL PARK
OCTOBER 4, 2012

NATURAL STONE ARCHES CAPTIVATE ME. I am trying to understand why. It cannot be that all arches on this planet are inherently pleasing to me. I do not swoon at the McDonald's logo. I suspect natural stone arches appeal to me because, perhaps more than any other geological feature, they look like designed, engineered objects despite having resulted from random, chaotic processes of nature.

Whatever the reasons, I loved stone arches. I could not have been more jazzed than to be entering a National Park with so many arches that it was named for them.

Natural stone arches are not all created equal. Some National Parks had rock formations called arches, but they were just eroded holes in cliffs. Those do not excite me much. Much better were arches where the top span is on the periphery of a rocky formation, so it looks like a flying buttress on an old cathedral. However, my favorite arches, by far, were ones where the arch is a completely free-standing structure like someone had driven a croquet wicket into the ground.

The archetype of my favorite arch type is the devastatingly gorgeous Delicate Arch in Arches National Park. Even if you do not know the name, you have likely seen it in photographs or illustrations because Utah uses it as a symbol of the state. For example, it is on Utah license plates and its recent state quarter design.

There is a viewpoint on the main park road from which one can get a decent, though distant, view of Delicate Arch. That was not going to work for me. I needed to see it up close, which required a three-mile round-trip hike that gained 450 feet of elevation on the way to the arch. It was the most popular trail in the park. Several previous visitors to Arches warned me they had struggled to find parking at its trailhead, so I set my alarm very early and started my one-hour drive to the park from Green River, Utah before dawn.

Upon arriving at the trailhead just before 7 AM, I found only two other cars in the parking lot and wondered if the reports of crowds were exaggerated. Since temperatures were predicted to hit 90 in the afternoon, it was still just as well that I was getting started early.

The trek to Delicate Arch was fun in and of itself. The trail passed through an area of almost entirely bare rock of the now familiar reddish Southwestern color scheme. Several smaller arches could be seen along the route. The trail had a perfect balance of being challenging without being draining or dangerous. For most of its length, it was not a trail per se, just a route over bare rock marked by cairns. Careful footing was sometimes required since most of the surface was a thin-grained sandstone nicknamed "slick rock."

As I crested a hill near the trail's end, I saw Delicate Arch slowly revealed from the top down. When I could see the bottom of the arch, I saw a young man and woman reclined against it, making out with gusto. As I tentatively approached the arch, they saw me and apologized in broken English and with an accent that sounded German to my ears. We exchanged pleasantries. I told them no apology was needed and to pretend I was not even there. As I wandered around the arch, I hoped they did not take that last statement too literally.

The couple left shortly after that leaving me alone with the arch. My first view of it had been a partial profile view striking, no doubt, due to its novelty. Once at its base, I stood directly under the arch to say I had. Still, I had yet to catch the perfect postcard view. There was a bowl-shaped area in front of the arch. I walked along it until I found a vantage point at which the arch looked just like it did on Utah's license plate.

While preparing to take a photo in this ideal spot, I realized that Delicate Arch looked like pants.

To clarify, it was not shaped like a neatly folded pair of pants or a worn pair discarded in a limp pile on the floor. It was shaped like a pair of pants with striding, muscular, disembodied legs filling them. As I faced it, the right base of the arch had a clean, continuous taper towards the top. The left base of the arch tapered to a thin spot about halfway up and then tapered back out again. The overall effect was that the right "leg" had just stomped its foot down while the left leg had stepped forward, bent at the knee. That evening, I was disappointed to learn via Internet research that I was not even close to being the first to think of this. Bloomers and Cowboy Chaps had been early nicknames before Delicate Arch became official.

A steady stream of hikers started arriving while I later sat and enjoyed the stunning view. I had just beat the rush. After I hiked back, I found the parking lot full and cars circling, looking for a spot to open. Before surrendering my now in-demand spot, I hiked a short spur trail to some striking Native American petroglyphs depicting a herd of bighorn sheep.

Delicate Arch was my favorite, but it was just the first of many arches I saw that day, many of which were also spectacular. I walked another eight miles that day. All trails led to at least one arch—and usually more. Minor masterpieces included Sand Dune Arch, located in a dune; Broken Arch, which had a crease that made it look cracked; Skyline Arch, located high above the trail on a ridge; two adjacent arches called The Windows; and Turret arch, which had a spire above it that looked like a castle turret. There were many other nice but lesser arches on these trails that I would have gladly hiked well out of my way to see in other parks due to my arch affinity. They barely attracted a second look here with such an embarrassment of riches.

I saw two less famous arches that I rank just behind Delicate Arch in beauty. One was Landscape Arch with a span of 290 feet long that was smoothly rounded throughout. Its stone looked so thin in places that it appeared in imminent danger of snapping, so I wondered if this arch should have been called Delicate.

Double Arch was the other arch I found to be a stone-cold masterpiece. While I had not known its name, I recognized it on sight because it had been a backdrop in the opening sequence of *Indiana Jones and the Last Crusade*. It was two arches of the "flying buttress" type coming from one cliff and meeting in a single central column on the other side. Myriad people lounged beneath its span in its relatively cool shadow. They first looked like ants as I approached this gorgeous 100-foot-tall wonder.

My final hike was through Park Avenue, a valley flanked by a cliff topped by towering sandstone fins that would look like a New York skyline if it had been in the sun too long. Although most were less picturesquely situated than those in Park Avenue, I had seen many other sandstone fins throughout the park.

On my way out of the park, I stopped in the Visitor Center, and exhibits indicated these fins were the arches' genesis. My fuzzy understanding of the process is that bulging underground salt deposits below split sandstone rock into these fins. The sandstone here is porous and has its sand grains cemented together with acid-soluble calcite. Like the process that can open a cave, water can absorb chemicals that make it acidic, seep into the rock, and dissolve calcite from the sandstone. Eventually, this weakens and cracks the bottom of the fins, which can eventually cause openings large enough to turn the fin into an arch. The large boulder piles beneath many of the arches I had seen were remnants of this process.

That weathering process does not stop when the arch is formed. Erosive forces keep attacking it, and when enough rock falls out of the hole, the span that tops the arch cannot support itself, and it collapses. When I had stood beside Landscape Arch and thought it looked like it could snap, I assumed that must be poetic fancy on my part. I now learned that it was not at all far-fetched. Three times since 1991, huge chunks of rock—one 70 feet long—fell from Landscape Arch's span. Visitors were once allowed to hike under it but now must stay behind a fence well behind it. More dramatically, in 2008, an arch named Wall Arch fully collapsed, sending thousands of tons of rock crashing to the ground.

Some people promote National Parks as timeless landscapes, but that phrase sounds off to my ears because it makes them sound static. These parks are dynamic environments changing with time. Trees die. New trees sprout. Mountains and canyons are slowly eroded. Volcanos are dormant for ages then erupt. Those changes are slow to happen or entirely unexpected, so they are only sometimes top of mind. Dynamism is more tangible in Arches since these stone stunners are nearer the end of their time than the beginning.

Arches National Park is one of my favorite National Parks, so I strongly recommend you visit it. The arches will probably still be there whenever you get around to going, but you might want to go sooner than later, just in case.

TWENTY-SIX
CANYONLANDS NATIONAL PARK
OCTOBER 5, 2012

MESA ARCH in Canyonlands is a free-standing arch with an opening long in span but with a height so short it looked like a bow—the arrow-firing kind—pointed at the sky. The arch was pretty and worth a walk, but it would not have cracked my top ten favorites in Arches National Park. It was still a pretty arch in the Islands of the Sky district of Canyonlands, but I was surprised to see many people photographing it before 7:30 AM.

Arriving early is one way I maximized my days in National Parks. My arrival time to any park varied, but I tried to arrive at each before 8 AM to take full advantage of the available daylight and because most parks were nearly deserted until 10 AM. Often, the entrance stations were not yet staffed when I drove into a park, and on my first hike of the day, if the trail went through woods, I took multiple spider webs to the face, meaning I was the first person—or at least the first person of my height —to traverse it that morning.

Mesa Arch was my first planned stop in Canyonlands. Since I had spent the previous night in nearby Moab, Utah, I arrived at its parking area at sunrise. The short trail to the arch was quiet, but I soon found a big gaggle of serious-looking photographers with expensive-looking cameras on tripods pointed at the arch.

What distinguishes Mesa Arch is that it sits atop a mesa cliff edge, so if you look down through it, you see into a deep canyon dotted with towering rock spires like those I had seen in Monument Valley. Photographers with good equipment and skills can get shots of those towering formations framed in the arch's curve. Serious photographers who are early risers like to get that shot with the sun rising into it, creating a sunburst effect. That was the aim of the crowd I found this early morning at Mesa Arch.

As I went to more parks, I was increasingly ruing that I had never taken time to truly learn photography since there were so many amazing things to photograph. Nonetheless, I took oodles of photos and occasionally produced a great one just by dint of the amazing locale and luck, not through any skill on my part.

Photos and writing notes had always been my primary means of documenting my time in a National Park. Sometime after I started my project, I learned many fellow park aficionados instead documented their progress through the system with National Park passports. These books sold in park souvenir stores have pages for each of the 400-plus sites run by the NPS, not just the National Parks. At each site's visitor centers, visitors can mark their passports with a rubber stamp indicating they have been to that spot.

Learning I was visiting National Parks but not filling out a passport book drove some fellow park aficionados nearly to apoplexy, but I was unmoved and stuck to photographs. I still took photos of myself in the park using the camera's timer. Since my camera took that nasty tumble at Guadalupe Mountains National Park, I started carrying a six-inch-tall tripod, so my new camera was less likely to fall. The tripod had bendable legs, so I could wrap it around part of a bench or a tree branch.

I would also take pictures of notable features of the park, keenly aware this was a little pointless as Ansel Adams and scores of other photographers had already captured these places in images far better than any I could ever produce with my meager equipment or skills.

Every night after a park visit, I would sit in my hotel room poring over pictures I had taken and post my favorites to Facebook. I had never done much on social media before my National Park trips began. I had found the whole concept silly. Many old quiz bowl teammates and friendly rivals at that game were early adopters of Facebook, so it became a means to keep in touch with them and other acquaintances with whom I would likely have otherwise lost contact. However, I mostly wanted to know their major status changes in life—when they moved, changed jobs, married, or had children—I found it frustrating that I could not filter these posts from posts about their political musings or pictures of pasta they made for dinner.

Whether my National Park photos were more interesting than a friend's pasta photos is debatable, but my park photos still generated more likes than anything I ever posted. As such, I found myself getting excited by "likes" but then feared that was pathetic. While fussing with my camera to get a better shot of a National Park beauty spot, I would wonder if I were spending time that way because I truly wanted a better picture or because I was subconsciously hoping a better picture would generate a few more thumbs-up symbols. I assuaged my concerns that I was addicted to likes by writing a commentary on the park and its attractions with my pictures, hoping that I was thus promoting the park as much as myself.

A perfect Mesa Arch shot with the sunrise shining through its opening might have generated a big like from my friends, but the good arch-photographing real estate was already taken by the early-rising serious photographers, and I did not have the skills or filters to get a good sunburst photo. As such, I retreated from Mesa Arch with the intent to return later. This had been my first stop since it was the most famous place in this unit of the park, but I was sure there had to be other less crowded wonders for me to find.

Canyonlands is 337,000 acres of sparsely vegetated, red rock desert southwest of Moab, Utah carved into an intricate maze of canyons by the Colorado and Green Rivers, which meet in the park. The park has three developed areas with visitor centers, campgrounds, and front-country trails that are close together as the crow flies. However, because the roads must wind around complex topography created by the maze of rivers and canyons, driving from any of these units to another takes hours behind the wheel.

As such, I eschewed the more remote and lower-elevation Needles and Maze districts and stuck to Island in the Sky, the district nearest Moab. Most trails I walked led to the top of cliffs on the edge of the mesa that gave Island in the Sky its name. From these cliffs, I saw breathtaking vistas of the lower elevation parts of the park, where canyons were nested into each other like bowls with telescoping bottoms. In places, there were four levels. I would be standing on a mesa looking down on the rim of a wide canyon with steep, sheer, bare stone walls. Those would end in a "floor," into which had been cut a narrower canyon, which had a narrower canyon cut into it. Finally, a narrow slot canyon was only a few feet wide at the bottom of it.

The widest canyons between mesas also held tall buttes with broad bases and spindly pinnacles like those in Monument Valley, but none were as memorably shaped as The Mittens. Most slot canyon bottoms appeared dry from this high vantage point, but I saw washes where water could travel whenever there was water to travel. The canyons appeared lifeless from here; it was just a symphony of ochre-colored bare rock except for the canyon surrounding the Green River, which was fringed with a vibrant green band.

Once I worked longer than I would care to admit trying to get a photo of me where the rim of the top edge of the canyon was below the picture's edge. Doing that would make me appear to be floating over the lower rims in the picture. One of the best views I saw was of White Rim Canyon. That canyon's top had a white-colored, scalloped rim that helped visually distinguish that layer from the ones above and below it.

I looked away from the magnificent canyons at times. I hiked up Whale Rock, a long, rounded sandstone formation atop a mesa. I heard a ranger describe the history of uranium mining in this area before it became a park. I went to a viewpoint offering a peek into Upheaval Dome, a 3-mile wide crater with some rock layers splayed upwards. It looked to my untrained eyes like an impact crater. An NPS sign said that a meteor strike was one hypothesized cause, but another was a massive shift in a subterranean salt layer.

My last stop in the park was a return to Mesa Arch. I took time to sit and look at the famed spot before taking photos, all of which proved to be awful. Although I could see the majestic monoliths below the arch with the naked eye, I never captured the full extent of the arch and the canyon floor below in a single photo. The glorious images still linger in my mind, though, which is the most important thing.

TWENTY-SEVEN
ROCKY MOUNTAIN NATIONAL PARK
OCTOBER 6, 2012

"IT'S FREEZING UP HERE," said a shivering woman in a family group that, like me, was walking the Tundra Communities Nature Trail 12,000 feet above sea level in Rocky Mountain National Park.

"I know. Who would have thought a tundra could be cold?" I asked snarkily, getting a well-deserved withering look in return.

Admittedly, I had not realized a tundra would be so cold this day. Since I was primarily hiking in Utah and Nevada deserts on this trip, I had not expected temperatures below 40°F in October, even in the Rockies, so I had not packed a winter coat. Thus, on this day, I had a leather jacket, a sweatshirt, and yet another shirt layered atop the shirt in which I had left the hotel that morning.

This National Park was not so chilly in its most popular areas at relatively lower elevation areas near Grand Lake on the west side of the park and Estes Park on the east, but I wanted to see the high country without working too hard. Thus, I drove up the amazing Trail Ridge Road.

The National Park Service claims Trail Ridge Road is the highest continuously paved road in the world. There must be some taller, only intermittently paved roads somewhere to necessitate the "continuously" qualifier, but whatever the case, Trail Ridge snakes through the Rockies until it climbs well above the tree line, topping out 12,100 feet above sea level. That a road of any type reaches those heights is amazing enough, but what is truly astonishing is that this well-paved road reaches such dizzying and oxygen-depriving heights and yet can easily and safely be driven in a standard car.

That said, a standard car can only be safely driven if the road is clear of snow or ice. At 12,000 feet, a road clear of snow and ice is virtually impossible outside of summer and early fall. Thus, the road is usually closed two-thirds of the year. As always, I had done my research and read that Trail Ridge Road was usually open roughly mid-June to late October, so I expected no issues accessing it during my early October trip.

While spending the night in Eagle, Colorado the night before I visited Rocky Mountain, I perfunctorily checked a Colorado road status website, which said Trail Ridge Road was closed due to snowfall. Crushed by the news, I started making a backup plan, but in the morning, the road was open again, so I made the two-hour drive to the western end of Trail Ridge Road, hoping it would not close again before I got there.

The previous day's snowfall had been completely cleared, so the road was open when I arrived. The only hazard I found was elk. The hazard was not the elk themselves but other drivers slamming on the brakes upon seeing an elk standing within eyesight of the road, stopping in the road, and taking a picture. Elk are magnificent creatures, but they were so prevalent in the park that unsafe stopping distances and using a two-lane mountain road as a parking lot hardly seemed justified. For example, at one point in the trip, I pulled into a picnic area to stretch and have a snack and found half a dozen elk grazing around the tables.

The name of Rocky Mountain National Park is presumptuous since the Rockies stretch for 3,000 miles across three countries, and several other National Parks are also located in the Rockies. This National Park protects just one small section of the Rockies in north-central Colorado. That being said, what a magnificent section it is. The 260,000-acre park contains 72 peaks over 12,000 feet tall. Its mighty Longs Peak is one of Colorado's "fourteeners."

As the road climbed into thin air at 12,000 feet, I stopped at many scenic turn-outs where I could see a sub-range called the Never Summer Mountains. They provided a clear demonstration of the term tree-line, the elevation above which trees cannot grow. From the road's vantage point, it was easy to see the sharp delineation between the dark green of the conifer forests and the light gray of the treeless mountain tops.

Near the road's highest point is the Alpine Visitor Center, which has exhibits about life above the tree line and was the starting point for the Tundra Communities Trail. Before this trip, I associated the word "tundra" only with the Arctic and Lambeau Field, but strictly speaking, the term means a biome cold enough that trees do not grow. This was specifically an alpine tundra since elevation, not latitude, was primarily responsible for the conditions preventing tree growth.

While walking this one-mile trail, I saw that despite a lack of trees, there was still plenty of life. The soil was covered with scrubby grasses and other short plants, which were now golden brown since the short growing season here had already passed. There were no signs of the tiny wildflowers that the visitor center briefly mentioned that brilliantly bloom here in summer. Those exposed rocks were covered with lichens and mosses ranging in colors from dull gray to rust orange to highlighter yellow. The trail also passed Mushroom Rocks, a cluster of rock formations composed of a layer of white granite below dark brown schist. The granite was eroding faster than the schist, causing them to look like mushrooms with dark, relatively wide "caps" on thinner, white "stems."

Some small, fuzzy creatures called pika do eke out a living here. A pika chews down grass during the brief warm stretch, eats some, and stores more grass in holes to eat during a brutal winter. I read the holes stocked by each pika, when combined, have the volume of a human bathtub. I saw a pika, a "cousin" of rabbits not much bigger than a hamster, while walking the trail. They are, according to a park interpretive sign, the "farmers of the tundra."

After finishing at the Alpine area, I continued driving east on Trail Ridge Road, and the pretty blue skies I had seen all day suddenly were dark with clouds. It started snowing at a pretty good clip, not enough to make driving difficult even on this twisty alpine road, but an October snow this hard was enough to impress even a Chicagoland resident. Fearing road conditions could eventually get treacherous, I stopped dawdling and stopping at turn-outs and just drove steadily down to the east end of the road from this point.

On its east side, Trail Ridge Road terminates in a valley near the town of Estes Park. The snow stopped once I reached this spot. I spent the rest of my time in the park walking short trails in the area, getting some cloud-obscured views of 14,000-foot-tall Longs Peak in the process. The most memorable trail passed through an area strewn with massive boulders that had been propelled there by a violent flood in the 1990s that resulted from the failure of a dam that predated the National Park.

As I neared the park exit, I saw a nearly full parking area. In front of it, many people had set up cameras on tripods with huge lenses in a scene reminiscent of what I had seen at Mesa Arch the day before. I could see no obvious attraction to photograph here, just a grassy plain and two small ponds. A sign at the parking area said the area was Sheep Lakes. Curious, I parked, exited the car, and asked a gentleman what he hoped to photograph. He indicated this was a good place to photograph bighorn sheep because they come here to drink out of the ponds here every afternoon.

Swiveling my head, I saw no sheep anywhere in visual range, and I did not have the patience or outerwear necessary to stand for some unspecified length in this cold waiting for bighorn sheep. Thus, I bid good day to the man who had kindly answered my question, returned to my car's warm interior, and exited the National Park. Passing through Estes Park, I saw eight bighorn sheep standing on a patch of grass in town. Apparently, no one had told them they had an appointment at Sheep Lakes.

TWENTY-EIGHT
CONGAREE NATIONAL PARK
NOVEMBER 10, 2012

LOUD RUSTLING STARTLED me as I hiked through the forested swamp that is South Carolina's Congaree National Park. It sounded like a large animal had been running through the forest and stopped just before reaching a spot on the trail fifty feet in front of me. I froze and tensed. Could it be a bear?

Several parks I had visited had bear populations, but I had always thought the chances of me seeing one were only slightly less remote than encountering a unicorn. Since seeing two bears while driving in Redwood, seeing a bear no longer seemed implausible. I had been on edge about encountering one since then.

My pre-trip readings never mentioned any bears in Congaree. The only animal warnings I saw for this park were about its epic mosquito swarms. The winged bloodsuckers get so bad around this park's swampy waters that there was a sign at the visitor center with a dial indicating the current level of mosquito activity, with settings ranging from "All Clear" to "War Zone." I selected this weekend for my Congaree trip partly because the park's website indicated November was usually not a problem time for mosquitos, and as predicted, the dial was at "All Clear" during my visit.

MY NATIONAL PARK DIET

No amount of mosquito activity could have made the noise in the brush that I had just heard, so my thoughts returned to bears. Even if bears were not typical in Congaree, Great Smoky Mountains National Park—the other park I would be visiting on this trip—most definitely had black bears and was only 200 miles away. Even if Congaree was not normal bear habitat, it was not unthinkable that one had ranged here.

On the other hand, I knew the noise was more likely to have been made by a deer or a well-fed raccoon. Also, I was barely a mile from the visitor center, so a visitor's Labrador retriever could have gone off-leash. I decided I was being paranoid and resumed walking.

That is when a large pig ran across the trail and bounded into the brush on the other side. Had I just seen a pig in a National Park?

Even before that incongruous image, my day in Congaree felt slightly different than my other National Park visits. Typically, I spent the day driving park roads to one trailhead, hiking the trail, driving to the next trailhead for the next hike, and so on, until I had done all the various hikes I had planned. In Congaree, virtually the whole trail system branched out from a single visitor center, so I parked the car once and spent the rest of the day on foot. I had planned a five-mile hike in the morning, a return to the visitor center for lunch, and a second five-mile hike in the afternoon.

My pig encounter was near the end of my first hike. Once I arrived back at the visitor center, I went inside and asked the ranger at the desk, "Am I going crazy, or did I just see a pig on the trail?"

"I am not qualified to diagnose you psychologically," she replied with a smirk, "but it is quite possible you saw a pig." The park ranger proceeded to expound upon the park's problematic porcine population. These were feral pigs that had escaped from farms or the offspring of such escapees. In addition to startling nerdy tourists like me, they were doing lasting damage to park vegetation because pigs root into the ground with their snouts. The ranger said the NPS was researching their impact and taking steps to control the park's population of profligate porkers.

The trails nearest the visitor center were on elevated boardwalks several feet above the forest floor. The swampy terrain in the park is in the floodplain of the Congaree River, so elevated boardwalks ensure visitors can usually see at least some of the area during periods of flooding, which are frequent here. Past the boardwalks, the trails were packed earth paths at ground level in the bottomland forest near the area's creeks, lakes, and swamps. The ranger in the visitor center had mentioned that the water level here on this day was about as low as it ever gets, but there were sizable pools of water and thick mud just off the trail.

Congaree is one of the newest National Parks. While forests in the surrounding area were heavily logged in the mid-twentieth century, the swampy terrain here meant it was relatively difficult to log. Thus, this parcel stayed in a pristine state long enough for locals in the 1970s to initiate conservation efforts that saved these old-growth trees from becoming furniture or lumber yard inventory. Congaree became a National Monument in 1976 and was "promoted" to being a National Park by Congress in 2003.

The trees were numerous, and their leaves formed a dense canopy. My pre-trip reading had indicated that this park was one of the few areas of virgin old-growth timber in the south, so I had expected to see some giants. Nothing sequoia sized, of course, but I thought I might see trees many feet in diameter and over 200 feet tall. Instead, most of the trees were downright skinny, but some of the conifers here, loblolly pines, according to the interpretive signs, did reach lofty heights above 150 feet.

While there are many other tree species here, the species making the biggest impression on me were the bald cypress. Their trunks usually had a wide, flared-out bottom that tapered quickly to a thin, cylindrical main trunk. They were surrounded by "knees," woody cones sticking up vertically from their roots. Scientists do not know for certain the purpose of these trees' knees. Some think they provide structural support in the soft, muddy ground. Others think knees help them absorb oxygen during floods. Whatever the case, I thought the many cypress knees made the forest floor look a little like a cave floor, except with the stalagmites made of wood instead of dissolved limestone.

The leaves above me were ablaze in autumnal colors, with yellow predominant and orange, red and brown leaves providing accents. It was a gloriously sunny day, but the thick forest canopy often kept the sun from reaching the trail, so I often walked in deep shadows amidst the black water and cypress knees while the yellow leaves above glowed brilliantly in the sunlight. Many trees had stringy Spanish moss hanging off branches, making the trees look like they had grown gray hair. These all combined to give the place an enchanted forest vibe like something in a fairy tale or fantasy novel, so I half expected to encounter Hobbits on a quest or seven whistling dwarves making their daily commute.

About halfway through my afternoon hike, I reached the banks of Wise Lake and sat on the trunk of a downed tree by the water's edge. Mostly, I wanted to rest my feet, but Congaree has a population of river otters. I hoped if I sat still by the water awhile, I might get lucky and see one. After fifteen minutes, I saw something long and fuzzy splash into the water across the lake from me and swim out of sight. I have chosen to believe that furry blur was an otter, but honestly, it was far enough away that it could have been a muskrat, a beaver, or even the rat equivalent of Michael Phelps, for all I know.

After finishing my second hike, I returned to my car and exited the park. Minutes later, I approached Columbia, South Carolina. I found myself in a giant traffic jam at the junction for the interstate that I needed to enter. I whimsically wondered if another feral pig was blocking traffic. While scanning local radio stations, I learned I had haplessly driven into the mass exodus of cars following a University of South Carolina football game.

A pig had not stopped me this time. Pigskin had.

TWENTY-NINE
GREAT SMOKY MOUNTAINS NATIONAL PARK
NOVEMBER 11, 2012

TEN MILLION PEOPLE visit Great Smoky Mountains National Park every year, making it the most visited National Park. Media citations of its visitation figures are often paired with the factoid that two-thirds of the nation's population lives within a day's drive of it. This implies that high visitation owes more to location than its natural features.

This is true to some extent. The Smoky Mountains have nothing so breathtakingly beautiful as Yosemite or the Grand Canyon. These mountains top out a mile above sea level, so they are tiny bumps compared to the mighty peaks in the western National Parks. Great Smoky Mountains National Park's main draw is that it is an enormous wilderness in the eastern part of the country, where wilderness is an anomaly.

This is not to say the park has nothing to offer. It has many rivers and creeks—most with one or more waterfalls, hundreds of miles of hiking trails—many leading to stunning panoramic views on mountain tops, and one of the most biologically diverse temperate forests on earth. The NPS website says 17,000 individual species have been documented here, including an astonishing 100 different tree species.

To enter the park from the west, I had to first bypass the tourist trap in Gatlinburg, Tennessee, a miles-long sprawl of souvenir shops, kitschy museums, and amusement parks that stops at the park boundary. Once inside the park, I was surprised that there was no entrance station. Some smaller National Parks do not have entrance stations, so you are supposed to pay your entry fee or show your pass at a Visitor Center.

Assuming that was the case here, I dutifully stopped at the first visitor center past the entrance and reported to its front desk with my park pass in hand. The man at the desk gruffly snapped, "This is a free park; you don't need that. I will stamp your hand if it makes you feel better."

Because most folks working in National Parks are so over-the-top friendly, his snarky tone was a surprise, but as a congenital smartass, I begrudgingly respected his patter. Because I am a cheapskate, I would ordinarily be thrilled to hear entry was free, but since I started spending eighty bucks a year on a National Park pass, I now felt cheated.

A waterfall named Laurel Falls just miles from that visitor center was the goal of my first hike, which required only a 2.5-mile round-trip walk from a roadside parking area via a paved trail, but the trail gained 300 feet of elevation on the way up. Laurel Falls was eighty-feet-tall and quite picturesque, with a small creek free-falling down a few feet over the very top of a cliff and then splitting into two gentle white cascades beautifully contrasted against the cliff's dark rock.

My main route for the day was driving highway US-441 through the middle of the park from Gatlinburg to Cherokee, North Carolina. This is the road most used to access some of the park's famous attractions. While driving the road, I stopped at several of its turn-outs to gaze at expansive mountain views, which were now enhanced with fall colors. While leaves appeared to be at peak levels of color during my visit to Congaree the day before, I seemed to be catching the tail end of fall colors here. Nonetheless, there were still plenty of reds and yellows in the foothills and on the lower reaches of the mountains. The tallest mountains had an almost banded appearance with warm autumn colors at the bottom, green conifers at the top, and the grays of deciduous trees that had already shed their leaves in the middle.

My longest planned hike that day was Alum Cave Trail, an in-and-back trail 4.5 miles long with 1,100 feet of elevation gain on the way up. It initially paralleled the Little Pigeon River, which was flowing quite energetically as a snowfall from the previous week melted. The trail then ascended a slope, and during this section, much to my delight, it passed right through the middle of a small stone arch called Arch Rock.

Finally, the trail reached the namesake "cave," which was not truly a cave but a one-hundred-foot-tall rocky bluff with a concave-shaped wall that meant one could stand at the bluff's base with a "shelf" of rock above your head. Despite standing directly under the cover of this rock shelf, I twice felt a splash of water hit the top of my head, and I looked up, puzzled to find the source. At the top of the bluffs, steady dribbles of water originating with melting snow on the rock atop the bluff were pouring over the shelf. On the way down, the water was blown to and fro by the afternoon's steady winds. The winds were swirling enough while I was there that the falling water changed stream directions so abruptly and erratically that it looked like giants were standing atop the bluffs urinating their names onto the trail below.

Sadly, when I think back on this hike, I remember most clearly not the surroundings but that I had to keep stopping every few hundred feet to pull my jeans upward. This annoyance was in part due to the bottom of the legs of these jeans becoming heavy with melted snow, but even more so, it was due to my insistence on wearing jeans that were too big. I had dropped thirty pounds at this point in my project, but ever a cheapskate, I was still trying to wear the 54-inch waist pants I had been wearing before I lost the weight. Doing so required repositioning them significantly, as I had previously worn my pants with the top tucked under my gut. With my new, slightly slimmer dimensions, my old pants were large enough to fit over the widest extremity of my abdomen, somewhere above my belly button.

MY NATIONAL PARK DIET

Wearing 54-inch jeans like this with a belt cinched as tight as possible had worked fine in sedentary situations, but during this hike, my pants would slowly slip down until they reached a point of no return at the bottom of my gut and then enter a free fall that required me to stop and pull them up lest I give someone an unwelcome view of my underwear. I was wearing a button-down shirt this day, so I tried to give myself a little more safety margin before semi-indecent exposure by untucking the shirt's tail.

The high point of my Smoky visit, quite literally, was my visit to Clingmans Dome. A seven-mile, winding road can take park visitors from highway 441 to a spot near the top of this 6,643-foot-elevation peak, the tallest both in the park and in Tennessee. Clingmans is the second-highest mountain in the Appalachians and, thus, the second-highest point east of the Mississippi. The two tallest mountains east of the Mississippi are both in a North Carolina state park and only top Clingmans by a mere one hundred feet.

While my ascent of Clingmans Dome was made almost entirely behind the wheel of my rental car, the final approach to the summit required leaving the car and walking a crowded and quite steep half-mile trail from the parking lot at the end of the road. At the top of the mountain, there was a large spiral walkway leading up a hideously ugly concrete observation tower, but the commanding, panoramic view of the Smokies available atop this tower made up for its aesthetic shortcomings.

My last stop in the park was to an old 19th Century grist mill near the highway, which had been built by people who had lived here before it was a park. It had a large wooden paddlewheel in a stream that turned the mill, which had been used to process grain. The whole building was now open for park visitors to tour. In addition to its historical value as an example of early American agricultural industry, this mill was a reminder that this National Park is a place that had been home to many people before it became a National Park.

Western National Parks were primarily created by re-classifying unsettled land owned by the federal government. By contrast, most eastern

National Parks required displacing residents living on those lands before the park was created.

Making the Great Smoky Mountains a National Park required displacing many unwilling-to-leave subsistence farmers from plots of land that their families had worked for several generations. The effort to make the area a park began in the early 1900s when logging companies bought large parcels of the Smokies and clear-cut forests so rapidly that conservation-minded locals feared the area would never recover.

Conservationists and area boosters who saw a National Park as a potential economic benefit convinced Congress in 1926 to pass a law allowing the creation of a Great Smoky Mountains National Park. However, the federal government would not purchase any land for it. The law only allowed the government to accept land donations into the park. It was up to private citizens or state governments to acquire the land.

A local fundraising effort netted a million dollars in small donations. The Rockefellers donated five million. A committee used these funds to buy Smokies land. Many sold willingly. A few who did that were even given leases allowing them to live on their land until their death after selling. However, many refused to sell, so the states pursued legal condemnation of some of the hold-outs that ended in forcible eviction. In total, 1,200 residents of the Smokies were relocated. The grist mill I saw was one of seventy buildings in the park today, mostly of log construction, that survive from the area's pre-park days.

A popular area on the park's western side, called Cades Cove, has many of these remaining buildings. I did not visit it on this first trip, but I have seen it subsequently during a later visit. This little valley is filled with charming houses, tiny churches, another grist mill, and cantilevered barns. These are interesting historical relics, but also a reminder that many lives were displaced to make this park.

This dark side of the park's history made me morosely think of "Uncle Frank," even though I do not have an Uncle Frank. That is a song by a favorite band of mine named Drive-By Truckers. Their songs often examine the complicated history and culture of the American South. "Uncle Frank" has lyrics describing an illiterate Alabama resident who "never held down a job or needed one in his life" because he used his army pay to buy "fifteen rocky acres he thought nobody else would want" and eked out a living there with subsistence farming and cutting timber. However, Uncle Frank's land is later taken from him by eminent domain so the TVA can build a dam that floods the property with a reservoir. In the last verse, Uncle Frank commits suicide, depressed over the loss of his property and unable to cope with life in a city.

Of course, another Drive-By Truckers song called "TVA" praises the construction of the same dam for creating economic opportunities and recreational activities for the region's many residents. As the band says in a different song, "Such is the duality of the Southern thing."

Like many things in American history, creating this park represents a duality: a conflict between individual rights and collective, national good. I tried to put myself in the mindset of those displaced Smokies residents. Would I enjoy this park so much if I knew the owner of this mill or a Cades Cove resident had been forced out and had a similar end to that of the fictional Uncle Frank?

As I walked from the grist mill back to my parked rental car, I saw other visitors intently watching something on the ground. Intrigued, I approached and saw them staring at a bright red salamander crossing the path at a steady but slow speed. I was delighted to have caught a glimpse of one. The Smokies have a huge variety of salamander species, so this range is called the "salamander capital of the world." This cute little red amphibian was a reminder of the incredible biodiversity that was likely saved by the creation of this park.

Thus, overall, I was delighted this park exists, but the story of Great Smoky Mountains National Park is incomplete without acknowledging those displaced to create it.

THIRTY
BISCAYNE NATIONAL PARK
JANUARY 20, 2013

BECAUSE "MACARENA" played as the Fort Lauderdale airport's baggage claim began turning, I feared my flight had traveled not just from Chicago to Florida but back in time. My cell phone screen still thought it was 2013, so I dismissed the notion, grabbed my checked bag once it was dropped, and left for my hotel.

Although the purpose of my trip was to visit the two National Parks near Miami, I had flown into Fort Lauderdale because flights here were two hundred dollars less than flights to Miami on this weekend for whatever reason, and it only added thirty miles of driving. My hotel for the weekend was in Homestead, a suburb of 60,000 south of Miami nestled between the two parks.

Biscayne, the first park on my itinerary, includes small islands east of Miami that are the northernmost of the Florida Keys and a mainland visitor center. Its primary mission is protecting an ocean area with coral reefs and grassy sea floors that support a wide array of marine life. Because my primary activity at National Parks had always been hiking, I was befuddled about how to experience Biscayne when planning my trip.

MY NATIONAL PARK DIET

A Jetty Trail at the visitor center was just a dock extending one-third of a mile into the bay so visitors could fish from it. Thus, it was hiking a trail just in name. There were also short hiking trails on some of the park's diminutive islands, but one had to get to the islands via boat to hike on them.

The NPS had an officially designated concessioner with offices and a dock by the Visitor Center. They offered several options to get out into the watery portion of the park, including a glass-bottom boat tour, a snorkeling tour, and a trip to one of the small islands, Boca Chita Key. Weeks before my trip, I pre-booked a glass-bottom boat tour ticket. I wanted to see the coral reefs but was leery of snorkeling since I had never done that before. I was not sure my maiden snorkeling voyage should be far out in ocean waters.

Two days before my flight, the concessioner called to tell me that the glass bottom boat had mechanical issues, so that trip was canceled. I could either switch to another tour or accept a refund. Still nervous about snorkeling, I transferred my ticket to the Boca Chita Key option, as it at least included a place to hike.

The morning of my visit, I boarded the concessioner's boat along with roughly thirty other people. Most, I soon learned, were not going to Boca Chita, but snorkeling because this boat was doing double duty. It would drop off those going to Boca Chita Key first, take the rest snorkeling, and then pick up those on the island while returning to the mainland after the snorkeling was done. The only other tourists on the boat going to Boca Chita Key were a family of four from South Carolina who had a goal to visit all the National Parks. They had been to nineteen parks, so we spent part of the ride comparing notes.

Upon reaching the island, the South Carolina family, a concessioner employee, and I disembarked the boat next to a campground filled with folks clearly in the park to party. Loud music blared from boat-based stereos while scantily clad people sunbathed and sipped potent potables. The vibe was more "Party Cove" than National Park. Nestor, the concessioner employee who joined us on the island, was ostensibly our tour guide but informed us he did not usually give this tour and did not know much about the island.

"Can you tell us anything about it?" I asked.

"I can tell you when the boat comes back to get you off it," he responded with a smirk, then added, "I also have a key to get you into that lighthouse" while gesturing at the pretty 65-foot-tall conical white stone lighthouse with a glass dome on top that we could see from the dock.

Having done my research before the trip, I informed the others while we walked to the lighthouse that the island had once been owned by Mark Honeywell, founder and first CEO of Honeywell. The lighthouse was purely decorative and not functional, but it was nonetheless used as the park's symbol and was on numerous postcards and magnets sold in park gift shops.

Nestor opened the lighthouse door. We all walked the stairs to the top and enjoyed a commanding view of the ocean and other tiny islands. After establishing when and where to meet for our return trip to the mainland, I left to hike the island's short trail. The campground and lighthouse were on the north end of the island that had been the site of Honeywell's vacation home, which was no longer standing. To get to the trail, I walked past the palm trees in the cleared lawn area and then passed through an arched gap in an ornamental stone wall that had formed the border of the Honeywell place's lawn.

Past that wall, the island was in a relatively natural state and filled with vegetation, especially mangrove trees, which I found fascinating. These trees live on ocean shorelines and thus have evolved to tolerate salt water, withstand battering from wind and waves, and are better able to handle soil beneath them being washed out than most trees. Their trunks typically ended several inches above ground level and then branched into their myriad of smaller roots above the surface, so they appeared to stand on stilts. Some mangroves were surrounded by tiny woody shoots sticking up into the air from below the water, making it look like someone had thrown hundreds of little brown drinking straws around the tree.

The Boca Chita Key hiking trail was only a half mile, so I walked it five times during our two hours on the island and could have done more, but I became nervous I might miss the boat. After returning to the dock, I sat at a picnic table with the tour guide and the parents of the family from South Carolina, whose kids were busily chasing nearby seagulls. While we waited for the boat, Nestor asked the parents what they had been doing in Florida. They mentioned their quest to visit all the National Parks and said they had been to Everglades National Park and were now visiting Biscayne National Park.

Nestor asked, "Aren't you going to any of the parks?"

The father of this family looked at the tour guide blankly for a beat before slowly repeating that they had been to Everglades and Biscayne National Parks.

"No," the tour guide clarified, "I meant theme parks, you know, like Disney?"

The South Carolina father said, "We prefer National Parks to theme parks."

These were my kind of people.

After an uneventful boat ride to the mainland, I was ashore before noon, and next walked the Jetty Trail twice. I enjoyed watching numerous tiny fish darting about the grassy bottom. After perusing the visitor center's small museum, I ate lunch and pondered what to do with the rest of my day. To meet my workday standard, I needed to walk two more miles and spend another four hours in the park. I could make three more round trips of the Jetty Trail, but that seemed pointless and would not take an hour.

During the boat ride back from Boca Chita Key, I noticed a large stretch of mangrove-lined shoreline on one side of the visitor center area. I asked a woman working in the center if there was a hiking trail there, but she said there was not. She instead recommended I could kayak to that area or some other small mangrove-lined islands by renting a kayak at the concessioner's office.

I had never been in a kayak. As with snorkeling, it seemed imprudent to make my first attempt at kayaking in the ocean, but I was out of other ideas. I walked into the concessioner's office. Nestor, my recent Boca Chita tour guide, was working behind the desk. I asked him if kayaking near the visitor center was difficult.

"It's a calm day. The water here is in a sheltered bay that never gets more than three feet deep as long as you stay in front of the little row of islands I'll show you," he countered. "You're a tall guy. If you fall in and lose your paddles and kayak, trust me, you could walk back."

"Okay," I said warily, "I guess I will try it, but I just ate, so aren't I supposed to wait an hour?"

"To kayak?" Nestor asked incredulously. "I think that's swimming."

"Yeah, but if I fall into the water, I might end up swimming," I countered.

I ultimately decided to give it a go without the one-hour delay. Once I paid, Nestor handed me a paddle and a life vest and led me to the kayak rack. He dragged one of the plastic crafts off it and into the water and then gave me a short lesson. After that, I set off.

My paddling was so awkward at first that I splashed water on myself four times, but I eventually found a rhythm. The concessioner tour guide had pointed out a line of small, mangrove-covered islands as a good place to paddle around, so I chose one as an objective and reached it in twenty minutes. There were huge numbers of birds on the top of the island's trees, and a squawking mass exodus ensued as I neared the island.

During my approach, I noticed that from here, several mangroves on the tiny island's shore had leaves that looked white. Earlier in the visitor center museum, I paid close attention to the mangrove exhibit. It mentioned three mangrove species in the park: red, black, and white. It had significant detail and pictures on the red and black types, which I recognized from seeing them along the Boca Chita Key trail. The display said nothing further about white mangroves.

These must be the white mangroves, I thought. I zeroed in on the closest one and paddled towards it for a closer look. After arriving, I laughed upon realizing that this was a red mangrove. It only appeared white because its leaves were coated in a half-inch-thick layer of bird crap.

I thought that mistaking a red mangrove befouled by birds for a white mangrove would make a funny Facebook post, so to illustrate it, I took a photo. Unsatisfied with my first attempt, I paddled to within inches of the tree and stopped to try and take a better shot.

While peering through the viewfinder, I did not notice gentle waves pushing me ever closer to the tree. The light current moved me enough that my forehead smacked into a branch, leaving a small mark, but far more distressingly, dislodging much of the dried bird crap from the branch, which now rained on me as if I was inside the world's most disgusting snow globe. Looking down, I saw I was covered in guano dandruff and frantically tried brushing it all off. I gave up when I realized I was streaking it all over my clothes and skin.

Although I desperately wanted a shower now, I had paid for another ninety minutes of this kayak. My cheapness would not let me return it so soon, so I paddled streaked in bird dung around more mangrove-lined islands and shorelines (thankfully, without further biological contamination) before returning to shore.

When I turned in my paddle at the concessioner's office, Nestor exclaimed, "Shit! What happened to you?"

"Exactly," I sighed, "Shit happened to me."

THIRTY-ONE
EVERGLADES NATIONAL PARK
JANUARY 20-21, 2013

ALLIGATORS WERE NAPPING on the trail I was walking, but I fretted more about leaving my rental car at the mercy of the rubber-devouring vultures.

I had just entered Everglades National Park, the 1.5 million acres of wetlands on Florida's southern tip that supports an astonishing array of plant and animal life, much of which could be seen at my first stop, Royal Palm, just past the park entrance near Homestead, Florida. A sign along the drive into Royal Palm's parking lot warned that vultures here could eat exposed vinyl and rubber on cars, like windshield wipers and window seals, so covering cars with a tarp was strongly recommended. I initially assumed this sign, like so many warning labels and signs, resulted from some past freak incident and an overreaction by lawyers.

Once I reached the lot, however, I saw a tarp-covered SUV with a crew of black vultures, each more than a foot tall, standing on its roof. Suddenly terrified, I scanned the lot and found dozens of other vultures seated on cars and others pacing on the lot near cars. None were actively pecking at windshield wipers, but I was sure I could see a hunger…nay, a ravenous lust…for rubber in their eyes.

It was just 8 AM, but the Royal Palm lot was already nearly full. Most other vehicles in the lot had blue tarps on them. Everglades—especially Royal Palm—is close enough to the Miami metro area that there certainly could be some locals who regularly come here, but most of these license plates were from far-flung locales. Had all these people driven here from Maryland and Ohio knowing in advance to bring a tarp?

In a nearby space, a family of four was busily tarp covering their minivan with a Tennessee license plate. I asked if they brought that tarp with them, and the mother turned and said, "No, there is a big brown bin with tarps and bungee cords you can borrow from the visitor center."

After thanking her, I scurried to the indicated spot but bitterly beheld a brown bin bereft of blue tarps and bare but for one lone bungee cord. Returning to my rental car, I anxiously scanned the lot, hoping to see someone removing a tarp from their car in preparation to leave. I found no one doing so and realized traffic would almost exclusively be arriving at this lot at an early hour.

Trying desperately to engineer a solution, I covered the windshield wipers with plastic bags I had acquired during an earlier shopping trip for food and beverages and two rubber bands I found in my laptop bag. Upon completion, I admired my handiwork for a moment before realizing this was pointless. If the vultures could eat chunks of a windshield wiper, how would a thin plastic bag foil them? Sighing, I left my uncovered rental car for the vultures and walked into Royal Palm.

Most National Park trails offer a chance to see wildlife, but the emphasis is on "chance." Sure, you might see some majestic creatures, but most of the time, you will just see plants and trees. By contrast, while I strolled on the Anhinga Trail, an easy, flat path at Royal Palm composed of paved and boardwalk sections that wind past a marsh and some ponds, I saw more individual animals than I have during some zoo visits. There were too many individual birds, reptiles, and fish to count.

The most striking feathered denizens of Royal Palm to my eyes were many of the trail's namesake, the anhinga, a black-and-white bird that hunted fish by diving into the water and then, after a successful sortie, ate their catch while lounging on tree branches and holding their long wings spread out wide to dry. There were also great blue herons, little blue herons, green herons, egrets, wood storks, double-crested cormorants, and so many other birds with names I do not know because I did not see them listed on the park interpretive signs. Many were standing in the water, staring intently into it for a fish to catch, and several times I saw one dart its head under and emerge with a wriggling bit of sashimi in its beak.

While most people here were casual tourists like me, I encountered three couples who were serious bird watchers monitoring the area with tripod-mounted cameras with telephoto lenses affixed roughly the size of a traffic cone. One elderly couple gushed to me in triumph about photographing a purple gallinule. After I admitted I had no idea what they were talking about, they let me look through their viewfinder at a roughly duck-sized bird with an almost psychedelic color scheme: a bright orange beak, raincoat-yellow feet, a navy-blue head, a forest green back, and most strikingly, an iridescent purple chest.

They assured me there were many other colorful species one could see here with lots of patience and the right lens, but as I had neither, I thanked them and went on my way.

There were so many less flighty animals to see here. I had always thought of the Everglades as a swamp full of murky water, but the water here was so clear I could often see to the bottom. Gars, largemouth bass, and many other fish species could easily be seen swimming in the water. Small snakes wriggled on the grassy banks. Many turtles sat on logs, often holding their four feet up in the air as if they had just painted their toenails.

Of course, I am burying the lede because alligators were the prime attraction. There were scores of them. All the gators I saw outside the water were motionless, most lying in direct sunlight a few feet out of the water in muddy chutes they had worn into the otherwise grassy banks from repeated use. From one boardwalk platform, I saw a dozen alligators, most over eight feet, apparently all snoozing.

I did encounter a few smaller alligators lying on the paved sections of the trail, which gave me pause. Docents strolled the walkway, assuring tourists that these alligators were not an issue as long as we gave them a respectful distance. One docent told me the alligators were only out of the water because they must warm up since they are cold-blooded. She then added, "They are water-based ambush hunters, so if you can see them, they are probably not hunting you."

That sentence was not as assuring to me as she likely meant it to be, but I kept going. After an hour, the only gators I ever saw move were in the water swimming. In one place, the boardwalk became a bridge over the deepest water in Royal Palm. While crossing it, I saw a gator swim towards, under, and away from the bridge, so I could observe it closely from above as it moved steadily by making tiny flicks of the base of its powerful tail.

The other Royal Palm trail led away from the water into a "hammock," essentially a "tree island," where the surface rock sticks high enough above the surrounding marshland that trees can grow there. Called the Gumbo Limbo Trail, it was named for a tropical tree plentiful here with reddish bark that peels off in flakes. It is nicknamed the "tourist tree" since its branches look like what would happen to my arm if I did not lather on sunscreen for a day in Florida. The base of the hammock was limestone, much of which was pocked with "solution holes," places where acidic water had dissolved a depression into the rock, in a more modestly scaled example of the same chemical process that led to the formation of caves like Carlsbad. Most of these holes held isolated pools of water used as home territory by amphibians.

After leaving Royal Palm, I spent the rest of the day driving to other nature trails, all accessed from parking lots along Main Park Road. Due to the soggy nature of the Everglades, most trails available to people who do not want to slog through foot-deep mud or wade through flooded prairies—are short nature trails on these hammocks or raised boardwalks. There was a series of nature trails, and each focused on one ecosystem in the park. My plan for the day from here was to visit them all. There were trails highlighting pine forests, a mahogany hammock, a mangrove-lined shore, and various types of flooded plains. All were around a half-mile in length and loaded with always informative NPS interpretive signs. Still, I found the park experience a little frustrating as it never really felt like I was hiking in nature, just strolling near it.

Main Park Road ended forty miles past Royal Palm at the Flamingo Visitor Center, near the southernmost point of mainland Florida. When I reached Flamingo, I parked and had a look around. It was on the north end of Florida Bay, the part of the Gulf of Mexico between mainland Florida and the Florida Keys. There was a busy marina offering boat tours and a visitor center with a small museum. While I wandered through exhibits in the latter, a ranger announced she was leading a nature walk about crocodiles, so I joined.

While alligators were once considered an endangered species, they have rebounded to a robust population of a million in Florida alone. Crocodiles are abundant in other parts of the world, but in the United States, crocodiles only live in Florida and are considered an endangered species, with only a few thousand left in the wild. After the ranger talk, I knew how to tell the two species apart. The easiest-to-spot differences were color and snout shape. Alligators had a squared-off snout, while crocodiles' snouts were pointy. The crocodiles were gray in color, and the alligators were almost black.

Florida crocodiles prefer saltwater and, thus, will usually only be seen in areas of the park close to the ocean, like Flamingo. The ranger walked us to a few points on the bay near the visitor center, but we saw no crocodiles. She mentioned spots to which one could hike where crocodiles might be seen. I later tried one but had no luck. Of course, some would consider not seeing a crocodile as lots of luck.

Since Flamingo was quite literally the end of the road and it was just early afternoon, I lingered in the area a while, walking several different trails, including strolls that took me along mangrove- and palm-lined shores, through grassy coastal prairies, and around a small body of water called Eco Pond, which was almost as crowded with birds as the

Anhinga Trail had been. Most memorably, I watched a pelican scoop a fish out of the water, which visibly wriggled on its way down that stretchy pouch below the pelican's beak. I also saw several hot-pink roseate spoonbills lounging in the trees.

While walking a paved walkway back to the visitor center after finishing those ambles, I saw a woman staring intently at a specific tree beside the trail. I stopped out of curiosity, and she said something to me in another language—I think it was German—in an agitated manner. She pointed at a specific spot on a tree, so I peered into the foliage and jumped about a foot back when I saw she was pointing at an eastern diamondback rattlesnake, the largest venomous snake in North America.

Diamondbacks are common in the park and rarely bother people, but I later read a news story saying a park ranger was bit by one while trying to remove it from a building that year, so it is not wise to get near one if you can avoid it. I was not sure what the presumably German woman wanted me to do. She kept talking emphatically at me and motioning towards the tree, so I told her in the most reassuring tone I could muster that I would tell someone at the visitor center and quickly left.

Minutes later, I saw a ranger in the visitor center. I told her what I had seen. "Are you sure it's a diamondback?" she asked.

I told her, "I'm not a herpetologist, but it had a rattle and diamonds on its back. I promised a German woman I would tell someone, so I have done my duty."

As I drove away from Flamingo on Main Park Road, I realized that this was the third time I had encountered someone speaking in a foreign accent that I believed was German. I now wondered if Germans were especially drawn to National Parks or if I incorrectly thought all foreign accents were German.

The next morning, I drove to another part of Everglades National Park called Shark Valley. Here, visitors can walk, take a tram tour, or ride bicycles on a fifteen-mile-long paved loop road into a sawgrass marsh. Ever the hiker, I chose to walk, but since I was flying back to Chicago late that afternoon, I could not cover the whole thing and had to turn around and start hiking back after hiking only the first three miles.

To my left, as I started walking, was a vast expanse of flooded prairie called a sawgrass marsh, arguably the signature Everglades habitat. Local Native Americans called this terrain Pa-Hay-o-kee, which loosely translates as "river of grass." Geologists call it a "slough" (pronounced "slew"). It is not technically a swamp because the water, in this case, the Shark River, is not stagnant, but flowing, albeit imperceptibly.

In Shark Valley, the slough stretched as far as I could see in virtually every direction, interrupted only sparsely by small "hammocks" covered in trees. Sawgrass, the dominant plant here, looked like grass to me, but it is technically a sedge, meaning it had tiny teeth on its blades, hence the "saw" in its name. The water around the sawgrass was rife with tangles of beige-colored, ropy-looking algae called periphyton.

On the right side of the trail were "borrow pits," ditches that had been dug by people to get dirt for use in building up the trail bed. These ditches were now filled with water, plant life, and animals like I had seen at Royal Palm. Baby alligators could be seen here in the grass, typically huddled closely together in groups of five or more. Baby alligators hid well here because they had yellow stripes for camouflage in the grasses during their vulnerable youth. I did not see any adult alligators close to these baby groups, but I gave them a wide berth since I had read that alligator mothers could be fiercely protective.

As I left Shark Valley, I passed a sign saying, "Stay on the trail. Stay eight feet from wildlife." While swerving into the grass to give an alligator lying on the trail a wide berth, I chuckled that those two instructions on the sign were not always geometrically possible in the wildlife-rich Everglades.

THIRTY-TWO
ISLE ROYALE AND VOYAGEURS NATIONAL PARKS
JUNE 14, 2013

ON A COLD JANUARY morning a week after my jaunt to the Everglades, I stooped to tie my shoes, and my shoes began spinning around me. That is what they appeared to be doing, anyway. I was reasonably confident my shoes were stationary in reality. They only appeared to spin in my eyes because I was experiencing vertigo.

Thanks to an Alfred Hitchcock movie, many think "vertigo" means fear of heights, but that is "acrophobia." Vertigo is a hallucination of rotational movement, often resulting from inner ear problems.

When my shoes spun, I suspected it was vertigo because I had experienced that a decade before. At that time, any time I moved my head, even in the slightest, everything in my field of vision appeared to rotate around me for a few minutes. My doctor told me this was because little crystals on hairs in my inner ear had come loose, impeding the flow of fluid in my ear and sending my brain confusing signals that caused one eye to move back and forth. He said it should clear up in two or three days, and it did. At first, I assumed this new bout of vertigo was another round of the same thing.

It soon became clear that this vertigo was a different type than what I had before. It did not stop in three days. Over the next three weeks, I had five or more vertigo incidents daily, each about ten minutes long. Vertigo had only happened when I turned my head before, but now it could happen at any moment, even if I held my head perfectly still for an hour. The previous time, the world spun slowly and horizontally from left to right, as if on a lazy Susan. This time, if things spun horizontally, the Susan was not lazy. Also, sometimes the world spun vertically as if it were riding a Ferris wheel, and I was on the central hub.

When not experiencing vertigo, I felt fine, but during vertigo, I was, for all practical purposes, debilitated. I could not focus my eyes on a thing without it appearing to move, which meant I could not walk, drive, or even read or watch TV. The only thing I could find to do during a vertigo episode was to stumble into bed, lie down, shut my eyes, and listen to something soothing. I soon became quite versant with the NPR schedule.

Soon my anxiety over what would happen if vertigo struck me at the wrong time became worse than vertigo itself. Had vertigo always happened on a set schedule, I could have gotten things done when the world was stationary and planned to be in bed when spinning started. I had no such schedule. I had to cancel business trips and work from home. For two weeks, I went nowhere but to the doctor's office.

My doctor had initially told me vertigo would stop in a few days, as the previous bout had. After vertigo continued for the third week, he ordered several tests: elaborate hearing checks, a physical therapist pushing my torso in various directions while yelling, "don't resist me," an MRI of my brain, and a visit to an ENT, who just sat at a computer for the entire visit typing everything I said after he asked me to describe my symptoms. When I was done with my descriptions, the ENT stopped typing and politely dismissed me. I exclaimed in dismay, "That's it? You did not even examine me!" He then perfunctorily shone one of those little doctor lights into my ear holes, but I assumed it was simply to placate me.

After all of this, my primary doctor told me he found no other problems that could cause vertigo from those tests, such as MS or a tumor, so I probably had Meniere's disease, meaning my body was shoving too much fluid into the inner ear. After all those tests, I wanted something more definitive than "probably." I asked in frustration, "Isn't there a test? Can't I pee on a stick, and if it starts spinning, I have Meniere's Disease?" The doctor said there was no such test. He indicated that medicine did not even know exactly what caused the condition, and there was no cure.

At this moment, I feared my life as I knew it was over. If vertigo did not stop, I did not know how I could safely do my business-travel-heavy job, hike in National Parks, or even drive to the grocery store. Amid this deep-seated fear and after spending gobs of money on tests, a doctor told me I "probably" had a condition of unknown cause. I found this deeply unsatisfying, as you can imagine.

The lack of diagnostic certainty became more frustrating when the doctor told me the best way to manage Meniere's disease was by reducing salt in my diet and eliminating alcohol and caffeine. Quite fond of that last one, I thought that wondrous substance was too much to sacrifice for something I "probably" had but desperate for improvement, I went cold turkey off both. Bringing my salt intake down to the recommended level initially sounded easy, as I do not care for salty snacks or shaking salt onto my food. When I started reading labels on foods I commonly ate, I found astonishing sodium levels in foods that did not seem salty.

The doctor also prescribed a diuretic, which he said would help regulate fluid levels in my ear. He also told me to take Zyrtec because he had read that allergies might contribute to Meniere's disease. Over the next few weeks, vertigo subsided and stopped. Life started returning to normal. I eventually resumed business travel and started walking outside again, although I did both with trepidation I had never experienced before.

In April, I learned I had a slowly leaking pipe in the bathroom next to my bedroom, and the drywall around the leak had started to mildew and then coat in black mold. I cleaned that mess and brought in mold abatement equipment to be safe. I eventually paid to have the entire bathroom remodeled. Since the doctor had mentioned allergies as a possible contributor to Meniere's disease, and my vertigo stopped about the same time I cleaned that moldy mess, I wondered if the two incidents were connected.

Even once vertigo had stopped, I had trouble shaking the fear that it could start again. I know enough science to realize the timing of the pipe leak being stopped and my vertigo stopping were, strictly speaking, coincidental. I had not established correlation, let alone causality. It made me feel more confident to believe a leaky pipe had caused all my issues, so I decided to go with that as a conclusion, no matter how irrational.

I had not dared to plan a National Park trip that vertiginous winter, but in early June, I had two vertigo-free months behind me and decided it was time to start visiting National Parks again. I made plans for a typical fly-then-drive trip later in the month, but first, I decided to make a relatively low-cost test run to Isle Royale and Voyageurs National Parks, which I collectively, but inaccurately, called "the Minnesota parks."

Isle Royale is an unpopulated island in Lake Superior, 45 miles long by 9 miles wide. Although part of Michigan, Isle Royale is not reachable by road. The shortest commercial boat ride to it leaves from Grand Portage, Minnesota, so I associated it with Minnesota. Voyageurs, which truly is part of Minnesota, was a vast tract of forests, lakes, and streams on the Canadian border just west of International Falls.

As I left Barrington to start the nine-hour drive to northern Minnesota, I realized that even though I had visited 32 National Parks in just over two years, most of those trips involved plane rides and then paying for rental cars. This trip would be the first time I visited a National Park in my personally owned car, an all-wheel-drive Ford Five Hundred that I loved. I suddenly felt guilty that my car had not seen the wonderful things I had seen, but I instantly felt silly for having that thought.

Somewhere between Beloit and Janesville, Wisconsin, I was in the fast lane cruising past some slow 18-wheelers on I-90 when I heard a loud crash followed by an inrush of air above my head. I looked up to see my sunroof had shattered into innumerable glass shards. Those were now falling on me like snow from a new, jagged, and rapidly expanding open portal in my car's roof.

Taking the next exit, I pulled into a gas station and used its coin-operated vacuum in a vain attempt to suck all the glass from the car's interior. Even after spending all twenty quarters that a cashier had given me in exchange for a five-dollar bill, the carpet glistened from glass bits as if coated by winter frost. I found no obvious cause for the sunroof's break, as no rock, steel chunk, or drone-fired missile was on the floor.

Perplexed and bleeding from two fingers pricked by shards as I cleaned, I drove to the nearest Ford dealership and asked if they could replace my sunroof. They did not have a sunroof in stock and said it would take days to get it. I called some glass repair places and other southern Wisconsin dealerships, but they said it would take days, too. The dealership kindly offered, free of charge, to do further vacuuming and cover the hole with flexible plastic sheeting that they claimed would stay in place at highway speeds for weeks until I could get the new sunroof.

Embarking on a multi-day trek with my belongings in a car with a gaping hole covered with something no thicker than Saran wrap seemed a poor idea, so I reluctantly returned to Barrington. It was just as well that I did so as the plastic sheet pulled partially loose not ten minutes after I left that dealership. It started flapping so noisily that I had to pull over and tear it off before I lost my mind. Luckily, it was a mild, sunny day, so apart from the noise, there was no major issue with driving with a hole in my sunroof. Upon getting home, I dropped my car off at my usual Ford dealership for repair. Then I rented a car.

On my second try, I arrived without incident in Grand Portage. There was an NPS-run National Monument and a state park nearby, so I originally planned to spend a full day sightseeing around Grand Portage before my boat tour to Isle Royale. My sunroof catastrophe cut that to an afternoon, but this proved sufficient. The National Monument was a reconstructed 18th Century fur-trading fort with exhibits on the history of early American fur trading. "Voyageurs," the name of the second park I would visit on this trip, was what the French called long-haul canoe paddlers who took furs from Grand Portage to Quebec for shipment to Europe.

Grand Portage State Park was even better as it featured a 120-foot-tall, almost perfectly vertical waterfall on the Pigeon River, which in these parts, was the boundary between the US and Canada. That was the highlight, but I also hiked a four-mile trail upstream to a smaller waterfall and, at one point, stood on the riverbank and tried to skip a rock to Canada, hoping to add a counterpoint to the time I skipped a rock across the Rio Grande to Mexico in Big Bend National Park. Alas, the Pigeon was roaring because it was so energetically overloaded by melting snow further north. Every time my skipped rocks hit the surface, they were churned underneath before making it halfway.

The next morning, I boarded a boat for the two-hour ride to Isle Royale. En route, the crew stopped the boat above the wreckage of a steamboat named the SS America, which had sunk after dropping off some passengers on the island in 1928. This was interesting until the boat crew spun the boat in a circle to make sure everyone had a chance to see the wreck. This was a little too close to vertigo for me at that moment.

As we approached, Isle Royale was pretty from the water, with its main landmass full of evergreen trees and its bare, rocky shorelines gray but stained with bright orange streaks. The boat docked at Windigo Ranger Station on Washington Harbor, an inlet of Lake Superior between the main part of the island and a thin peninsula. Windigo had been the site of human activity on Isle Royale for some time as the area was unsuccessfully used for copper mining in the late 1800s and was the site of a hunting lodge in the early 1900s. It is now one of three developed areas in the National Park with a visitor center and a campground.

The boat spinning incident reminded me it might be a good idea to tell a crew member where I was planning to hike just in case vertigo returned, and I could not get back to the boat. While we disembarked, a crew member stood at the exit with a clipboard checking each passenger's name off a list as they exited. When I reached the clipboard man, I told him my name and that I was by myself. I then asked him to write down the two trails I planned to hike, but he snidely said he did not need to know what I was doing, just that I got off the boat. I asked him to write down the trails so he could tell the NPS rangers if I did not return. He gave me an annoyed look and wrote something. I suspect he wrote, "This guy is a pain in my ass," but it made me feel better to have told someone.

Most of the boat's passengers stuffed into the small visitor center after disembarking, but I immediately began a 3.6-mile hike on the Feldtmann Lake Trail to a place called Grace Creek overlook. The trail passed through a forest but had nice views of the harbor to my right. As the trail climbed steadily to the overlook, I once heard a large splash of water well below me, and I looked down to catch a brief glimpse of a moose emerging from the lake and disappearing into the trees.

Isle Royale's moose—and the wolves that hunt them—are famous and have been thoroughly studied by biologists since 1958. As Isle Royale is a relatively small piece of land and closed off to other land animals, it allows for a study of the interaction between a single predator-prey pairing. I was surprised to learn that the wolves and the moose are recent arrivals. Caribou and other large animals that had lived on the island in the nineteenth century were slaughtered into oblivion by miners or hunters. The resulting void of large animals on the island was filled in the early 20th Century by moose that swam here from Canada and wolves, who walked here via an ice bridge.

The island's moose population was a robust 1,000 individuals during my visit, but the wolf population had declined to under ten, down from a high of fifty. As their numbers shrank, the wolves were becoming inbred and sickly. In April 2015, I read an Associated Press story that reported the wolf population was down to only three individuals. A debate began on whether the NPS should let nature run its course and let the wolves die out or intervene and introduce new wolves to bolster the wolf population and genetic diversity.

At the top of the ridge, I enjoyed a commanding view of the harbor, a creek, and its surrounding wetlands and then returned to the visitor center. I ached for a closer moose sighting—or a distant wolf sighting—

MY NATIONAL PARK DIET

but I experienced neither. I had to settle for seeing the taxidermy wolf and the moose skeleton displayed in the visitor center.

On the Windigo Nature Trail, a level, 1.2-mile loop through the woods near the ranger station, I enjoyed strolling past white, yellow, and lavender-colored wildflowers until I arrived, quite unexpectedly, at an area of vegetation behind an extremely sturdy fence. A sign explained it was a "moose exclosure" used for scientific research. Since moose are relative newcomers to the island, biologists are studying if the vegetation in the forest is altered by moose, who feed on the island's trees. The exclosure served as a control spot in this research. While I assumed moose must have an impact, as I peered through the fence, I could see no differences big enough to be noticed by my untrained eye.

Keeping my visit to a day trip meant I only had four hours on the island, so that was my last hike. When I returned to the boat, the man with the clipboard sarcastically said he was glad I made it back alive while checking my name off the list. The return boat ride took a different route, so we saw a black-and-white lighthouse called Rock of Ages on Isle Royale. Any enjoyment I took in viewing it was undermined when the captain sent the boat into another too-close-to-vertigo-for-my-tastes 360, so everyone on board could see it.

That night, I drove three-quarters of the way to Voyageurs National Park and then stayed in a hotel. The next morning, I stopped for gas at a station outside the park boundary and noticed big signs listing both gas prices and the price of dry ice. Perplexed, I asked about this when I paid. The cashier explained that fishermen use dry ice to freeze and preserve their catches. This gas station also had a large room with tanks offering an astonishing variety of freshwater aquatic species for sale as bait.

Due to its proximity to the Canadian border and the abundance of lakes and streams, the park and surrounding areas are called "Boundary Waters." Over forty percent of Voyageurs National Park is underwater. I am not sure how many of Minnesota's 10,000 lakes are in Voyageurs, but if you look at a detailed map, you will see the park is contributing its fair share. Once inside the park, I drove to the nearest visitor center to get trail maps and found the parking lot filled with trucks hitched to boat trailers instead of the usual RVs and hatchbacks with luggage boxes on top. I saw many boats on the water and people casting fishing lines throughout the day. Water sports appeared to be the attraction for most park visitors.

Of course, I was in Voyageurs to hike, so I spent my day walking eight miles of trails with names like Oberholtzer, Blind Ash Bay, Echo Bay, and Rainy Lake. They passed shimmering blue lakes and climbed densely forested hills, where the only ground not covered with plant life were enormous chunks of granite studded in the surface—and even those were often covered with mosses and lichens. The park teemed with wildlife, too. I saw many different birds, squirrels, and deer, along with one coyote. Insects were busier here than in any other National Park I had visited, too, so I had doused myself with insect repellent. The trails were empty of humans except for me during all of my hikes on this day, so apart from the occasional distant roar of an outboard engine, the forests were quiet, and I felt I was hiking a true wilderness.

Park interpretive materials highlighted enormous boulders called "erratics" that a trail description said had been carried here by glaciers. One short trail went to an overlook from which you saw a beaver pond. From another trail, I saw a rookery, or group of nests, used by blue herons. These hikes all seemed low-key compared to the staggeringly deep canyons and two-hundred-foot-tall trees I saw in other National Parks.

While planning my trip, I read there were rocks at the surface in Voyageurs two billion years old, far more ancient than those at the bottom of the Grand Canyon. Seeing these proved disappointing as they had not been slowly exposed by erosion like the layers of the Grand Canyon but raised to the surface by seismic forces. When I saw some of these old rock layers on the ground at Voyageurs, it did not pack the emotional wallop of the Grand Canyon, where billion-year-old rock layers viscerally felt like they must be a billion years old as they were part of an organized mile of rock layers.

When I returned to my car after my last hike that day, I rolled my windows down, hung my left arm out the window, cranked some tunes, and cruised winding roads back to the highway to start my long drive home. Minutes later, I noticed two different ticks strolling on my left arm. Fearing they would latch on and transmit Lyme disease, with the fingers of my right hand, I flicked both ticks off my arm and into the wind, sending them on an aerial thrill ride that I imagine was the highlight of their brief tick lives.

With my right hand still in flick position, I scanned for more ticks to flick until I realized I was going thirty miles per hour with no hands on the steering wheel. I returned my hands to 10 and 2, drove to the nearest visitor center, went in a bathroom stall, disrobed, and inspected myself for bloodsuckers, fortunately finding none.

Since my Voyageurs visit was landlocked and my time on Isle Royale was a brief four hours, I experienced neither of them to their fullest. I saw enough to know neither park has the jaw-dropping wonders that most western parks have. Still, I never had the "why is this a National Park" vibe of Cuyahoga Valley. Both were wonderful natural places that I am glad are protected and well worth a visit.

After the angst of my vertiginous winter, frankly, I was satisfied to be in any National Park—or any place at all—that was not spinning around my eyes.

THIRTY-THREE
WIND CAVE NATIONAL PARK
JUNE 30, 2013

WHEN I PICKED up a rental car at the Denver airport, I expected it would take me to the three National Parks in the Dakotas. I did not expect it to become a scratching post for a half-ton animal.

Wind Cave National Park in western South Dakota was the first Dakota park on my itinerary. Since I love caves, I naturally started my visit with a ranger-guided tour of the park's namesake feature, the sixth-longest cave in the world. Wind Cave is named for air currents that pass through its natural entrance, a two-foot-diameter hole in a rock outcrop. The cave equalizes its pressure to the outside air through this small hole, so air can shoot out the hole or be sucked into it. In rare occurrences, 70-mile-per-hour winds burst out of the cave's natural entrance, but only a wispy breeze blew this day. Wind or no wind, I could not have wriggled through that small hole, so thankfully, our tour entered the cave via a far larger manufactured entrance.

Wind Cave has little water dripping into it, so there are relatively few speleothems and no spectacular multi-story ones like those I had loved at Carlsbad. The one formation Wind Cave has in abundance is "boxwork," a rare one composed of hundreds of thin, planar calcite crystals that hang straight down from the cave's "ceiling" and intersect in a manner that they form little upside-down, open-topped "boxes." Boxwork was academically interesting since I had not seen it before, but not exactly aesthetically appealing

Without pretty rock formations, I realized for the first time as my ninety-minute tour ended that the rock formations in caves were what I loved, not the caves themselves. Without speleothems, a cave is just an underground tunnel. I began to fear this whole park would be a bust, but there was a park above ground here, too. I planned to hike for six hours to complete my workday standard. Still, I was not optimistic about that prospect since most of the park is covered in gently rolling, grassy prairie.

On the six miles of trails that I walked, I saw no stunning landscapes, but the prairie held small surprises. Colorful wildflowers brightened the wide swaths of green grass, including the bright yellow buds on the prickly pear cactus that I was surprised to find growing this far north. I was far more surprised on one trail when I found a massive bison bull napping two hundred feet in front of me. I cut that hike short and slowly retreated. That and other close encounters with wildlife in Wind Cave National Park would prove far more memorable for me than the park's namesake cave.

Bison were the most memorable animals I saw in this park. They are often called "buffalo" in the US. They are enormous ungulates ranging from 1,000 to 2,000 pounds as adults. Scientists estimate that 20 million bison once roamed North America in vast herds from Mexico to Alaska, but habitat loss and intentional slaughters brought their population as low as a few thousand by 1900. Conservation efforts have helped the bison rebound; today, there are half a million alive. Many of those are domesticated for meat production and have been cross-bred with cattle. Wild, genetically pure bison are now generally only found in National Parks, state parks, and wildlife preserves. Wind Cave is one of the best places for a tourist to see them as it has a herd of over 300 wild bison roaming a small National Park.

Because bison are grazers, many people think they are just big cows and feel comfortable getting within a few feet of bison herds. During a later park visit, I saw a teenager walk up to a bison and throw his arm around it. These people would be more careful if, as I had before coming to Wind Cave, they had read a study on animal-caused injuries in Yellowstone National Park. It showed that bison injured four times more people there than bears in the 1980s and 1990s. Only one of the bison attacks mentioned in that report was fatal, but those attacked by a bison often had severe injuries.

A bison is an herbivore that will not eat you, but it can run 35 miles an hour and weigh between a half-ton and a ton, so it can apply significant kinetic energy to make you go away if they want that to happen. Bison bulls have pointy horns on their enormous heads built like battering rams so they can bash head-first into other males while fighting for mates. I had come to Wind Cave with a healthy respect for them.

In one spot in Wind Cave, I was taking pictures of bison grazing on top of a hill visible from the road. I did so from the NPS's recommended safe distance and while hanging out the door of my still-running car in case I needed to get out of dodge in a hurry. A couple in a car soon parked next to me, and the man got out of the car and started running up the hill toward the bison. Deciding to share my wisdom, I said, "Hey, you should keep your distance. They weigh a ton, have battering rams for heads, and run 35 miles per hour."

He made a dismissive gesture and scoffed, "They can't possibly run 35 miles per hour very long."

"They can run 35 miles per hour longer than you can," I retorted before driving away.

Many other members of the animal kingdom call the park home. I was delighted to observe a prairie dog town in the park, where hundreds of holes pockmarked a plain about the size of a city block. Prairie dogs are a species of ground squirrel about a foot long. They build networks of tunnels with multiple holes at ground level for access that are collectively nicknamed "towns." Numerous prairie dogs would be grazing in the town, and a smaller group appeared to be on high alert as if they were on sentry duty. If one of the "sentries" started chittering, the other nearby rodents would dash back into one of the holes for cover. As I watched for a long while, the prairie dogs would frequently pop out of their holes and then back into their holes for reasons I could not discern. It began to feel like watching the world's biggest Whack-a-Mole game.

On one hike, I saw an animal that looked a little like a deer, but instead of antlers, it had two horns on its top that formed a V shape. Halfway up the V, a smaller horn stuck out forward. This was a pronghorn, sometimes called a pronghorn antelope. These are the "antelopes" at play in the song "Home on the Range." They are the fastest creatures in North America and the second fastest in the world after the cheetah. They can hit a top speed of 65 miles per hour, but after eyeing me warily for a couple of minutes, this one left at a leisurely trot. While I did not want to stress the animal, I idly wished I looked more threatening because how cool would it be to see a wild animal run 65 miles an hour in a National Park firsthand?

After finishing at Wind Cave, I decided to drive to nearby Mount Rushmore, the famous massive mountainside sculpture of the heads of four American presidents. The fastest route between the two involved passing through a bit of South Dakota's nearby Custer State Park. Just past the entrance to the state park, I found a group of at least fifty bison completely blocking the road ahead. Unsure of what to do, I pulled into a turn-out and stopped my car behind a van. Within minutes, long lines of cars were backed up on each side of the herd.

After several more minutes of gridlock, a man in a red pickup with a South Dakota State Park logo drove towards the herd from what would normally be the wrong lane in the other direction. He was yelling at the bison and slapping his hand on the side of his truck in an apparent effort to direct the herd to move. I was initially relieved someone was breaking up the traffic impediment, but my relief turned to fear when I found the herd moving towards—and then surrounding—my car and the other vehicles behind me.

Literal tons of hairy beasts were adjacent to my car on all sides. The one to my left unnerved me most at first when it peered into my car. One to my right soon got my attention when I heard a thunk in that direction. The bison there was scratching her head on the passenger-side rearview mirror, which was one of those that were designed to fold in, and the noise I had heard was the sound of that mirror folding in.

The man in the state park truck succeeded in moving the herd, but for the next several minutes, my car was surrounded by bison, and my heart threatened to leap out of my chest. As the last of the herd passed, I began to feel more confident I would escape this situation without injury or telling a long story at the rental car counter. Then I saw a teenager open a window on the van parked ahead of me, lean out the window, and give a bison an open-handed smack on the rear end. This bison made a startled noise and scampered headlong towards my car, but the bison luckily veered to go around it.

Sadly, this would not be the last traffic snarl during my drive to Mount Rushmore, but humans were responsible for all the others. A few times in the state park, a distant view of Rushmore could be seen from the road, and inevitably, this would cause a traffic jam as someone would slam on their brakes, stop right in the middle of the narrow road, get out of the car, and take their own sweet time getting a photo.

Thus, I arrived at Mount Rushmore irritated with humanity and my first moments at the famous sculpture did little to lower my stress level. While the NPS runs Mount Rushmore because it is a National Memorial, a concessioner runs the multi-story parking garage that you must use to park on-site legally. Thus, while the park is technically free, I had to pay $15 to park because my park pass did not waive or reduce the fee. Grumbling out of the garage, I walked into an area that looked like a shopping mall with restaurants, a bookstore, and a souvenir shop. These shops were all filled with herds of humans denser than the bison herd I had just escaped.

Past the shops, though, I found a quiet amphitheater directly across from the mountain where I could sit and take in the iconic sculpture. Later, I perused the nice museum, which displays original concept art for the project—including a preliminary smaller sculpture in which the presidents have carved clothed torsos, not just faces—and has interpretive exhibits on how the sculptor, Gutzon Borglum, and his crew created the tableaux with, insomuch as such a thing is possible, careful use of explosives.

Images of Mount Rushmore are so common and familiar that I had expected to come here and say, "yep, that's it, looks nice," and then get back on the road. Instead, I was enthralled. Four of my favorite subjects—art, history, engineering, and geology—were intersected in this thing. Seeing it in person gave me a new appreciation for how it was made, its beauty, and its enormity.

Then I realized how it was made, its beauty, and its enormity were also things I newly appreciated about my country by visiting National Parks.

THIRTY-FOUR
BADLANDS NATIONAL PARK
JULY 1, 2013

"IT MUST BE TERRIFYING to have a one-ton animal roll around on your roof," I said to the other tourists standing at one end of a prairie dog town near the west entrance to Badlands National Park.

A bison herd twice as big as the one that engulfed my car the day before was grazing beyond the prairie dog town. One particularly large bull strode into the other end of the prairie dog town, threw himself on the ground, and rolled around, kicking up a small dust storm. Before this, most prairie dogs had been grazing on all fours while a few others stood upright at attention in their holes, scanning for threats. Once that bison strode into their domain, the rodents all squeaked, and most took cover in a hole.

The bison and prairie dogs had been on a flat, grassy plain, but soon after leaving them, I found a viewpoint from which I could see the unusual terrain that had made this place a National Park. Like the Painted Desert in Petrified Forest, a large area of hills was composed of multi-colored layers of soft sedimentary rock. The biggest difference here relative to the Painted Desert is that the red, yellow, and brown hills of Badlands National Park are not surrounded by arid deserts but by grassy prairies.

These badlands are mostly buttes with steep, barren slopes. Some are topped with tall, thin pinnacles that make them look like earthen church steeples. These hills began as sediment that settled at the bottom of an inland sea 40 to 70 million years ago. Cross-sections of the rock formed by those ancient sediment deposits have been revealed by the slow work of wind, precipitation, and other erosive forces. Some buttes were barren, while others had flat tops supporting fields of green grasses in this vast expanse of crumbly rock.

I spent my day in Badlands driving the park's main scenic road from west to east, occasionally stopping for hikes into those hills. I wondered if someone was re-modeling their house when they named these trails because there was a Door Trail, a Window Trail, and a Shelf Trail, all of which were short, easy walks into the badlands. Another easy trail passed through an area rich in fossils and had interpretive signs about them.

Those were all nice, but my two favorite hikes in the park were a 4.5-mile amble combining the Saddle Pass Trail and Medicine Root Trail and a 1.5-mile in-and-back jaunt on the Notch Trail.

The Saddle Pass Trail was only half a mile long, but it climbed 150 feet up to the top of one of the buttes. Not only was it steep, but getting traction was challenging because the trail surface was crumbling into little bits of rock, barely harder than dried mud. Those bits were coming loose under my feet and acting like ball bearings under the soles of my shoes.

Once I crested the top of the butte, I found it flat and covered in grass except for some spots where small and steep rocky pinnacles poked skyward. Trail guides said that several mammals, like deer, bighorn sheep, and pronghorn, liked to graze on high plains like these since a bison cannot usually clamber up the steep inclines. The only animal I saw here was one bighorn sheep I startled while hiking the Medicine Root Trail.

Gaining traction on the Saddle Pass trail was even tougher going down. After involuntarily doing the splits while attempting to avoid an uncontrolled tumble, I finally decided dignity was overrated and scooted down the last third of the trail on my butt.

Thankfully less terrifying was the Notch Trail, a 1.5-mile hike with about 130 feet of elevation gain on the way to the namesake break in the badlands, which yielded a nice overlook with a view of a river valley. For the steepest section of this trail, the "dirt ball bearings" effect I had experienced on Saddle Pass was ameliorated by the addition of a 50-rung log ladder lying on the slope.

After finishing at Badlands in the late afternoon, I drove to another National Park Service unit outside Badlands called Minuteman Missile National Historic Site. At the height of the Cold War, the US had hundreds of Minuteman missiles ready to launch in silos across the country. Minuteman was the first solid-fueled intercontinental ballistic missile that, if needed, could have delivered nuclear bombs to far-flung spots around the globe. Since the Soviet Union would presumably try to destroy these missile bases if war broke out, they were usually placed in sparsely populated areas.

Many sites have been closed following the arms reduction treaties of recent decades. Once this one near Badlands was decommissioned, it was turned over to the National Park Service. Visitors can get tours of a command center that managed multiple remote silos. One of the silos can be visited on your own.

While peering down at the top of the missile during my walk around the silo, I wished one of the Minuteman silos in my native Missouri could have instead become the National Park Service site to interpret the history of this missile program. There were once 150 of these silos in western Missouri, some just miles from my hometown. I have clear memories of watching the 1983 TV movie *The Day After*, which depicted the aftermath of a fictional nuclear war between the US and the Soviets. The film was set in the area around Kansas City, which was devastated in the film because the USSR bombed the many missile sites there. My hometown felt perverse pride when Clinton was listed as one of the towns destroyed. Homerism and childhood memories aside, I begrudgingly admit it is more efficient to have made a National Park site out of a Minuteman silo so near an existing National Park.

I spent that night in Spearfish, South Dakota, and over dinner, sculpted my mashed potatoes into a column with a flared bottom and announced, to no one in particular, "this means something!" It meant that I had seen *Close Encounters of the Third Kind* one too many times and that I planned to enter Wyoming in the morning to visit Devils Tower National Monument, a natural wonder in that film.

Devils Tower is a giant pillar of rock about 1,250 feet tall, the same height as the Empire State Building, that juts abruptly from the Great Plains so that it can be seen from miles away. It is composed of porphyry, an igneous rock, which is thought by most geologists to have formed when magma pushed its way into layers of older, subterranean, soft sedimentary rock. Those sedimentary rocks later eroded, leaving us with today's tower sticking above the plain like a sore thumb.

The tower was visible long before I reached the National Park Service entrance station, but I kept going to see the thing up close. I parked at the visitor center and then walked a trail around the tower, finding it to be made up of individual rock columns that made it appear grooved. A huge pile of rocky debris below the tower suggests the Tower was once wider. As I walked among some of that debris, I saw those individual columns mostly had a hexagonal cross-section and a width roughly as tall as me.

Devils Tower has a special place in the history of the National Park system because it was the first place to be named a National Monument. Coincidentally, when I left Devils Tower, I started driving towards the National Park named after the same president who had made Devils Tower a National Monument.

THIRTY-FIVE
THEODORE ROOSEVELT NATIONAL PARK
JULY 2-3, 2013

IN 1883, a wealthy young New York City politician read that bison might soon go extinct. Alarmed, he quickly took action. Did he pass legislation to start a conservation program? No, he traveled to North Dakota, hired a guide, and shot a bison to ensure he had one's head mounted on his wall before they were all gone.

Eighteen years later, that bison-bagging politician, Theodore Roosevelt, became President of the United States. His thoughts had changed enough by then that he arguably did more for the National Park idea than any other president has since. Visitors to the National Park named for him can explore that story by seeing the land that inspired Roosevelt or ignore his story and instead enjoy a beautiful landscape supporting much wildlife, including some cranky wild horses.

From Devils Tower, I drove 250 miles to Medora, North Dakota, a little town just outside the main entrance to the south unit of Theodore Roosevelt National Park. The last leg of this drive was on I-94, which passes through the east end of the National Park, and there was an interstate rest area inside the park on the rim of a place called Painted Canyon. I stopped, parked, and found the rest area housed a small NPS visitor center. It was also the trailhead for a hike into the canyon.

The Visitor Center was already closed when I arrived just after 5 PM, but I walked the trail into the canyon, which looked like a greener Badlands National Park. Similar colorfully banded earthen buttes were here, but the floor of the canyon and some sides of the banded hills were dotted with scrubby grasses and short evergreen trees. The more prevalent greenery meant it was less visually striking than the mostly bare Badlands of South Dakota, but it also made it seem like a more inviting place to amble.

After spending the night at a hotel in Medora, I entered the National Park Wednesday morning at its main entrance. I stopped by the visitor center there, which had the usual extensive exhibits on the park's flora, fauna, and geology, along with exhibits on Teddy Roosevelt's time here, including an odd wooden sculpture of the former president on horseback that looked like it had been made of popsicle sticks.

After shooting his bison, Roosevelt learned about a cattle ranching boom around Medora and decided to invest, buying a ranch with two locals, and he was not a silent partner. Despite being a New York state legislator, he returned to North Dakota for extended stays. He threw himself into ranch work and lived what he would later call "the strenuous life." He later bought a second ranch about thirty miles north of Medora.

I was only visiting the park's South Unit, which contains some of Roosevelt's first ranch. His second ranch is the non-contiguous North Unit of the park. The first ranch's cabin is just outside the South Unit's visitor center near Medora, but it now sits seven miles from its original location. The NPS did not move the building from its original location; it was already well-traveled before this land became a National Park. During Roosevelt's presidency, the cabin was moved to St. Louis for display at the 1904 World's Fair, and it went on to be displayed in several other places before returning to North Dakota.

Roosevelt divested his ranches after a brutal winter in 1887 killed half of his herd, but this period still had a big impact on him, so much so that Roosevelt went so far as to say that he would never have been president without his time in North Dakota. His time working with real-life cowboys inspired him to create the "Rough Riders" volunteer cavalry unit, which made him a household name in the Spanish American War. Also, understanding life in the West helped him politically appeal to a new demographic that would have otherwise been tough for a bookish, rich New Yorker to reach.

Most importantly to a National Park fan, though, Roosevelt's first-hand experience with the rapidly dwindling game populations in the Dakotas made him a passionate conservationist. He co-founded the Boone and Crockett club, one of the first conservation organizations, and then as president, used executive orders to create the National Wildlife Refuge system and name a host of threatened places and National Monuments, many of which became National Parks, such as the Grand Canyon.

After finishing at the visitor center, I drove the main 35-mile loop road through the park's South Unit and walked various short trails to overlooks from which one could see these badlands.

One trail went to and through Wind Canyon, where a short cliff face of white sandstone had eroded into interesting shapes, including some curvy white sandstone pillars that looked a bit like cartoon ghosts. There were also wonderful views of the Little Missouri River here as it gently arced past some bare rock cliffs. I walked various short trails to other less dramatic overlooks during the day, seeing lots of wildlife along the way. Most animals I saw were of species I had seen at Wind Cave or Badlands, like deer, bison, and prairie dogs. One animal was new here, however: wild horses. A significant population of them lived in the park, and several times, I saw groups of unbridled horses far above, with manes often flowing majestically with the wind. It was quite a sight.

Later, while walking a short path from a parking lot to the park's tallest point, Buck Hill, I had a much closer wild horse encounter. Three wild horses were standing a few feet from the parking lot. Four people were nearby snapping photos. I passed by, walked to an overlook on Buck Hill, and lingered there awhile, admiring a majestic near-panoramic view of these North Dakota badlands.When I turned to return to my car, I found my path blocked by those same three wild horses I had seen near the parking area. They stood single file on the short trail, which in that spot passed through a short trench between two small rocky ridges two feet tall. I was standing on a point that jotted out from the hill. My choices were to jump over the cliff behind me and fall to a certain death, go over one of the steep hillsides to my left or right to certain injury (and possible death), or stand my ground and risk a likely trampling.

The horses and I held our positions for a few minutes—but what felt like hours—until the horses started neighing and snorting in obvious agitation. The front one stamped its hoofs. Hoping it would signal I wanted to get out of their way, I stepped onto the rocks forming the shallow trench around the path. As soon as I had, the front two ran down the trail and headed down the hillside to my left.

Relieved, I watched them gallop majestically down the hill and then realized I was only watching two horses. I turned to find the third horse in the original line, which was reddish brown and had a blonde mane, still standing in my way. It reared its front legs up into the air and neighed loudly. Then it began stamping its hoof and snorting.

"This is it," I thought. "I am going to be stomped to death by a horse."

One's life is supposed to flash before their eyes in such a moment, I thought, but instead, I could only ponder how embarrassing this would be. Being devoured by a grizzly, a wolf pack, or a cougar was not desirable, but at least it would sound kind of badass. Being stomped to death by a horse, however? People would think things went wrong on a trip I made to a farm. Such thoughts proved premature. After what seemed like an eternity, the blond horse followed the other two. The trail was clear at last.

The last few trails I hiked while completing my drive along the main park road were thick with sagebrush. I had heard the term many times in Westerns but had never known what it was, so I was glad to put a leaf with a name. Sagebrush plants were two- or three-foot-tall bushes with small leaves on spindly stalks than fanned out a couple of feet from the roots. The leaves were a pale green that almost looked silver from a distance, and it had a strong, pungent aroma. Park interpretive signs said Native Americans used it to disguise their scent on hunts. I had no trouble believing that worked.

One trail entered an area with exposed veins of coal. Prairie fires or lightning can cause exposed coal to catch fire, and veins can continue burning underground for years. A coal vein here caught fire in 1951 and burned underground into the late 1970s. An interpretive sign claimed park visitors used heat from this coal vein fire to cook marshmallows. Coal fires can bake clay-based rock near the coal into a natural brick that geologists call "clinker" but North Dakotans call "scoria." Some of this scoria was so dark red that it looked like someone had created the layers out of building bricks. As coal burns away, the rock layers above it fall into the void in a phenomenon called a "slump."

By noon, I had finished all the nature trails along the main park road. I wanted to do more hiking but was unsure what to do next. On the extreme western end of the park, I had read that some badlands had eroded to reveal a large array of petrified wood. This area was reachable from a trailhead on the park loop road but only by a 10-mile-hike called the Petrified Forest Trail. All the trails I had done so far on the day were easy, but I had already put five miles on my feet that day, and I was not sure I had another ten in me.

At the visitor center, I asked a ranger if there was any shorter way to get to the petrified wood. He gave me directions to a park trailhead that could only be reached by driving on roads outside the park. From this trailhead, the petrified wood was only a four-mile round-trip hike. While driving this recommended route, I passed many oil wells just barely outside the park boundary. North Dakota's 1880s cattle boom was long over, but these wells were evidence of the state's 2010's oil boom that had given North Dakota a rapid influx of investment and the lowest unemployment rate of any state at the time.

From the trailhead, I passed two miles of badlands resembling what I had seen all day before cresting the top of a hill and seeing enormous pieces of petrified wood scattered throughout the valley below. Much of the petrified wood I had seen in Petrified Forest National Park was lying along paved trails as if I was walking through a landscaped rock garden, but here, along this natural surface trail, I was looking at tree stumps with flared bases and even roots. While most specimens in Petrified Forest National Park were facsimiles of trees that had already fallen and been washed downstream before being petrified, these stumps are thought to have been buried by deep mud in ancient floods before death, so now the trunks still stand as they did in life.

These stumps were enormous—some were over ten feet wide—because they were copies of mighty redwoods that lived sixty million years ago when North Dakota was a subtropical forest. They were relatives of the coastal redwoods and Sequoias I had hiked under in California.

The National Parks, where human impact is intentionally minimized, had often felt timeless on past visits. Of course, as I also voraciously read about the dynamic nature of our planet as revealed through geology on display in places like National Parks, It is silly to call a place timeless as I have already written that thought. The earth is ever-changing, albeit usually quite slowly, and our day is just one snapshot in its history.

"Wouldn't it be cool," I thought as I hiked back to the trailhead, "if sixty million years from now, vacationing hikers who live in a North Dakota redwood forest saw stone copies of the Giant Sequoias eroding out of a Californian desert hill?" Later, when I drove from the trailhead to the interstate, I passed those steadily pumping fossil fuel rigs and hoped we did not turn California into that desert in only sixty years.

THIRTY-SIX
YELLOWSTONE NATIONAL PARK
SEPTEMBER 3-5, 2013

"WHERE SHOULD WE GO FIRST?" Robert Wright asked as we entered the world's first National Park.

That question is more challenging to answer in Yellowstone than in any other National Park. Most parks have a main road or two that direct you to the most popular features in a logical sequence. In Yellowstone, key features are far more numerous, sometimes only sporadically erupt, and are spread over a figure-eight-shaped road system. Yellowstone is enormous at 2.2 million acres, making it larger in area than Delaware and Rhode Island combined. We had three days to explore it, but we would barely scratch the surface.

Soon after entering the park in West Yellowstone, Idaho, we crossed the state line into Wyoming, and I recommended that we follow my, as usual, carefully scripted trip itinerary and spend our first day here in the southwest section of the park, which has the highest concentration of the geothermal features that make Yellowstone so justly famous.

Yellowstone has been scientifically shown to have sprouted an enormous "super volcano" more than once. It is assumed that will happen again. Thus, magma is atypically near the surface in Yellowstone (distances range from four to ten miles). That leads to very hot groundwater doing some fascinating things. While walking Yellowstone's trails this day, we saw mud bubbling like a witch's kettle, bursts of steam pouring out of holes in the ground, geysers flinging water one hundred feet in the air, and searing hot pools of water. The latter were in various colors like milky white, sapphire blue, or emerald green.

Our first sight of these features—and the first smell of them since the geothermal areas all had a strong sulfur odor—was in the Norris Geyser Basin. We walked a one-mile trail through Porcelain Basin, named for the smooth, white silica deposits covering the ground there. The white, in turn, was dotted with pools of hot water, many of which looked a little like that blue milk Luke Skywalker drank in Star Wars and streaked with rust-orange or lime-green extremophile bacteria that could tolerate the heat of scalding pools. The area was also replete with fumaroles, holes in the earth's surface from which steam jetted into the air.

Most hydrothermal features had old-fashioned-looking labels by them with colorful names. I purchased a pamphlet with descriptions of the named features. While many of the names seemed inexplicable, we encountered an aptly named gray oval of sludge emitting nothing but hot air that was called Congress Pool.

I had seen most of these things on a smaller scale at Bumpass Hell in Lassen Volcanic National Park, so I was most excited to see Yellowstone's world-famous enormous geysers, which had not been present in Lassen.

Like most everyone, I was familiar with images of the park's most famous geyser, Old Faithful, shooting water one hundred feet in the air, but I was disappointed to learn that while there are some similarly spectacular geysers, most of the geysers in the park—and all I saw in the Porcelain Basin—are much less spectacular. Many, from the surface, are just hot pools that occasionally splash water two or three feet into the air as if a small creature had done a cannonball into them.

Although small, some geysers here were memorable, like Whirlygig Geyser, which had small eruptions accompanied by a rhythmic chuffing that sounded like a steam engine. On another Norris Trail that led into a place called Back Basin, we saw Vixen Geyser every few minutes fire thin jets of water fifteen feet into the air as if some subterranean creature was shooting a Super Soaker.

Back Basin did have one of the big ones, called Steamboat Geyser, which can spray water three hundred feet into the air, making it the tallest of any active geyser on earth. We, unfortunately, did not see it do anything. Scientists can reliably predict how often some of Yellowstone's geysers will erupt, but Steamboat's eruptions remain unpredictable and can be weeks or months apart. It was once dormant for fifty years and then resumed erupting periodically.

Such is an example of the potential for frustration—and magic—in Yellowstone. The natural environments in all parks are dynamic, but if you go to the Grand Canyon or Crater Lake, you can be pretty sure that you will at least see the Grand Canyon or Crater Lake. Those geological wonders rarely do anything highly different on a typical day. You just want to see them. In Yellowstone, by contrast, any geyser will be there, but you may hike to one and see a stationary pool of water while you are hoping for a magnificent eruption. On the other hand, you might see something that has been a stationary pool of water for weeks, months, or even decades suddenly send a plume of water thirty stories into the sky.

Norris had a small museum, and we perused it once we had walked the area trails. There we learned that the NPS runs a geyser prediction hotline, a phone number visitors can call to hear the predicted eruption times for various big geysers in the park. My phone's coverage indicator displayed one lonely bar, but I called and got through. The most famous geyser in the park, Old Faithful, erupts quite predictably roughly every hour and a half, so a hotline is not needed for it, but the recording started by stating its next time. Then the hotline recording ran through times for several other big geysers, and most did not predict an exact specific time but a possible window of several hours. The next predicted eruption window for Grand Geyser, the tallest of the predictable geysers listed on the hotline, had just started.

Grand Geyser is close to Old Faithful in the Upper Geyser Basin. The world-famous Old Faithful was in our plans, although I had penciled it in for later in the day. However, I called an audible and suggested to Robert that we should head to that area now and catch both. He agreed, so we walked towards the big geysers about an hour after a drive to that area. Half our drive was taken up by finding a spot in the Upper Basin's massive parking lot. While we hastily moved toward Grand Geyser, we saw a jet of water project 150 feet into the air. We were still a tenth of a mile away, but it was quite a show, even from that distance. We arrived at the back of the crowd and watched several smaller spurts and mighty puffs of steam that trailed the eruption's main plume.

Once Grand Geyser was through, we still had thirty minutes until Old Faithful next did its thing, so we wandered through a bit of the Upper Basin, seeing various hot pools and smaller, less spectacular geysers as we had at Norris. Signs throughout both geyser basins we had visited—and all the others we would see later in the trip—warned not to step off the trail because they were a "Thin Crust Area." I turned to Robert after we had seen about half a dozen of these signs and said, "As a long-time resident of the Chicago area, I feel there should be a Deep-Dish Area for equal time." Robert groaned in response.

My horrible jokes aside, these warnings are serious as rock or soil is thin around geothermal features. It is possible to fall into scalding acidic water if you put too much weight on one spot. Because of this, you must walk through most geyser basins on raised boardwalks instead of ground-level trails. Many park visitors seemed to want to fall into scalding pools of acidic water as I saw people step off the boardwalks and onto the ground surrounding geysers or hot springs several times.

We arrived at the main Old Faithful viewing area ten minutes before its predicted time, but we waited just over fifteen minutes for the eruption. There was a huge crowd of camera-toting tourists sitting on benches, grumbling that the geyser was minutes late as the predicted eruption time passed. The vibe was more like people waiting for a tardy dolphin show starting at Sea World than a natural phenomenon at a National Park.

Old Faithful is world-famous, arguably the second-most famous feature of a US national park after the Grand Canyon. Like the Grand Canyon, Old Faithful gained that fame without a simple superlative. It is not the biggest, most predictable, or most frequently erupting geyser. It is just the most frequent and predictable of Yellowstone's big geysers. It erupts every ninety minutes, while the other hundred-footers erupt no more than three times a day. Thus, if you only have a few hours in the park, Old Faithful is the one big geyser you can be sure to see erupt.

While Old Faithful is more predictable than the other big geysers and has always erupted close to its predicted timing, it is not so regular that you can set your watch on it, and the eruptions are now slowly trending farther apart. Over the park's recorded history, the latency period has gradually expanded from around 60 minutes in the 1930s to the ninety-minute average today.

When Old Faithful finally erupted slightly late after our arrival, it did not disappoint, eliciting oohs and ahs from those waiting. The wind had kicked up a bit, and this blew some of the water laterally from the geyser eruption's 100-foot apex, which spread the water droplets at the top, giving the water spray some width and body that made it more visually striking than the more columnar eruption we had seen from Grand Geyser.

Once Old Faithful petered out, we resumed our explorations in Upper Geyser Basin. We saw geysers with large, shapely cones of mineral deposits around them with names like Castle Geyser and Grotto Geyser and smaller, less showy geysers with memorable names like Economic Geyser and Spiteful Geyser. There were also more colorful hot water pools. My favorite feature was the spiral-shaped Chromatic Pool, which had two long arcs of water branching from a circular central pool. It made me think of pictures of galaxies. It was relatively shallow, had a blue core, and had yellow and rusty orange areas around it.

Morning Glory Pool had a roughly similar color scheme but greater visible depth. An interpretive sign explained that the color of this pool has slowly changed from a deep blue to the same orange-yellow-blue scheme of Chromatic Pool due to people throwing things in it. This sign indicated that the color changes are due to contamination and to those tossed objects restricting the opening at the bottom of the pool, which changes water circulation and temperature.

Before leaving the Upper Geyser Basin, Robert and I walked into the Old Faithful Inn. We had wanted to stay here, but it was fully reserved long before we selected our trip dates. Built in 1904, the Old Faithful Inn claims to be the largest log structure in the world. Its four-story-tall lobby had a massive stone fireplace. The curvy, knotty wood we could see in the many upper-level staircase rails visible from the lobby gave the place an M.C.-Escher-meets-Lincoln-Logs vibe.

Since we could not get a room at the Old Faithful Inn, Robert and I spent our three Yellowstone nights at the lodge in Grant Village, a cluster of buildings along the banks of Yellowstone Lake, the large lake in the southeast section of the park. Grant Village had a post office, a gas station, an auto repair shop, and restaurants. Although it was just twenty miles from Old Faithful, getting there took us over the Continental Divide…twice. Old Faithful and the Grant Village area were at an elevation of just over 7,000 feet, but the road between them climbed through two mountain passes at 8,300 feet.

We checked into our lodge at Grant Village and found our room, which looked like a basic, modern hotel room, except it had no TV. Our windows offered only a view of the parking lot and trees surrounding it, but we were only a short walk from the lakeshore. We ate dinner in restaurants in the village each night, which had dining rooms with lake views and menus featuring many elk and bison items, presumably thinking that seeing them in the park would make us want to taste them.

We started our Tuesday by driving north through the Hayden Valley. This flat, grassy valley is seven miles wide and seven miles long. Many animals graze here, so it is one of the best places in the park to view wildlife. We had seen several individual bison along park roads while driving the day before, but in this valley, we saw a large herd of them even bigger than the one that surrounded my car at Wind Cave. This bison herd had decided to cross the road but lingered on the pavement for a while before finishing, which caused a major traffic jam that a ranger was trying to manage. One bison, which had already crossed the road, now walked back onto the pavement, and briefly stood right next to our car. "I hope he does not know about that bison burger I ate last night," I fretted.

Even after the ranger directed us past the bison traffic jam, the going was slow because every few feet, someone spotted a deer, bison, or elk near the road, stomped on their brakes, and turned onto the shoulder. Half the cars behind that first car would decide that whatever that first person had seen must be amazing, stomp on their brakes, and look around. This was so common that a Pavlovian reflex still caused me to look for wildlife at the sight of brake lights for a week after returning to Chicago.

We made several short stops in the morning. We saw geothermal areas that were less spectacular than what we had already seen. Past visitors must have tried to compensate for that by giving them more spectacular names, such as Mud Volcano and the Black Dragon's Caldron. This area was rife with mud pots, pits of gloppy mud that had bubbles plop out of them at irregular intervals as steam forced its way to the surface.

Our headline stop for the day was Mammoth Hot Springs on the park's north side. The hot water from these springs does not shoot out of the ground; it just trickles slowly and steadily. However, the water goes through limestone along the way and dissolves calcium carbonate. After it seeps out of the ground and cools, some calcium carbonate crystallizes on the rock outside, leaving travertine deposits. "It's like an outdoor cave!" I exclaimed upon seeing small stalactite-like travertine deposits and smooth dripstones at the first such spring we saw.

The most beautiful of the Mammoth Hot Springs was Palette Springs. Its hot water ran down a ridge with little steps coated in a textured, brilliant white layer of sparkly travertine. It looked like someone made a pyramid out of checkers and then sprayed it with whatever they used to make the popcorn ceilings in 1970s houses. The heat-tolerant bacteria we had seen at other geothermal areas made rust-orange streaks on it.

We spent about three hours wandering the Mammoth Hot Springs area. I loved it, but most of the individual active springs looked essentially alike. One interesting phenomenon near several hot springs was that travertine deposits had built around some trees over time and killed them. In some cases, the trees absorbed the calcium carbonate, leaving their trunks a ghostly white. While we had seen orange or red stains from the heat-loving bacteria in many of these geothermal areas, in one spot here, a boardwalk went directly over a stream of hot water. We could see another extremophile bacteria there that had formed thick, almost ropy-looking mats. In other places, the hot pools of water had a thin skin of minerals plating out on them that looked almost like someone had left a creamy soup sitting too long.

Mammoth Hot Springs was also the site of Fort Yellowstone, the fort used by the Army when it patrolled Yellowstone before the National Park Service was formed in 1916, and visitors can tour some of its buildings. Congress created Yellowstone National Park in 1872, but for the next few decades, they rarely appropriated any money for its protection and management. Poachers openly shot wildlife. Native Americans attacked some early tourists. General Phillip Sheridan, who had that section of the west under his military purview, decided to protect the park and stationed cavalry there. Sheridan became an advocate for the park and recommended expanding it to better protect bison herds and once lobbied Congress to prevent a company from building a proposed railroad through the park.

I also talked Robert into driving to the north entrance to the park at Gardiner, Montana, so I could see another piece of Yellowstone history. In 1903, Gardiner built a stone arch over the entrance to the National Park. Since the rail line came to Gardiner, this was the typical entrance for early tourists.

Theodore Roosevelt visited Yellowstone during his presidency. During that trip, he gave a dedication speech for this arch in which he articulated a strong link between National Parks and democracy itself. Of Yellowstone, Roosevelt said, "The scheme of its preservation is noteworthy in its essential democracy. Private game preserves, though they may be handled in such a way as to be not only good things for themselves but good things for the surrounding community, can yet never be more than poor substitutes, from the standpoint of the public, for great national playgrounds such as this Yellowstone Park. This Park was created and is now administered for the benefit and enjoyment of the people." That last phrase, a quote from the 1872 law that made Yellowstone a National Park, is inscribed on the top of the arch.

After re-entering the park through the arch in Gardiner, we visited a strange swimming hole called Boiling River. The hot water from Mammoth Hot Springs runs into a creek that flows into the Gardiner River. At the place where they meet, the cold water of the Gardiner (temperatures in the sixties are typical) merges with the 140°F water of the creek. By carefully picking spots, you can swim or wade in pleasantly warm waters or stand with one foot in very hot water and another in very cool water.

Boiling River is accessed via a flat 1.25-mile trail just north of the Montana-Wyoming border. We had brought trunks for this, and there was a place in which to change at the parking lot. Robert and I decided to roll up our shorts and wade. Ominous signs warned that the thermal waters of Yellowstone might host organisms that could cause rashes, infections, meningitis, and Legionnaire's Disease and recommended not sticking your head below water. I did not plan on getting water above my knee, so this was no problem. A large group of elk was also enjoying the warm water just downstream of the human tourists.

The hot springs and geysers are here because Yellowstone is a "super volcano" that has erupted explosively every 650,000 years or so. The NPS Yellowstone brochure illustrates the shape of the most recent eruption's caldera. It is enormous, roughly 45 miles by 30 miles, and includes much of the park. As we drove south from the Mammoth Hot Springs area, the road passed through Golden Gate Canyon, one of the best places to see the 500-foot-thick layers of material belched from an eruption of the Yellowstone volcano 2.1 million years ago. That same eruption sent enough ash into the air that geologists have found layers of it in places as far away as Los Angeles and St. Louis.

We started our Thursday by visiting a small geothermal area near our lodge, West Thumb Geyser Basin. The geysers and hot springs were less spectacular than the areas we saw on Tuesday, but the lakeside setting made the experience novel. The most beautiful feature was Abyss Pool, a light blue pool with green forest, steaming fumaroles, and a big lake behind it. It was such a striking scene that Robert and I observed it silently for several minutes before making jokes about the James Cameron movie.

The most famous feature in West Thumb is an unspectacular-looking hot spring called Fishing Cone in the lake, a few feet from the shore, rising just above the water's surface. In the park's early days, fishermen are said to have caught fish in the lake and swung them, still on the line, into this hot spring to cook them. This is no longer allowed, a sign indicated, to protect the hot spring, but not, apparently, the fish.

The highlight of our third day was a visit to the Grand Canyon…but not that one. Strictly speaking, the one in Arizona is the Grand Canyon of the Colorado River, but it is so grand that nobody bothers to say the rest. Yellowstone National Park has the Grand Canyon of the Yellowstone, a 24-mile-long 1,200-foot-deep gorge along the Yellowstone River.

The Grand Canyon in Arizona may be way longer and four times deeper, but Yellowstone's Grand Canyon is just as pretty. We started our visit at the most popular place to view the canyon, Artist's Point, and found its khaki-colored walls were mostly bare rock but dotted with color from evergreen trees and red, yellow, and orange streaks—and sometimes even puffs of steam—from geothermal features on the canyon walls. In the center, the white water of the Yellowstone surges along the canyon floor after tumbling 300 feet down from the Lower Falls, which sent mist and a rainbow far up the canyon walls. Several people have insisted that my picture taken at Artist's Point is so pretty that it cannot be real, but I assure you it is real and spectacular.

We continued to marvel at the canyon as we walked the South Rim Trail and then hiked Uncle Tom's Trail into the canyon to get a closer view of the falls. Uncle Tom's Trail quickly descends five hundred feet into the canyon via steep inclines and 300 stairs. After spending several minutes feeling the power of the spray from the falls and taking pictures of the rainbow in its mist, we reluctantly began climbing out of the canyon.

I hate walking upward on stairs; these were no exception, especially since they took me away from a great view. I liked them a little better when we were near the top. I noticed Robert was not immediately behind me but was a full flight below, red-faced with his hands on his knees and panting. I gloated because Robert had ribbed me for being the one panting during our first trip to National Parks. I decided to be mature and let it go without comment. Minutes later, I decided to comment and teased him for being slow for most of the walk back to the car.

We spent the rest of our afternoon in the park's southwest section to see other geyser basins we had not seen Tuesday, like the Black Sand, Midway, and Biscuit basins. We saw another dizzying array of geysers, fumaroles, and hot springs.

The highlight of these last hours of ogling geothermal wonders was the Grand Prismatic Spring, the largest hot spring in the US and the third largest in the world. As long as a football field, this spring's waters have distinct rings of color mimicking the pattern of colors in a rainbow: a deep blue center, green and yellow bands from sulfur deposits, and a red outer ring from the now familiar rust-red bacteria.

We got a general impression of the spring's immense size at ground level, but we were too close to it to fully appreciate the rainbow color scheme or see its full extent in one gaze. I had seen aerial photos that perfectly showed the spring's full shape and rainbow colors. I wanted to see that. We learned that a viewpoint for Grand Prismatic Spring could be accessed by walking partway down the Fairy Falls Trail and then climbing a hill along it. We did this and found the magnificent view I wanted.

A few weeks after our visit, I read that a tourist had crashed a drone into Grand Prismatic Spring and experts feared this could restrict its water flow and alter its color scheme. Infuriated that one visitor's carelessness might ruin such a beautiful natural wonder that belonged to all Americans, I thought back to the sign I had seen on our first day in the park that said pale blue Morning Glory Pool had once been a deep sapphire blue. Its colors were altered by people throwing coins into the pool's opening. Then I thought about the fools wantonly walking on "thin crust" areas, risking both damages to themselves and the geothermal features. Another interpretive sign we had seen on a trail called Forces of the Northern Range mentioned a destructive fire caused by a camper's carelessness.

Such thoughts made me so angry that I wanted to volunteer to patrol Yellowstone's geyser basins wielding a baseball bat.

Theodore Roosevelt's 1903 speech to dedicate the Gardiner Arch included him saying, "The only way that the people as a whole can secure to themselves and their children the enjoyment in perpetuity of what the Yellowstone National Park has to give, is by assuming the ownership in the name of the nation and jealously safeguarding and preserving the scenery, the forests and the wild creatures."

Most hands-on, day-to-day "jealously safeguarding" falls to National Park rangers. These civil servants may give helpful advice to tourists one minute and participate in a dangerous search-and-rescue operation the next minute, possibly because a tourist ignored a ranger's practical advice. Many rangers are law enforcement professionals who fight and solve "ordinary" crimes in the park and work to protect the park's wonders and creatures from malfeasance like poaching or vandalism.

Robert and I visited the Museum of the National Park Ranger as one of our last stops in Yellowstone. Exhibits here explained a park ranger's job and how it has changed over time. I strongly recommend it as a museum and a small way to pay tribute to those doing this vital job.

Rangers do not want or need park visitors turning vigilante, so I put aside my *Walking Tall* in a National Park fantasy. That said, while rangers are employees of the National Park system, all Americans co-own it. Such damage would not occur if National Park visitors acted like proud, responsible co-owners of these unique places with a vested interest in protecting their natural wonders and beauty.

THIRTY-SEVEN
GRAND TETON NATIONAL PARK
SEPTEMBER 6, 2013

"COME ON, get out there. You won't get stuck," I crowed to Robert Wright.

The Yellowstone visit Robert and I made in the previous chapter was the centerpiece of our longer trip that started with us flying to Salt Lake City, Utah on Saturday, August 31st. Robert admitted the Mustang he rented on our last joint trip had been constraining, so he selected a Ford Taurus Limited this time.

We then drove west two hours on I-80 to The Bonneville Salt Flats, where drivers set world speed records during Speed Week events held every summer and fall. If no race events are underway, visitors can drive on the salt at their own risk. Before our trip, Robert talked boldly about driving our rental car on the salt flat.

Much like Badwater Basin in Death Valley, the Bonneville Salt Flats are broad, flat valleys between mountains covered by a layer of dirt topped with a salt crystal crust. The long, uninterrupted flat surfaces made this an ideal place for bringing souped-up cars to maximum speed.

Today's Great Salt Lake, which we had seen from the interstate while driving here, was created by a much larger body of saltwater thousands of years ago. We were looking at salt the lake's slow contraction has left behind. A light but steady rain fell during our drive. This rare desert precipitation left a thin layer of water on the salt and dissolved Robert's resolve. Although the rain had been light, Robert insisted there was too significant a risk of getting stuck. Naturally, I responded by teasing him about being a chicken.

"No way I'm going out there now," Robert insisted, not bowing to my taunting. "The water can seep through the salt and turn the dirt below it into mud. I have read too many racing blog stories about racing cars getting stuck in that stuff after rain."

We were standing on a paved parking lot adjacent to the flats just off I-80. The only other person there was a middle-aged man wearing a straw hat seated on a lawn chair in front of a van, silently staring toward the mountains just as he had been since we had arrived.

"He's right," intoned the man by the van without breaking his stare across the salt. "I wouldn't go out there unless you know what you're doing. I saw a car get stuck about a half mile out there," he said, pointing in a specific direction, "and before it was all said and done, it took three tow trucks to get him out."

"Three tow trucks?" I asked incredulously.

He then told a lengthy, richly layered tale that I cannot recall in full detail, but the gist was that a race car got stuck there once after a run in the rain. A tow truck was called that also got stuck. A second tow truck was summoned and suffered the same fate. Finally, a third more massive tow rig freed all three stuck rides.

As Robert listened to more Bonneville stories that man recounted after he finished describing the tow truck threesome, I wandered away intending to hike a salt flat again. I hoped to relive the magic of crossing Badwater Basin but soon abandoned the notion as every step on the lightly watered crust splashed brine. I returned to the parking lot with soggy shoes that later developed a white crust on the soles after drying.

We spent that night in Salt Lake City, then started Sunday by driving to the north side of Great Salt Lake. We were here to see three attractions, the first of which was the Golden Spike National Historic Site. In 1869, at this spot in the now defunct town of Promontory, a golden railroad spike was driven into a wooden tie during a ceremony held to mark the meeting of the Central Pacific and Union Pacific railroads. Driving the golden spike marked the completion of the United States' first transcontinental rail line.

Rail lines were later routed further south, so the original track was salvaged for scrap metal. The National Park Service has rebuilt this section of track and daily re-enacts the Golden Spike ceremony with train engines painstakingly restored to resemble the actual ones that met in Promontory for the ceremony in 1869. Robert and I watched both engines arrive and then perused the site's museum, which had many artifacts, but not the actual Golden Spike because it is on display at Stanford.

Because they were nearby, we stopped at a sculpture on the north side of the Great Salt Lake and a display of rockets in front of a rocket plant owned by the company ATK. The rockets were reminiscent of the "missile gallery" we had seen in Albuquerque and gave Robert a chance to go into aerospace geek mode.

The sculpture, however, was quite unusual. Called Spiral Jetty, it was created in 1970 by Robert Smithson and was composed of 6,000 tons of local black stones arranged into a 15-foot wide, 1,500-foot long, counter-clockwise spiral. Depending on the lake level on a given day, you might find the sculpture entirely above water (as it was during our visit), partially underwater, or wholly submerged. Robert and I walked to the center of the spiral and then past it to the mucky edge of the Great Salt Lake's water, which, from our vantage point, looked pink from the color of salt-loving microbes living in it.

Once finished near the Great Salt Lake, we continued driving into Idaho and spent the night in a little town called Burley. The following day, before heading to our next stop, we bought a few things in a Walmart, and upon returning to our car, I was stung by a bee. Whenever someone asks me if I am afraid of hiking in National Parks because wild animals live there, I tell them that no animal in a National Park has injured me, but I have been injured by an animal in a Walmart parking lot.

From there, we drove to Shoshone Falls, an enormous waterfall near Twin Falls, Idaho. Here, the Snake River plunges 200 feet down a rocky cliff one thousand feet wide. The falls are inside a steep canyon with 500-foot-tall walls. We had driven into the canyon and parked at a city park with an overlook away from the falls, but the roar of the water was loud enough that we had to raise our voices for the conversation that ensued.

"This is awesome," Robert said as we gazed at the roaring falls.

"This isn't a National Park, is it?"

"No," I answered, "It's just a city park with an enormous waterfall."

"Then how did you find out about this place?" Robert wanted to know.

"I saw a video of it during a *Jeopardy!* clue," I responded.

"We're here because of the Clue Crew?" Robert asked.

"Yeah, Sarah was very convincing," I acknowledged.

"Wait a minute," Robert said. "If that's the Snake River in the canyon, this is the Snake River Canyon, right?"

"Stands to reason," I admitted. I planned this stop to see a waterfall after seeing the waterfall here on *Jeopardy!*, but I had never seen the canyon named in my pre-trip research, and I was not sure where Robert was going with this.

Robert demanded, "Well, isn't this where Evel did that jump? Well, or tried to, anyway?"

I realized Robert meant an ill-fated 1974 attempt by daredevil Evel Knievel to jump over Snake River Canyon in Skycycle X-2, a vehicle he called a motorcycle but was a rocket with token wheels on the back.

Knievel's basic idea and math for the jump were sound—as sound as strapping oneself to a rocket could be—but a malfunction caused the parachute to open early, sending Skycycle crashing to the canyon floor.

Robert found an interpretive sign in the park that confirmed the jump did occur just outside this park, and the sizeable earthen ramp Knievel used could be viewed from the end of a two-mile hiking trail in the park that led to the top of the canyon. We agreed we had to see this ramp. Forty-five minutes of walking later, we were looking at the ramp, which sat just a few feet behind a barbed wire fence.

We did not have a rocket on our rental car, but we still traveled next from Twin Falls to the Craters of the Moon. Along US Highway 26, between Carey and Arco, Idaho, sits Craters of the Moon National Monument, a National Park Service-protected ancient basaltic lava field of more than 600 square miles in area with more than twenty volcanic cones and craters that collectively inspired the place's name.

We hiked trails here for six hours through vast swaths of black rock formed by old aa and pahoehoe lava flows and saw rock "molds" of trees, formed when a tree was covered in a lava flow and burned away, and volcanic "bombs," smooth volcanic rocks that had been flung from volcanos during eruptions. We climbed two ancient volcanoes: 160-foot-tall Inferno Cone, an ancient cinder cone that looked smooth from a distance but was composed of small loose cinder rocks that shifted beneath my feet as I walked, and Snow Cone, a spatter cone so named because its interior stays cool enough to retain ice inside year-round.

My favorite places here were the lava tube caves. Lava tube caves form when lava flows from a volcanic eruption are so big that the outside of the flow cools back into rock, creating, in essence, a lava pipe. Once the lava flow stops, a hollow tube of cooled lava rock is left behind. While Carlsbad and Wind Cave were examples of solution caves, meaning acidic water had dissolved a tunnel out of a pre-existing solid layer of rock, lava tube caves are called primary caves, meaning this rock initially formed in the shape of this cave.

Lava tube caves did not have stalactites, but I loved exploring them because none were electrically lit like Carlsbad, so you had to do some actual spelunking wearing headlamps and carrying flashlights. Getting inside some required negotiating large rubble piles, and I managed to scrape my knee on one, adding a second minor injury on the day to the bee sting I suffered earlier. Some of the caves stayed cool enough that there were sections of the floor covered in ice. Going inside these caves felt exciting, yet never dangerous—apart from my knee scrape—because the NPS had detailed guides telling you exactly how long each one was and how best to travel in them.

The next morning, we drove to Yellowstone for the three fabulous days I described in the previous chapter. We checked out of that lodge in Yellowstone the morning of Friday, September 6th, drove out of Yellowstone's south end, and, only ten miles later, entered the north end of Grand Teton National Park.

This National Park covers the steep, glacier-covered peaks of the forty-mile-long Teton mountain range and a lovely valley to the east called Jackson Hole. The park takes its name from the tallest peak in the range, Grand Teton, which tops out at 13,700 feet. What makes this place so striking is the contrast of Jackson Hole to the peaks. This valley is 7,000 feet below the top of Grand Teton. There is an abrupt transition from that flat valley to the towering mountains.

There is a large lake on the north side of the park called Jackson Lake, and there is a developed area called Colter Bay Village with a lodge, campgrounds, a store, and a marina between two small peninsulas projecting into that lake. A two-mile Lakeshore Trail meanders around one of those peninsulas. Robert and I started our morning by hiking it. It was a nice walk in the woods, and we saw a bit of wildlife, but nothing exotic, just deer and rabbits. We were about to write it off as just a nice leg stretch when we reached a spot on the lake's shore and were treated to seeing a line of jagged Teton peaks perfectly reflected in the clear lake waters. This stunning view was worth the walk.

We spent most of our time in the park's most popular area, Jenny Lake. There is a visitor center with a small museum on one side of this pretty lake. Some hiking trails go all the way around the lake on the shore, and another trail is on a slope well above the shore. There is also a frequently running ferry boat across the lake that takes visitors, for a small fee, to the Cascade Canyon trailhead, where visitors can access the park's most popular trail.

We took the ferry and started hiking this trail, which ascended the lower elevations of one mountain slope, and after half a mile arrived at a one-hundred-foot-tall waterfall. Roughly another half mile took us to a viewpoint over Jenny Lake called Inspiration Point. In this stretch, the trail gained about two hundred feet of elevation and was very crowded, with steady streams of hikers moving in both directions. It was narrow, and its surface was studded with rough, shifting rocks. Thus, our progress was slow.

Inspiration Point yielded a nice lake view. Many hikers immediately turned and hiked back to the lake, but Robert and I continued into Cascade Canyon. This was not a steep-walled canyon, just a "wrinkle" between two mountains with a creek passing between them. This was a nice hike through a mountain forest, but it did not lead anywhere spectacular. When raindrops started falling, we returned to Inspiration Point.

We decided to hike back to the car via the two-mile trail on the south end of Jenny Lake instead of returning on the boat. There is a trail directly on the shore, but it was closed for maintenance, so the only option was a trail higher up the slope that was a dual-use hiking and equestrian trail. As such, we had to spend some of our energy stepping around multitudinous mounds of manure deposited by some literal horse's ass.

After finishing that trail, we were both tired and decided to call it a day. It was just as well as a huge downpour started during our drive to the hotel in Jackson, Wyoming, where we spent the night.

That evening, we ate at a popular local brew pub. I laughed out loud when I noticed that one of the large tanks in the brewery area had "Rob

Still Sucks" painted on its side. I smirked as my friends in the dorm and I had usually just called Robert "Rob" during our college days. "How did they know you were coming here," I asked Robert, barely able to speak that sentence between short bursts of laughter.

Several years after our graduations, my closest college friends annually reunited at Rolla during the university's St. Patrick's Day festival, which was the biggest party at our alma mater. Rolla students say Saint Patrick is the patron saint of engineers, so each year, four days around Saint Patrick's Day contain a parade, a concert, binge drinking, and unusual rituals. Fraternity pledges walk the campus carrying a shillelagh and, when ordered to do so by senior frat members, attempt to decapitate plastic snakes with them.

After graduation, this seemed like the best time to have an annual informal reunion. The first time we did this, Robert had a conflict and could not join us. To properly punish him for his absence, my friends and I called Robert that night. We loudly yelled into the phone, in near-perfect unison, "Rob, you suck."

More than a decade later, this brewpub in Wyoming had heard that message. If I do say so myself, I showed remarkable restraint and good manners after seeing that message on the brew tank. I only texted three of our shared friends about it and brought it up only eight times during dinner.

Robert seemed to be taking it in stride, but as we walked back to our hotel after dinner, I tried to take a conciliatory tone and conceded, "You may still suck, Robert, but traveling with you hasn't."

THIRTY-EIGHT
OLYMPIC NATIONAL PARK
FEBRUARY 1-2, 2014

NO PERIOD in my life had felt longer than the seconds I spent stopping the blaring alarm on my rental car just after 6 AM on a Saturday in a residential neighborhood of Aberdeen, Washington.

My visit to Olympic National Park was between two consecutive weeks I spent working on a project at a Tumwater, Washington beverage plant. Since I needed to be at the plant late on Friday the first week and early on Monday the second week, I chose to stay in Washington for the weekend. That saved PepsiCo the cost of two flights and saved me ten hours of being crammed into an airline seat.

Since Washington had three National Parks I had yet to visit, I wanted to visit one that weekend. Each was drivable from Tumwater but centered on mountains snow packed in February. Slogging through snow held little appeal. Also, the NPS website said visiting Mount Rainier or North Cascades National Parks in February required tire chains, which I did not have. Regardless, it was not wise to drive somewhere that required them in a rental car.

That left Olympic National Park as the only option. While it also had 7,000-foot peaks that required tire chains to visit in February, Olympic had some low-elevation stretches near the Pacific coast that stayed warm enough in winter that snow was rare. Rain was not rare there, however, as this part of the park annually receives 12 feet of rain on average, making it the wettest place in the contiguous 48 states and the only place in the lower 48 with rain forests.

Hiking through rainforests sounded exotic, so I excitedly made reservations and an itinerary. My resolve to hike in Olympic National Park that weekend waivered during my first week working in Tumwater due to the weather. The high temperatures in the 50s were a welcome change from frigid Chicagoland, but it constantly rained that week, and Tumwater was generally not nearly as rainy as the rain forests. What was I getting myself into? Still, I had made plans and packed a poncho, so I stayed the course.

Tumwater and Olympic National Park are on the Olympic Peninsula, that northwestern part of Washington that on a map looks like a battering ram on the front of the state. The tire-chain-requiring Olympic Mountains filled the center of the peninsula, so I would avoid those by driving a loop around the outside of the peninsula, stopping for hikes in the National Park along the peninsula's west and north coasts.

When I finished work Friday night, I drove across the south end of the peninsula from Tumwater to Aberdeen, Washington, a port city a little south of the National Park, and I spent the night in a hotel there. Aberdeen is arguably most famous as having been the hometown of Kurt Cobain, the late lead singer and songwriter of Nirvana. This rock band was a generational touchstone for me since their success ushered in the 1990s alternative rock scene that was the soundtrack of my college years. The first time I remember feeling old was the day I heard a radio DJ say Nirvana's album *Nevermind* was twenty years old.

The "welcome to Aberdeen" sign I passed while driving into town said "Come as you are" on it, a reference to a Nirvana song. As I checked into my hotel, I wondered if Aberdeen had erected a Cobain memorial. While preparing for bed, I read online that it had done so at a spot near a bridge over the Wishkah River that had been a hangout spot for Cobain in his teens. Despite not knowing it existed just seconds ago, I suddenly ached to see it, but I was unwilling to sacrifice any daylight time in the National Park, especially on a short winter day. Thus, I decided I would try and see the memorial before sunrise.

When I found the memorial before 6 AM the following day, I was surprised it was not in ample green space but on a thin strip of grass along the banks of the muddy Wishkah directly across from a row of houses. After parking in front of one of those houses, I walked around the memorial, which was composed of a metal sculpture of Cobain's Fender Jaguar guitar atop a stone plinth and a metal ribbon engraved with "One more special message to go, and then I'm done, and I can go home," a lyric from the Nirvana song "On a Plain." I loved the understated design that kept the focus on Cobain's music.

Returning to my rental car misty-eyed in the still dark, misty morning, I accidentally hit the "panic button" on the key fob instead of the button that unlocked the doors. The car alarm began blaring. As I desperately tried to shut it off, I managed to drop the keys on the wet pavement. Thus, I had to drop to my knees to retrieve them and shut off the alarm. I quickly scrambled to my feet and into the car. I sped away, fearing someone I had just woken in one of those houses might emerge any moment and do something that would necessitate the construction of a Jeremy White memorial.

While periodically checking my rearview mirror to ensure I was not being followed by a shotgun-waving, prematurely roused Aberdeen resident, I drove to the Quinault rain forest, my first planned stop in the National Park, faster than Google Maps had predicted. During this drive, the rain dissipated, and a sunny morning dawned, the first sun I had seen in five days. I could not believe my luck. The sun shone for my entire time in the park. That poncho never left my backpack.

While "rain forest" had conjured mental images of an Amazon jungle, Quinault did not have triple canopies, long vines, or monkeys. Quinault was a temperate rainforest. Like the rest of coastal Washington, most trees were not hardwoods but conifers. The two immediately apparent differences between this rainforest and non-rain-forest wooded areas near Seattle were the size of the trees—they were much bigger here—and the abundant mosses that covered—nay, smothered virtually every trunk, branch, and twig.

Walking here felt like striding through an enchanted forest from a fairy tale. Wispy, yellow-green moss hung down from branches as if the trees had grown out their hair. Fuzzy dark green moss so blanketed some tree trunks that they looked like the limbs of green stuffed animals. Long dead trees on the forest floor had substantial young trees growing on them. Other trees had trunks stopping three feet above the ground with partially exposed spindly roots that, from a distance, made them look like they were walking on spider legs.

Two of the four trails I walked in this area led to enormous trees, one a spruce and the other a red cedar, said to be the world's largest example of their species. The cedar had a hollowed area in its trunk so vast that I could stand inside it and wave my arms without hitting anything. Tendrils of wood hung down from the top of the hollow, like stalactites in a wooden cave.

After leaving the forest, I entered an area of the National Park directly on the Pacific coast with several beaches. These did not have hiking trails, but I parked at each and walked to the water's edge. These were not manicured swim beaches but thin strips of sand strewn with driftwood and boulders beneath rocky cliffs. At some, the ocean surface was pierced by "sea stacks," tiny rocky islands topped with columnar spires that looked like they could be smokestacks of factories.

Sea birds soared above me and various marine life scuttled in tidal pools here, but I spent most of my time scoping those sea stacks and the rock layers in the cliffs. Rocks along one beach were pockmarked with shallow holes that had been bored into them by clams. Another beach had vertical sedimentary rock layers at the base of its shoreline cliff. Since sediment is usually deposited in horizontal layers, I inspected this spot, wondering if some seismic event had folded them upward.

While staring at the rocks, I did not notice a little wave about to crash ashore. I left that beach with a wet left pant leg. With the heater at full blast and the vents aimed at my dripping jeans, I drove out of the park and into a town called Forks, which sounded familiar. I could not think of why I knew the name until I saw multiple storefronts in its business district offering *"Twilight* tours" or *Twilight* souvenirs. Yes, Forks was the setting of that Stephanie Meyer novel series and subsequent movies about a whiny teen girl and her love triangle with a mopey vampire and a muscle-bound teen who transforms into a wolf. I had not read the book, but I had seen that film due to a personal policy that had backfired.

One of my favorite places in Barrington was a movie theater called The Catlow. It was built in 1927, had been designed to resemble a Jacobean dining hall, and had a fountain in its lobby sculpted by Alfonso Iannelli. The Catlow had an excellent sandwich shop in its lobby which was then called Boloney's. You could bring one of their sandwich creations to your seat and eat it during a movie. Dinner, a film, art, and architecture… What's not to love? As such, upon moving to Barrington for a job in the late 1990s, I made a personal policy to watch any movie screened there that I had not already seen. I followed it unquestioningly until the night in 2008 when I reported dutifully to the Catlow to watch *Twilight*. I have seen worse movies, but something about the brooding teens in *Twilight* irritated me more than any other film I have ever seen. Knowing it had sequels on the way, my policy was amended to exclude all films with "Twilight" in the title.

I bought my lunch in Forks but feared *Twilight* associations would make me lose it. Thus, I drove swiftly back into the National Park to eat my lunch and to see another rainforest, this one in the Hoh river valley. This area was like Quinault, with nature trails into dense forests with trees blanketed by moss.

Hoh was busier than Quinault and had more interpretive materials, including exhibits in the visitor center and more frequent interpretive signs. The vibe of my hikes in Quinault had been an awed reverie through a fantasy environment. By contrast, the Hoh valley felt like walking through the world's best biology textbook, explaining the wonders I had pondered in the morning.

For example, I learned those hanging mosses were "epiphytic," meaning they took nutrients from rain or the air. Those trees with spider legs started life on a "nurse log," a rotting chunk of wood from a dead tree that gives nutrients and structural support to living plants. If a tree begins life on a nurse log, its root system starts feet off the ground, leaving its top exposed when the log eventually rots away.

I backtracked and spent that night in the park at the Kalaloch Lodge, located on a Pacific beach site near those I visited earlier. This beach was smoother and flatter than the ones I had seen earlier. The Seattle Seahawks were playing in the Super Bowl the next day, and someone had drawn a 10-foot-wide version of the team's logo in the sand. Sitting on the beach at a respectful distance from this artwork, I watched a spectacularly colorful sunset over the Pacific.

The following day, I drove back through Forks on US-101, turning east and re-entering the National Park. From there, the road was immediately next to Lake Crescent, a gorgeous lake that filled a glacier-carved valley between steep mountains. In this northern part of the park, I hiked along that lake and to a lovely 120-foot-tall waterfall called Marymere Falls.

It was sunny through those hikes, and as I drove out of the park and down the eastern side of the peninsula, but clouds gathered as I reached Tumwater. It began immediately raining while I walked into my hotel. I can only assume this was nature's way of reminding me how fortunate I had been to experience two precipitation-free days in the rainiest place in the lower 48 states.

THIRTY-NINE
HOT SPRINGS NATIONAL PARK
MAY 27, 2014

HOT SPRINGS WAS the only National Park I had ever visited in a year before starting my National Park Diet. My parents once took my two sisters and me to Hot Springs, Arkansas while I was in high school.

Thrilled to go somewhere new at that age, I spent weeks reading about attractions in that city and was delighted to learn that a National Park was just a few miles from where we would be. Back then, I had not thought too deeply about what National Parks were meant to be, but I knew natural wonders like Old Faithful and the Grand Canyon were in National Parks, so I assumed this park would have things on a similar scale. When I got to visit it with family then, Hot Springs National Park fell far short of what I imagined.

Hot Springs National Park is an oddball among National Parks. Cuyahoga Valley had seemed odd to me since it was nestled amidst suburbs, but Hot Springs National Park seemed even stranger as it was located downtown in a city of 35,000 people. The park's most visited area is at the base of Hot Springs Mountain. Well, they call it a mountain. It seemed big enough in high school since I had yet to see the Rockies or the Appalachians, but it was just a hill only 600 feet tall.

The mountain, town, and National Park were all named for natural hot springs on a mountain from which 140°F water seeps out of the ground. Hot Springs sometimes claims to be the first National Park. While this is not technically true, there is some truth to it. The federal government set aside these hot springs for public use as the Hot Springs Reservation in 1832, forty years before Yellowstone was named a National Park. Hot Springs was the first place to be set aside by the federal government for recreational purposes, but it was not officially designated a National Park until Congress renamed it in the 1930s.

In the mountain's original natural state, hot spring water flowed down its slopes to a creek at its base. Businesses leased land along that creek from the federal government and built bathhouses on their plots that utilized the naturally occurring hot water. The area became a tourist attraction. Some visitors just sought a spa day and other cures since the spring waters were purported to have medicinal properties.

The sizable town quickly grew around the reservation. A military hospital and more bathhouses were built. Elaborate landscaping was added to the mountainside. The springs were capped, and their water was piped directly to the bathhouses and hospital. The creek was even routed underground into a tunnel. The place eventually bore little resemblance to its original natural appearance.

Circa 1900, the early wooden bathhouses were replaced with grand brick or stone structures. Although most still stand, only the Buckstaff is still an operating bathhouse. The other buildings are now owned by the government and are rented to businesses or used as National Park facilities. The Fordyce Bathhouse, built in 1899, has been restored to period glory and is the National Park's main visitor center and museum.

During my family's visit to the park in 1992, we toured the Fordyce. The building's interior had gorgeous designs, like bronze sculptures, intricate tile work on baths, and stained-glass windows in changing rooms. The various bathing pools and equipment are displayed and explained, including some later debunked devices that were viewed as cutting-edge therapy at the time of their use.

We walked a half-mile red-brick promenade above Bathhouse Row, where visitors in Hot Springs' glory days strolled in their most fashionable attire after a day of bathing. We saw the Thermal Cascade, a manufactured waterfall in which hot spring water was routed down a slope into a steamy-tiered pool retained by cobblestone walls. We turned the handle of a water fountain that dispensed hot spring water, first built so visitors could take a jug home. One hot spring is left uncapped. My clearest memory of that 1992 visit is of sticking my hands into the waters emerging from it and feeling the heat on my fingers, seeing the steam on my glasses, and marveling that water could emerge from the earth at that temperature.

The high point of that day was driving to the top of Hot Springs Mountain, where my father bought tickets allowing us to ride an elevator to the top of the 200-foot-tall observation tower on the mountain. Here we saw a commanding view of Hot Springs and the surrounding mountains. My father snapped a photo of his three children standing on that tower.

When I started my National Park Diet, I put a fuzzy "maybe" on revisiting Hot Springs since my family's trip to that National Park in my teens meant I had been there before. Late in 2013, though, I realized this thought was dubious. I had not been telling people, "In my entire life, I will eventually have visited all the National Parks in the contiguous 48 states." No, I had been saying, "I will visit all the National Parks in the 48 contiguous states in only 48 months." Semantically, I was thus obligated to return to Hot Springs.

Once I resigned myself to re-visiting Hot Springs, I decided to append my visit to my already planned 2014 Memorial Day weekend trip to visit my parents. When I mentioned returning to Hot Springs National Park, my mother dug into her photo archives and gave me that picture my father had taken of my sisters and me standing on the observation tower in that park in 1992.

On Memorial Day afternoon, I drove most of the way to Hot Springs, then reached the park early Tuesday morning. I wanted to do everything I remembered from my teenage visit and hike a trail on the mountain. The weather forecast showed a strong chance of afternoon rain, so I decided the bathhouse should wait until a rainy afternoon. I parked near Bathhouse Row and then walked the Peak Trail, a steep, half-mile path to the top of the mountain.

The Peak Trail ended at the observation tower. Since I intended to go up it at some point, I decided it might as well happen while I was already here. The tower was a paid attraction run by a concessioner on National Park grounds. I bought a ticket from the concessioner that ran it and rode the elevator to the top. After enjoying the view, I pulled out a scanned copy I had made of that picture Mom had given me of my sisters and me standing here. I spent many minutes playing with my camera and tripod, trying to take a picture in which I stood in the same spot as in that earlier picture.

Upon returning to the base of the observation tower, I started walking a 1.7-mile loop trail atop the mountain, but halfway through my walk, it started raining. I had not brought a poncho or an umbrella on the hike, so I aborted this plan and returned to my car by the shortest route I could find. After retrieving an umbrella from the car, I walked the paved Grand Promenade behind Bathhouse Row. I stopped at the various outdoor sites I remembered as a teen, like the eagle-bedecked hot water fountain, the uncapped hot spring, and the human-designed and engineered Thermal Cascade waterfall. It all seemed pathetic now. A fake twenty-foot waterfall was puny compared to Yosemite Falls.

While thus musing, I had taken little note of a man wearing cowboy boots and a heavily worn trench coat sitting on a bench near the pool at the base of the Thermal Cascade. He said hello, and I turned and said the same to him. I then asked how he was doing. Upon looking at him, I assumed, based solely on his appearance, that he was homeless. Then again, maybe he was a millionaire into shabby chic.

"You must be a good person," the man said to me, "because most people are too stuck-up to talk to me."

Although initially flattered, I grew concerned when he continued angrily, "Most people think they are better than me. The rude people will get their just desserts someday. You just wait." After a pause, he stared off to the west and intoned ominously, "A hard rain is gonna fall."

Was he quoting Bob Dylan or foreshadowing some apocalyptic revenge? Then, he turned to me and spoke, with a hand shielding his mouth as if relaying a secret, "I have special powers that enable me to predict a storm, and it is about to storm."

Turning to look in the direction he had been staring, I saw the biggest, darkest cumulonimbus I had ever seen, fast approaching the bathhouse area. His special powers must have been contagious because now I also knew a hard rain was going to fall. I told the man I had to leave, and speed walked to the Fordyce.

I did not walk speedily enough. After getting caught in the opening minutes of a downpour, I toured the Fordyce dripping wet as if I had spent the morning luxuriating in a bathhouse and forgot to towel off when done. Little had changed in the Fordyce since 1992, but its Gilded Age splendor was more interesting to me now that I had far more interest in antiques and art than in my teens. When I left the Fordyce, the rain lessened in intensity, but it was still coming down too hard for me to want to hike. It was just mid-afternoon, so I cheated two hours on my workday standard when I gave up and hit the road.

Hot Springs is an interesting place, but it does not seem to deserve the same classification as natural wonders like Yellowstone and the Grand Canyon. If I were in charge, I would re-label Hot Springs as something else besides "National Park." National Historical Park or National Recreation Area seem like more fitting designations compared to the other nomenclature for NPS units. Of course, that change in nomenclature would be viewed by Arkansas and the city around the park as a severe demotion. They would fight tooth and nail to stop it, so it will likely never happen.

After driving across Arkansas in pounding rain for a few hours, I stopped to spend the night in a hotel. That evening, I reviewed photos I had taken that day and posted my favorites to Facebook. In a fit of nostalgia, I posted the picture I had taken of me standing alone on top of the observation tower on this day next to a scan of that picture my mother had given me where I stood next to my sisters as a teen in the same spot.

A Facebook friend made me chuckle when she riffed on the plot of the film ***Back to the Future*** by asking if I had gone back in time in a Delorean and somehow stopped my parents from meeting altogether or had split them before they gave birth to my sisters.

FORTY
NORTH CASCADES NATIONAL PARK
JULY 4-5, 2014

MY RIGHT LEG was submerged in mud to my knee, and I could not extract it. My left knee and the can of bear-repelling spray attached to my belt were embedded in the sloped side of a snowbank two feet tall. This hike into North Cascades National Park had become something I had desperately hoped to avoid: an adventure.

Friends would frequently ask me questions about my "National Park adventures," and I would reply politely, but that three-word phrase irked me because I am a very literal person who knew a Merriam-Webster dictionary definition for "adventure" is "an undertaking involving danger, and unknown risks." "Unknown risks" and "danger" were things I never sought in life and certainly did not want on vacation.

My ideal day in a National Park involved walking to amazing things in sunny, temperate weather on trails that were challenging but within my abilities. I wanted my nature experiences coddled and curated. I had no interest in testing my mettle in the wilderness, doing extreme sports, or putting myself in harm's way. Risks were impossible to eliminate in the outdoors entirely, but I strove to avoid any "unknown risks" by researching each known natural hazard at every park before arriving, asking National Park rangers if I had remaining concerns upon arrival, and adapting the best ways I had learned to avoid or mitigate them.

With 41 parks under my belt, I was prepared for most hiking hazards. My backpack was pushing twenty pounds on most hikes with things I had purchased in response to various hiking calamities I had researched or imagined. As I planned my eleven-day road trip to North Cascades, Glacier, and Mount Rainier National Parks, I read that North Cascades might have and Glacier did have grizzly bear populations.

Nothing in my previous pack loads would repel a grizzly. As those bears can weigh half a ton and have sharp claws and teeth, they were the new hazard on which I fixated before this trip. Numerous websites promised information to make hikers "bear aware," and I read most before this trip. All agreed the best way to avoid bears while hiking was steadily making noise. Bears, they said, would avoid humans if they heard them coming. Attacks usually occurred only when a bear was surprised by a hiker and needed to defend cubs or food. Outdoor stores sold bear bells one could wear while walking, but the best technique was said to be simply talking aloud, especially when approaching bends in the trail where you cannot see what lies ahead. Most sites specifically suggested shouting "Hey bear!" as if bears spoke English.

The websites' advice turned confusing if noises failed and you encountered a bear on a trail. All agreed that the first step was to determine the species. Was it the smaller black bear or the larger grizzly? Identifying the species was not straightforward. Black bears were usually darker and smaller than grizzlies, but individuals in both species came in various hues and sizes. One site suggested identifying the species by determining the snout angle as if the beast would wait for me to assess it with a protractor. Claw length was cited as a distinguishing trait, but I feared that if I could see a bear's claws, it was too late to matter.

Once the species was determined, websites recommended different courses of action for each. They suggested quiet, slow retreats from a grizzly but aggressive noisemaking and arm-waving for a black bear.

If all else fails and a bear charges, you should use "bear spray," pressurized canisters of extra-powerful pepper spray. The capsaicin in pepper spray was said to irritate bears' sensitive noses so they would flee the scene. The stuff cost fifty bucks, heavily taxing my cheapskate ways, and a can of pepper spray seemed a ridiculously puny defense against a half-ton creature. Still, I had seen them use this stuff on an actual grizzly on a MythBusters episode once. It had worked like gangbusters, so it was better than nothing.

It was illegal to take bear spray on a commercial flight, even in checked luggage, so I bought some after landing in Seattle at a Cabela's between the airport and my hotel. That night, I opened the package in my room. The package included the actual can and a "training can" with which one could practice before entering the woods. Instructions indicated that bear spray cans had a safety that had to be removed before firing. Since this could be tricky, users were encouraged to rehearse removing a safety using the training can.

To make my practice run as authentic as possible, I placed the training can in the provided bear spray holster, which I had clipped to my belt. Standing in front of the tallest mirror in the hotel room, I did my best quick draw, removing the safety in one smooth motion, and pressed the trigger with gusto. My heart nearly stopped when a loud blast of air burst from the can with sufficient pressure to briefly wiggle the mirror in its wall mounts. For an instant, I feared I had just pepper sprayed myself, would soon be in agony, and facing a lifetime Marriott ban. I had assumed the training can was empty, but I soon read that the training can was fully pressurized. It was just missing the pepper. My heart resumed beating after reading that fact.

The next morning, I drove into North Cascades National Park, which protects part of the Cascade Mountain Range in northern Washington near the Canadian border. The most famous Cascades are tall, active volcanoes further south, like Mount Saint Helens and Mount Rainier. The North Cascades are less well-known than their southern cousins because they are not as tall and have not erupted recently. There may also be a PR problem since the North Cascades have unwelcoming names like Mount Terror, Forbidden Peak, Mount Despair, and Damnation Peak.

Technically speaking, I never drove my rental car into the National Park because North Cascades is organized differently than any park I had yet visited. Almost the entire official National Park is a designated wilderness with no facilities and only rough backcountry trails. The places typical tourists go when in National Parks—visitor centers, lodges, roads, manicured front-country hiking trails, campgrounds—are not in the National Park here, officially speaking, but in two adjacent, NPS-run National Recreation Areas.

I was driving into Ross Lake National Recreation Area, a narrow, east-west oriented strip of land along Washington state highway 20 that bisects the official National Park. The National Park and the two National Recreation Areas share joint management and are collectively called the North Cascades National Park Complex on brochures and signs. Because of this unusual designation, most people who visit North Cascades National Park Complex never technically enter the National Park. According to 2013 visitation statistics, only 21,000 people entered the National Park that year, while three-quarters of a million only visited Ross Lake.

No average person would be troubled by such nuance. They would consider a day spent in Ross Lake National Recreation Area a visit to North Cascades National Park. I had, however, pledged to visit every National Park in the lower 48, not every National Recreation Area. Thus, I had to break the plane into the official National Park to ensure my National Park Diet had no asterisks.

Entering the National Park boundaries required long hikes from Ross Lake or an adjacent National Forest. I had chosen to tackle the Thornton Lakes Trail, a backcountry trail of ten miles, round trip, with 2,500 feet of elevation gain. While I had hiked more than ten miles in a day several times, I had always done so on a series of relatively easy one- or two-mile trails over the course of a day, with breaks between each trail. This would easily be the longest single hike I had ever tackled.

It was also a backcountry trail, meaning it would be the most lightly trafficked hike I had done, so it could take longer for someone to come by and help me if I had problems. I kept thinking this was a bad idea, but I had to ensure I officially entered the National Park. I had chosen this trail because it was one of the shorter ways to reach the National Park boundary and because it ended at a viewpoint that looked incomprehensibly spectacular in an NPS website photo in which a hiker stood on a ridge far above a sapphire mountain lake nestled at the base of jagged, snow-covered peaks.

My car was the first to arrive at the trailhead parking area, underscoring that I was heading into a less-traveled territory. I soon learned that the trail differed from those I had grown accustomed to in National Parks. It was almost overgrown by tall grass and weeds except for a thin gravel strip down the middle. At one point, there was a literal two-foot-wide sinkhole in the trail. I had to cross several small streams without bridges. Then two miles in, the trail started climbing steeply via switchbacks. This part was at least clear of brush, but water from snow melting above was flowing down the rutted path so fast that it looked more like a shallow creek than a trail.

This was my first long hike using trek poles, the metal walking sticks that look like ski poles. The advertised benefits of trek poles were that users expended less energy climbing slopes and reduced pressure on their joints when descending slopes. I tended to fatigue after more than five miles in my early hikes. I had bought a cheap pair of trek poles, found them of no help, and stopped using them. Now that I had recently achieved my goal weight of 300 pounds, I was routinely logging ten miles a day in a National Park. In recent trips, sore ankles supplanted exhaustion as the factor that limited how far I could walk.

Several hikers with whom I discussed this problem said trek poles solved their ankle pain. At first, I resisted, insisting I should not need equipment to walk, but after doing some research, the engineer in me was convinced of their efficacy. I purchased a more expensive pair of shock-absorbing trek poles for this trip. They worked quite well; as the trail climbed, walking seemed easier than on past steep hikes.

Three miles into the hike, I crested a slope and entered a meadow still so thoroughly snow-covered that I could not find where the trail continued. Not wanting to get lost in the Cascades, I marked the last place I knew was the trail by sticking one of my trek poles in the snow and started wandering the meadow, searching where the trail continued. At one edge of the snow-covered meadow, I saw a lane clear of vegetation through some trees. I thought that must be the trail, but it looked extremely muddy. Before stepping down onto that mud, I checked its depth with the other trek pole still in my hand.

When I leaned down to do that, I slipped. My right leg shot like a torpedo into the muddy spot I meant to poke with the trek pole. Once I stopped moving, my left leg was bent at the knee, which was wedged into the edge of the snowbank. My fully extended right leg was buried in mud past my knee.

My first three tries at pulling my right leg out of that muck were unsuccessful; it felt like some unseen force was pulling me from below the earth's surface when I tried to move it. Panic started. I might be irrevocably stuck until another hiker came along, which was not a pleasant thought because I had not seen another hiker yet. I took deep breaths for a few minutes and then drove the one trek pole still in my hand as far as I could into the top of the snow. I pulled up on it several times until, finally, my leg came free.

Back atop the snow covering most of the meadow, I decided that even if trek poles did not help my ankle pain, they had just paid for themselves. After removing my suddenly hefty right boot, I poured out a volume of goop that seemed geometrically impossible since my foot had just been in there. Then I used handfuls of snow in a successful attempt to wash the muck off my right leg.

While doing this, I stewed and cursed myself for pushing my limits too far with this hike. I was alone on a remote trail and could have easily been stuck for hours without help. I had taken this risk for what? To say I had technically entered the National Park, a distinction that should be of interest only to legal scholars of public land designations. Feeling ashamed, I decided to bail on this trail and find a safer place to hike. When I returned to retrieve the trek pole I had used as a trail marker, I scanned the meadow that had so recently entrapped me and suddenly saw where the trail continued. It was on the other side of a creek. How had I missed that?

Suddenly with a clear path forward, my confidence returned to its meager baseline level. I decided to finish this hike. Probably overcompensating to put the spot of my earlier panic far behind me, I strode steadily up this final section of the trail. I soon passed the sign marking the official boundary of the National Park. Less than an hour later, I crested the ridge I had seen in that amazing website photo.

Unfortunately, I found a very different vista than the one online. Thornton Lake was not an azure stunner on this day because it had not yet melted out—it was still a frigid, white oval. The jagged mountain peaks above the snow pile below still made for a fantastic view by any usual standard, but it paled in comparison to the one I thought would reward me for my long walk. I glumly started my return hike.

Even though my bladder seemed the size of a walnut, I had somehow never yet had to answer nature's call on a trail. Of course, I had never done a hike so long before. Half a mile down from the ridge, I needed to urinate urgently. I would have walked a few feet off the trail and stood behind a tree, but I had seen no hikers all day and had fallen into a mud hole the last time I left the trail. Thus, I took care of business standing on the trail, directing the stream into the snow on one side of the path. When I heard voices approaching, I finished hastily, zipped my fly, and had everything tucked back into its proper place when I saw the two men and one woman hiking. It would have been nice had they arrived when I was stuck in a mud pit instead of as I was relieving myself, I mused. Still, I felt much better knowing that I would probably have been rescued in a timely fashion had I been unable to free myself from that mud.

The rest of the hike down was uneventful. I spent the rest of the afternoon in the Ross Lake National Recreation Area on more fun and less taxing activities. A short trail led me from the visitor center into a lush riverside forest. I stood at viewpoints on US-20 and admired two mountain-framed lakes filled with milky, turquoise-colored water and the distinctively shaped Liberty Bell Mountain, which seemed a fitting end to a July 4th National Park visit.

Once I passed the Cascades, I was shocked at how quickly the vegetation changed. The evergreen forests were replaced by golden scrubby grasses reminiscent of central California. After arriving at my hotel for the night in Chelan, Washington, I was so tired that all I did before bed was eat a quick dinner and shower the boot that had been fully immersed in mud.

The next day, I visited the third unit of the North Cascades complex, Lake Chelan National Recreation Area, which is named for a fifty-mile-long lake wedged between two rows of mountains that is narrow enough to look like a river on a map. Chelan, the town where I spent the previous night, was amid a significant apple-producing area on the lake's southeast end. The National Recreation Area was on the north end of the lake and was an expanse of wilderness apart from a village with tourist services called Stehekin.

No roads connected the recreation area to Chelan or anywhere else, so unless you wanted to make a fifty-mile hike, it could only be reached by seaplane or boat. Concessioners offered trips by both means daily. Tickets for the thirty-minute seaplane trip cost ninety dollars. The four-hour boat tour cost twenty dollars. I had bought a ticket for the plane in the morning and a ticket for the boat back in the afternoon, an attempt to compromise between my twin loves of saving time and money.

Flying on a seaplane sounded exciting when I bought the tickets since I had flown often on jets for business trips and vacation trips my entire adult life but boarding this pontoon-enhanced Buddy Holly killer triggered unexpected anxieties that were not at all calmed when the plane's engines started and roared so loud the pilot had to give us noise-canceling headphones to protect our hearing.

Once in the air, I was distracted for a time by fabulous aerial views of the lake. Our headphones had integral mikes, so we could talk to the pilot if needed. One of the three other passengers on the plane brought my anxieties back when she began using her mike to pepper the pilot with a seemingly unending series of questions about our destination. What was there to see? Where should one eat? Where should one hike? Could you rent a bicycle?

Irritated because she had not done any pre-trip research—I had a stack of papers in my backpack with answers to all these questions and many more—and fearing she would distract the pilot, whom I felt should be exclusively focused on flying this contraption, I spent the waning minutes of the flight in nervous agitation until the pilot smoothly landed on the north end of the lake and docked in Stehekin.

My five hours in Lake Chelan National Recreation Area were terrific. To make the most of my time, I rented a bicycle near the dock and rode it through the quaint village, along the Stehekin River, and to a roaring, 200-foot-tall waterfall called Rainbow Falls. After an excellent lunch at a bakery, I returned the bike and hiked a trail along the lake, which filled the narrow V-shaped crease between two parallel rows of towering green, snow-capped mountains. This stunning scene reminded me of pictures I have seen in books and documentaries of Norway's fjords.

Even though I had been anxious while on the seaplane and a second flight on one would have cost more, I wished I had sprung for the return seaplane ride shortly into my boat ride back to Chelan. It was tedious since we were traveling away from the picturesque end of the lake and heading toward the east end, surrounded by brown hills, orchards, and towns. As we approached Chelan, the lake, which had been quiet in the morning, was abuzz with boat traffic. The boat ride's best moment came just before we reached the docks when two cocky jet-ski riders tried to "get air" on the boat's wake and took spectacular spills.

When I returned to my car in Chelan, I opened the trunk to put my backpack in it. My nose was assaulted with an offensive olfactory onslaught more potent than any I have encountered. I say that as someone who used to use porta potties at Lollapalooza annually. Tentative, gag-interrupted explorations revealed the foul smell emanating from my hiking boot that had been mud immersed after I fell off that snow bank the day before. My attempt at boot sanitation had not felled some malicious microorganism in that muck. After a day in the car trunk, it had developed chemical warfare.

FORTY-ONE
GLACIER NATIONAL PARK
JULY 7-9, 2014

"EVERYWHERE YOU LOOK, it looks like a beer commercial," is how a co-worker named Rick Kraft reverentially described Glacier National Park. Everyone else I knew who had been there also raved about it, so I dedicated three days to exploring it. Still, I was surprised when my mere mention of the park prompted a woman to start a conversation with a pair of footwear.

The day after visiting Lake Chelan, I drove 400 miles to a hotel near the west edge of Glacier. En route, I ate lunch and stopped at Dick's Sporting Goods in Spokane, Washington. I went into Dick's to buy a replacement for my hiking boot that had been befouled because my bumbling left it baptized in North Cascades mud. After selecting a sturdy and comfortable pair of Merrell boots, I approached a register.

The cashier beamed at me and asked, "Are you going hiking?"

Every fiber of my being wanted to reply sarcastically with something akin to Bill Engvall's "Here's your sign" catchphrase, but I controlled the urge. I told her a thumbnail sketch of my Cascades misadventure and concluded by saying I was now traveling to Glacier National Park. Thus, I urgently needed fresh kicks.

The cashier gasped, looked directly at the boots, and said, "Glacier? You guys are in for a treat!" She continued talking to the boots about Glacier National Park as she processed the transaction.

The following day, I entered Glacier National Park from the west. I immediately turned onto the park's main scenic drive, Going-to-the-Sun Road, which zigzags through the park in a roughly east-west orientation. I had read this road was a scenic wonder, but I was unimpressed twenty miles into it when I parked at the trailhead for my first planned hike.

The 4.5-mile round-trip trail to Avalanche Lake is one of the park's most popular. Multiple friends had recommended it. It was pleasant at first as it paralleled a creek rushing through a box canyon, but from there, the trail left the stream and climbed hills deeply shadowed by evergreen branches far above. I only saw dusty ground, roots, and browned pine needles for two miles. This hike was a breeze compared to the Thornton Lakes trail, but it was not easy, and all I was getting out of it was boredom.

All was forgiven once the trail ended in a forest clearing. Before me was a near-vertical mountain wall of bare rock with a shimmering lake at its base of beguiling turquoise color. The lake's water arrived via three narrow waterfalls crashing hundreds of feet down that cliff. This was right out of a beer commercial, but I had not brought beer and instead enjoyed the scene by sitting on a log and staring for half an hour while sipping Gatorade from the 28-ounce bottle I had developed. Naturally, I had brought a Glacier Cherry.

After reluctantly leaving the lake edge and hiking back to my car, I resumed driving east on Going to the Sun Road, which soon lived up to its sterling reputation. Since it tops out at 6,600 feet, roughly half of the head-spinning 12,000 feet elevation I attained by driving Trail Ridge Road in Rocky Mountain National Park, Going-to-the-Sun Road did not initially sound that impressive. What it lacked in height, however, was more than compensated by its near-constant array of stunning vistas of crystal-clear lakes and streams beneath 9,000-foot peaks that glaciers have been sculpting for millennia.

Although less than 15 miles long, I spent hours traversing the highest section of Going-to-the-Sun because I kept stopping at turnouts to gawk at the mountains, lakes, and river valleys far below me. The scenery here blew me away, but I was having trouble putting my finger on exactly why. I had seen mountains—many far taller than these—in other parks. None had entranced me quite like this.

The only thing I could see that was different here was that the mountains seemed more dramatic. They were often bare rock and thin, almost blade-like at the top. Their sides were gouged and lined as if sculpted by a chisel. In a way, they had been sculpted, but not by chisel. Instead, the mountains' shape resulted from 7,000 years of erosion from the movement of the many alpine glaciers that gave the park its name. The park had 150 glaciers when first mapped in the mid-1800s, but now only 39 are left due to global warming.

During my time in the park, I saw distant views of some of the park's remaining glaciers from viewpoints. NPS interpretive signs displayed pictures of those same glaciers at different times in history. All were dramatically smaller than in the early 1900s. The average glacier is 40 percent smaller. Some have shrunk as much as 85 percent. The pictures also show the tree line advancing up the mountains. Experts predict that soon—possibly as early as 2030—Glacier will have no glaciers.

Whatever the future may hold, the park was stunning this day. I enjoyed every minute as the road twisted toward its high point. I was thankful to have a chance to drive this section because it recently looked like it might be closed when I arrived. The road's highest elevation portion only opens in summer because high-altitude snowfalls bury it in winter. The NPS plows open the road as early as they can each year, but the exact date varies. When I had planned my trip, I found a chart on the Internet listing the road's opening day over the past years. Few opening days were past mid-June, so arriving on July 7th seemed safe.

That surety withered on June 17th when Glacier's high country was pummeled with a late-season storm that dumped two feet of snow. As my trip approached, Going-to-the-Sun had not yet opened. I started checking the road plowing updates the park posted on Facebook so often that an observer might have thought I was under the delusion that my page views were helping relocate the snow. My worrying was unwarranted as the road opened on the day of my flight to Seattle. The late snow fed small but powerful temporary waterfalls that crashed down mountainsides and onto the hoods and roofs of cars on the road. One cliff face that usually has several of these is affectionately called the "car wash" by tourists.

After leaving the scenic road's most amazing section, I parked and started a hike to make a four-mile round trip to two larger waterfalls called St. Mary Falls and Virginia Falls. A half mile into the trail, I realized I had forgotten my bear spray. Upon noticing this, I wondered if it was safe to continue, but the bear safety sites said bears would avoid humans if they heard them talking. This trail was crowded with loquacious walkers, so I decided it was safe to continue. I reached St. Mary Falls soon after, which was a pretty, 35-foot-tall, three-tiered cascade. Much of the walk here had been in direct sunlight, so I lingered around the falls for a while to cool off as it was shaded and bathed in mist from the falls.

A chill colder than anything shade and mist could generate went down my spine when I realized there was a danger in not having a can of bear spray on my hip besides risk from bear attacks. The bear spray package had warned that the can could rupture if it reached 120°F. My packaging career had more than once required me to collect data on conditions inside shipping trailers. Hence, I knew that on sunny days, temperatures in a vehicle could far exceed outside air temperatures. With bright sun cooking black leather seats on an 80-degree day, I knew reaching 120 inside my rental car was unlikely but far from impossible.

If that bear spray can ruptured inside the car, I knew it would flood the car with a nasal irritant that would leave the mud-soaked boot that had so troubled me two days before seeming like a scented candle by comparison. Now sweating from mentally generated heat, I decided to forgo

Virginia Falls and hustled back to the car. Fortunately, I found the can intact.

I had intended to make my last hike of the day to a spot called Sun Point, but there was much construction in this section of the road. An orange sign said Sun Point was closed, so I kept driving to St. Mary, the tiny town on the east side of the park, where I was staying the night at a lodge.

The main lodge was a three-story building in a rustic style with rooms, a souvenir store, and a restaurant. The lodge complex was augmented with other buildings that had guest rooms, cabins, and a one-story motel where I was staying. My room was basic and without the lodge's rustic charm but clean and comfortable, with a mountain view out the window. The motel rooms were also among the few in the lodge with TVs. I am slightly ashamed of being happy to have a TV while staying at a National Park, but hey, I could not see the mountain after dark.

I saw a sign for a Red Eagle trail and followed it to a trailhead next to two log cabins built in 1913 that had been one of the park's original ranger stations. From there, I walked a 3.6-mile loop through fields abloom with wildflowers of myriad colors to places where I could catch more stunning views of St. Mary Lake. It was a lovely way to end the day. I would not have found it had I been driving to another park instead of staying at the lodge. Maybe there was something to gain by staying at these parks after all.

My entire Tuesday plan was to hike in the area often cited as the most beautiful part of the park, the Many Glacier Valley. The lodge was only twenty miles from Many Glacier, but fearing the parking lot would fill up, I woke as early as ever and made a beeline for the parking lot at the trailhead for the Grinnell Glacier Trail.

This trail was nearly eleven miles long round trip and gained 1,800 feet of elevation on the way out. It leads to an alpine glacier on a wall of mountains at the end of the Many Glacier Valley. In the park's early days, hikers could walk on that glacier, but that is now discouraged because the glacier's accelerating melting from global warming has made some of it too unstable to support hikers safely.

After reading the trail alerts posted at the trailhead, I learned I would not even be able to get to the base of the glacier this day, much less walk on it. The last mile and a half of the trail were closed because deep snow on that final stretch of trail, remnants of that previously mentioned late storm, made it unsafe to hike the trail unless you knew how to use specific pieces of mountaineering gear. Some of that gear had names I did not know how to pronounce, much less use, so sadly, I realized I would have to stop walking before the base of the glacier, trimming this to a seven-and-a-half-mile hike.

All the hikes I had done the day before were crowded with other people before I arrived, but I noticed my car was the only one parked at this trailhead. The thought that I might be more likely to encounter a grizzly if I was the first hiker of the day began to unsettle me. Another car with a couple in it pulled into the lot while I read the trail alerts. Since I hate getting stuck behind slower hikers and am generally mildly misanthropic, ordinarily, the arrival of others at the trailhead would have spurred me to hastily launch myself down the trail so I would not have to follow them. This time, however, I decided I should let them go first because I hoped they would make enough noise to scare off any bears before I arrived. If all else failed, hopefully, the bears would be distracted by mauling this couple long enough for me to get away safely. Returning to the car and pretending to search for something in the trunk, I dallied long enough for that couple to depart ahead of me.

The trail initially hugged the banks of two small lakes fed by snow and glacier melt called Swiftcurrent Lake and Lake Josephine. This section was shaded by forest, which obstructed views, but there were frequent clearings. One such spot was the Lake Josephine boat dock, where I captured what is likely my best photo. I am a terrible photographer, so this is nothing to brag about, but I think this one was a worthy effort by anyone's standards. It captured two beautiful mountains and a boat almost perfectly mirrored by the lake's surface. After this trip, that picture had a long run as my desktop background at work until I removed it in the name of productivity because I spent too much time wistfully staring at it.

After the trail left the shores of those two lakes, it climbed fast. There were only short, sparse trees on this part of the trail, which was essentially on a ledge in the slope. This meant there was none of the pleasant shade along the lakes, but the increase in sunburn risk was more than offset by the now constant supply of awe-inspiring views, which were striking due to a mix of many gorgeous elements in a compact area. At the base of that mountain wall that towered above the valley was a third small lake called Grinnell Lake, which had that beautiful turquoise color. Water from glacier melt above entered that lake through a tall, powerful waterfall. The brilliant white Grinnell Glacier and another glacier higher up the mountain called the Salamander gleamed in contrast against the gray and browns of that mountain wall. While seeming solid gray or brown from a distance, as I progressed on the trail, I could see the mountains had bands of varying color, and their tops had been eroded into delicate, wavy fins. Finally, to add a little color to the foreground, the trail here had nearby brightly colored wildflowers.

Far too soon, I came to a sign the NPS had installed to inform hikers of the trail closing. Brief transgressive daydreams of crossing that rope crossed my mind, but I trusted the NPS knew what they were doing when they closed the trail. I dejectedly turned to start my return trip.

I have been back to Glacier since the trip described here and walked to Grinnell Glacier that time, so I now have seen what I would have seen that day had the trail's end not been closed. The glacier was a vast expanse of ice covering 200 acres, and at its base was another small lake, but this lake had several small icebergs floating in it. Grinnell Glacier is shrinking with rising global temperatures. The small lake is growing bigger for that reason.

Even without being able to walk to the glacier on this trip, the Grinnell Glacier Trail had already taken its place as my favorite hike. The near-constant gorgeous views along this trail are simply stunning. In my opinion, the only things I have seen in a National Park—or elsewhere—that rival this spot in beauty are the two grand canyons: the Grand Canyon in Arizona and the Grand Canyon of the Yellowstone.

About fifteen minutes after I had turned around at the trail closing sign, hikers started coming up the mountain in droves. The trail was only wide enough for one hiker to walk in most places comfortably, so someone usually had to step aside and let those coming in the other direction pass. Hiking etiquette recommends giving the right of way to those climbing. I followed the etiquette, meaning the return trip was a long slog. This would generally irritate me, but on this trail, I was happy to have an excuse to stop and enjoy the views.

Later, a gigantic tour group came through, hogging the entire trail. I stepped aside and let them pass. While I waited, a man and two tween girls walked up behind me and waited for that same group to pass. We exchanged pleasantries. One of the girls then asked me why I had a spray can on my belt. I explained that it was bear spray and how it worked. After the large tour group passed, I started walking again. Behind me, I heard one girl say she wanted to see a bear. The other replied, "Yeah, me, too, but that jerk ahead of us is going to spray it before we see it."

After returning to the trailhead and eating lunch in the picnic area next to the Grinnell Glacier trailhead, I walked the Swiftcurrent Nature Trail, a three-mile primarily level trail that loops around Swiftcurrent Lake. In the early afternoon, the trail was crowded. Many other people were on the lake in canoes and kayaks. Halfway around the lake, I came to the Many Glacier Hotel, where I had wanted to stay on this trip, but it was booked so far in advance that I had to settle for St. Mary Lodge instead.

The Many Glacier Hotel is situated so that it has a fantastic view with an almost pyramidal mountain directly across the lake and a series of other peaks as a backdrop. The hotel had a snack bar with seating in front, so if I could not stay there, I could at least enjoy the view for a few minutes. After buying a huckleberry soda (you can buy almost anything huckleberry flavored in Glacier, as that berry is common here), I sipped it on a bench while chatting with some people staying in the hotel. Within a few minutes, I realized I did not want to stay at the Many Glacier Hotel. I wanted to live in it…well, only for the summer.

The astounding views mainly prompted my silly urge to reside here, but I was also charmed by its architectural style. From later reading, I learned it was based on a Swiss alpine chalet. In the park's early days, the Great Northern Railroad, which ran the train routes that early tourists would have had to take to Glacier, marketed it as America's Alps. Thus, early accommodations often had Swiss themes. The Great Northern also used the slogan "See America First" to encourage wealthy travelers to come to a National Park via railroad instead of spending their vacation dollars taking a ship to Europe.

It was only 3 PM, and I had already finished my two planned hikes for the day. Wanting to walk a little more, but not much more since I had done 11 miles, I reviewed a brochure listing Many Glacier hikes hoping to find something just right. The only even remotely short trail listed was a 1.7-mile round-trip hike to a waterfall named Apikuni Falls. That sounded like an excellent easy way to end the day.

That hike list should have mentioned the Apikuni Falls trail gains over 600 feet of elevation in the 0.8 distance to the waterfall. That was not the leisurely walk I wanted at that moment. Nonetheless, I made it to the 100-foot falls after thirty minutes of sweaty huffing and puffing. When I arrived, a couple was standing at the base of the falls, but they were staring at a cliff opposite the falls. Upon noticing me, they showed me they were looking at two mountain goats walking far above our heads. I stared in wonderment as the white goats deftly trotted downward on the cliff face on little rock ledges that scarcely looked wider than they were.

My plan for Wednesday was to drive Going-to-the-Sun Road across the park—west-to-east this time—and stop for hikes before leaving Glacier and starting the drive to my next National Park. My main hiking goal for the day was to complete the famous Hidden Lake Trail at Logan Pass, but the lodge staff had shown me how to hike to Sun Point from another parking area called Sunrift Gorge. This required only a 2-mile round-trip hike that also passed another small waterfall called Baring Falls.

Most trails in Glacier were crowded and noisy enough that I had started neglecting my bear safety techniques apart from carrying the spray. However, the trail was empty and spookily quiet when I began my walk to Sun Point at 7 AM. It also had several blind turns. Quiet, blind turns were supposed to be the most likely scenario for a bad bear encounter, so I started nervously smacking my trek poles against each other and yelling, "Hey!" as I approached each bend.

After doing this, before one turn in the trail, I rounded the corner to find an elderly couple moving to the side of it. The woman angrily pointed at me and said that if I wanted them to move out of the way, I should have asked them politely and not yelled at them. After apologizing profusely, I explained I was following bear safety advice, and my yell was not directed at them because I had no idea they were around the corner. To avoid future confusion, maybe I should yell, "Hey bear," as the websites had suggested.

The view from Sun Point was spectacular, with yet another row of rocky peaks reflected in a lake, but the wind rippled the water's surface enough that I could not generate the perfect mirror image photos I had been so happy to get in my Many Glacier pictures. This was only a minor disappointment. Happily, I managed to make it back to the car without angering any other elderly ladies.

The parking lot at Logan Pass was virtually empty when I arrived at 8:30 AM. The visitor center was not yet open, so I headed straight for the snow-covered Hidden Lake Trail. It is an in-and-back trail. While one can turn around any time they want, most hikers either go to an overlook above the namesake lake for a 2.7-mile round-trip hike with 500 feet of elevation change, or some continue from there down to Hidden Lake itself for a 5.4-mile round trip. I planned on hiking to the lake but quickly found walking quite difficult on slippery snow. Half a mile into the walk, I thought the overlook might need to be sufficient.

At this elevation, there were few trees, so there were mountain views at virtually every step. The trail passed some small, eroded peaks and did so much closer than my previous walks had. The many sedimentary rock strata with subtly varying colors in the peaks were more visible at this closer distance. Although the overall impression was still gray, individual layers with reddish and greenish casts were visible.

These meadows through which I was walking would typically sport rare alpine wildflowers this time of year, but the late snow meant no such flora was yet to be on display. The trail did offer fauna. I saw several large ground squirrels called hoary marmots darting about on some rock ledges near the trail, but they tended to make alarmed whistling noises and scurry away before I could get a good look. Soon after, I saw mountain goats descending a cliff to the right of the trail and stopped to take pictures. They were far away, so even after zooming as far as my little point-and-shoot camera would go, I captured only blurry images. A group of hikers from the other direction saw me with my camera. One smirked and said, "If you round that bend ahead, you can get a much better goat picture."

Thinking that hiker meant I would come to a place where I saw the goats on that cliff more clearly, I resumed walking but rounded the next bend and found four other mountain goats—three adults and one kid—walking the trail towards me. I moved to the side and let them pass. Soon after they did, they turned into a stand of short trees. Their coats were mostly shaggy and thick, but all had spots where it was shorter, as if someone tore out a handful of hair. I wondered if they were shedding into a thinner summer coat.

Soon after, I arrived at Hidden Lake Overlook, walked to the edge, and saw not a lake below me but a snow pile at the base of a mountain. A shark-fin-shaped peak named Bearhat Mountain had been partially visible throughout the hike, but the small lake typically surrounding its base in warm weather is only visible once you reach this overlook, hence the name Hidden Lake. With the lake replaced with snow, I saw no reason to continue slipping and sliding down a trail to where a lake would have been.

After turning around, I found several hikers surrounding the four mountain goats I had observed previously. One man had the long lens of an expensive camera pointed inches from the face of one goat, which snorted and looked agitated. The NPS recommends staying eight feet from wildlife, but this guy was not eight inches from a goat. I tarried, hoping the goat would head butt the guy in the camera or crotch, but the man eventually moved to a more respectful distance. I resumed my walk. One man on the trail was using cross-country skis, which made his going much easier than what we other hikers were experiencing.

After leaving Logan Pass, I resumed my westward drive across Going-to-the-Sun Road, frequently stopping to admire the beauty spots again. Near the road's western end, I stopped at the Apgar visitor center and turned in my bear spray to a ranger. Glacier's visitor centers accept bear spray canisters and either recycle them or dispose of them free of charge. Although I would be in Mount Rainier National Park later in the trip, that park's website did not indicate bear spray was needed. With 100-degree temperatures predicted in the area that I would drive through en route to Rainier, I was more terrified of the can exploding in the car than bears.

In the visitor center parking lot, I took off my boots and changed into sneakers for the drive. This place had a hold on me, so I had never been more reluctant to leave a National Park. As I placed my boots in their box, I said to them, "She was right. You guys were in for a treat."

FORTY-TWO
MOUNT RAINIER NATIONAL PARK
JULY 11-12, 2014

AT AN ENTRANCE STATION for Mount Rainier, a park ranger handed me the usual park brochure and a separate note indicating marijuana was legal in Washington state, but possessing it violated federal laws, and National Parks were on federal land. I am not a marijuana user and had no intention of toking in a park, but I chuckled at this example of the complexity of our system distributing powers between federal and state governments.

I chuckled harder when I thought, "I'll bet at least one stoner has used this as a rolling paper."

This park's namesake 14,000-foot-tall mountain had not smoked in over a century, but it is an active volcano. Although I enjoyed lovely views of the mountain through the windshield while driving to the park, I could not see it as I started my first planned hike for the day, which led to a stand of giant, ancient trees called the Grove of the Patriarchs. After initially following the Ohanapecosh River, the path crossed it via a cable suspension bridge that looked like a metal version of that swinging bridge at the end of *Indiana Jones and the Temple of Doom*, albeit closer to the water and with fewer priests on it removing still-beating hearts.

A sign before the bridge indicated that only one hiker should cross at a time. Although I had reached my goal weight of 300 just before starting this trip, I still weighed nearly twice as much as two average hikers and thus had the willies when I set foot on the bridge. My queasiness grew as it bounced and swayed disconcertingly while I walked on it, but I made it across. I soon stood beneath a canopy of cedars, Douglas firs, and hemlocks, all hundreds of years old, towering 200 feet above with trunk diameters up to fifteen feet wide.

For the rest of the morning, I drove the main park road west towards the center of the park, stopping to walk various trails to waterfalls, box canyons, and more big trees. My longest morning hike on the 2.5-mile Bench and Snow Lakes Trail gained 700 feet of elevation en route to two beautiful mountain lakes nestled in a cirque. While retracing my steps back to my car, it was hard to pay attention to my footing because I could constantly see mighty Rainier towering above me in this direction.

Soon after finishing that hike, I arrived in Paradise. No, the walk had not killed me; Paradise was the name of the small village near the mountain that is the site of the park's main visitor center and lodge. Besides its mountain proximity, Paradise is most famous for its meadow at a 5,000 feet elevation that fills with thousands of wildflowers of every hue and size in early summer and offers spectacular year-round views of Rainier and the peaks of the nearby Tatoosh Range. Paradise is also the starting point for a maze of different trails, from short strolls to intricately technical mountain climbs.

While planning the trip, the websites I had read said wildflower coverage in Paradise should be at its height in late June and early July, so I planned my trip accordingly. It was readily apparent soon after my arrival that Paradise had experienced late-season snowfalls on par with those that had also smothered the high country in Glacier. Heartbroken, I realized hiking here would likely be miserable, and those meadows famed for wildflowers would not be awash in any color but white.

The Skyline Trail, a 5.5-mile hike with 1,700 feet of elevation change, had been my planned capper for the day because it passes through the wildflower meadows before going to a Rainier viewpoint called Panorama Point. Even with my trek poles and new boots, I slipped in the still-deep but rapidly melting snow with regularity. After struggling up the first of the steep sections, it was already late afternoon, and I called it quits because I realized there was little chance I would get through 5.5 miles of this mess before dark. Besides, with no wildflowers to see, there was no reason to risk straining my ankles slipping on this slick trail.

During my return walk, I took a spur to a waterfall called Myrtle Falls and finally found some fully melted-out spots revealing small patches, most just a few feet in diameter, where yellow and white wildflowers bloomed above green grass. In every single one of these spots, at least two large ground squirrels, called hoary marmots, were busily devouring the greenery. These marmots must be used to people walking near them because as hikers passed by, they did not stop eating or show any signs of concern, let alone flee.

At the visitor center, I asked a ranger if any Paradise trails were not snow-covered. After he stopped laughing, he said the Nisqually Vista Trail had the least snow cover. I walked to its trailhead and started hiking this 1.2-mile loop that seemed to be every bit as snow-covered as the Skyline Trail. Its main attraction was an overlook that afforded a good look at the Nisqually Glacier, one of 25 glaciers on Rainier. Each glacier was named for the creek or river that originated with meltwater from that glacier.

After I was tired of hiking, I checked in to the Paradise Inn, the wooden lodge in Paradise built in 1916, where I stayed the night. While it has had some updates over the years, it retains its original rustic character and lacks many modern amenities. There was no elevator, and my tiny room had no bathroom, so ablutions and calls of nature required a trudge down the hall to shared facilities. There was also no TV, Wi-Fi, or cell coverage to provide entertainment, so after a delightful dinner in the lodge's restaurant, I listened to a ranger talk on the park's history and watched the sunset over some jagged distant peaks from the porch.

Although I planned to spend a second day in Rainier making a ten-mile hike around the Paradise system, as I ate breakfast Saturday morning, I chucked that plan. The previous day's slipping and sliding had sapped my desire to hike snow-covered trails. I resolved to leave the park and see Mount Saint Helens instead. While driving west out of the park, I made several short hikes, two to lovely waterfalls (Comet and Christine Falls) and another through the ruins of a 19th Century spa built by some hot springs west of Rainier.

Although Mount Saint Helens is dwarfed in size by Rainier, it rivals the bigger mountain in fame since its major eruption in 1980 that produced massive steam vents, a 5.1-magnitude earthquake, and a collapse of the north side of the mountain leading to an avalanche of scalding pyroclastic material and an explosion that downed trees nineteen miles away. More than fifty people were killed, and hundreds of homes and miles of highway were damaged. I was five years old at the time, and I clearly remember being both fascinated and terrified by the images of the eruption on TV.

Rainier and Mount Saint Helens are only thirty miles apart, but from the western exit of the National Park, it was a 120-mile drive to the other volcano since the roads must curve around the mountainous terrain. After its eruption, Ronald Reagan made Mount St. Helens a National Monument, but the US Forest Service ran it since the volcano was already inside Gifford Pinchot National Forest. As was the case in my drive to Rainier, the mountain I wanted to see was visible during much of the trip, but I wanted to see the Johnston Ridge Observatory, the main National Forest Service Museum from which one can best view the side of the mountain that collapsed in 1980.

Several miles before Johnston Ridge, the half-a-dozen cars I had been following on the two-lane highway to the volcano turned into the driveway for a building called the Forest Learning Center. Curious, I pulled in for a look and found it was a museum on forestry and Mount Saint Helens run by Weyerhaeuser, the lumber company that had been given a contract by the National Forest Service to re-plant some of the forests that had been devastated by the eruption.

The National Forest Service has a very different mission than the National Park Service. The lands it administers are not meant as parks but sites for resource extraction. Private companies log, mine, and drill National Forests, activities not allowed in National Parks. The Forest Service is charged with making sure these activities are done sustainably. Weyerhaeuser was re-planting this devastated forest not entirely out of altruism but to later log it. The Forest Learning Center was ostensibly educational, but it became clear that the main goal was to communicate that Weyerhaeuser is awesome.

I have no axe to grind against Weyerhaeuser or the lumber industry in general. I have worked for nearly two decades in engineering packaging focused on plastics, but that is an industry that relies on many materials made from wood. I am also currently typing these words sitting in a wooden chair, hoping that these words will one day be printed on paper. Still, seeing a pro-lumber-company museum on federal land galled me for some reason. That aside, it was a nice enough place. Mount St. Helens was visible from viewing platforms here, and it had fine exhibits on the eruption and forestry. Since the place was so crowded, I wondered if most tourists mistakenly thought this was the Johnston Ridge Observatory.

My wonder proved unfounded. Plenty of tourists were at Johnston Ridge when I arrived there. There was a long line to get into the place, and once inside, it seemed other visitors were constantly jostling me. While I know this cannot be true, it sure felt like there were more people in its gift shop alone than I had seen in all three National Parks I had visited on this trip. The nice museum also had a theater showing a well-done movie on the eruption. After experiencing those, I walked to the outdoor observation deck.

From a distance, Mount St. Helens looked shorter but similar to Rainier. Here at Johnston Ridge, however, I could see it had an irregularly shaped mile-wide divot in its side. It looked like the mountain was the top of a chocolate ice cream cone, and someone had given it a lick. This was the scar left by the 1980 avalanche that dropped the mountain's height by 1,300 feet. From this vantage point, it was not hard to imagine the kind of power this cataclysm must have generated. The seemingly innumerable felled trees still littering the hills around the visitor center further drove that point home.

I was fascinated and terrified all over again.

At the observatory, I learned there was a hiking trail into the "hummocks," the giant piles of debris far below that had been created by the 1980 eruption and avalanche. I drove down to the trailhead and, along the 2.5-mile walk, found that even ten miles from the crater and three decades of erosion from the eruption, these rubble piles were many times taller than me. While grasses and small trees covered some, many could still be seen in cross-sections, revealing they were composed of a jumbled mess of soil, rock, and ash.

Near the trail's end, I looked behind me to get one last look at the mountain. I noticed that although the skies were otherwise clear, a few wispy, vertically oriented white clouds were sitting right above Mount Saint Helens such that they appeared to be emerging from the crater. I assumed this could not be the case and that these were ordinary clouds in the sky that had hit the perfect spot to create an optical illusion.

After leaving Mount St. Helens, I drove to Seattle and spent a pleasant evening there before catching my return flight to Chicago Sunday morning. During my five hours in the air, I rued that I had to leave the beautiful Pacific Northwest and return to work the next day. I bought some airline Wi-Fi, checked my work e-mail to mentally prepare for what awaited me, and then read some websites on Mount St. Helens.

I encountered a news article saying that puffs of steam had started coming from the crater this summer, to the alarm of some living nearby. The article showed pictures of these steam emissions. I now realized those "clouds" I had seen had emerged from the crater. A geologist quoted in this article emphasized that periodic minor steam venting was typical for an active volcano and in no way indicated imminent eruption.

I am sure these geologists know their stuff, but it felt good that I was going home just in case.

FORTY-THREE
MAMMOTH CAVE NATIONAL PARK

AUGUST 9, 2014

AS A CAVE LOVER, I was jazzed about entering the National Park containing the world's longest cave. Although a very brief self-guided tour is sometimes available, going far into Mammoth Cave requires a ticket for a ranger-guided tour. Those can range from one-hour "discovery tours" to epic eight-hour excursions.

Mammoth Cave is the only National Park besides Hot Springs that I had visited before inventing my National Park diet. A business trip in January of 2011 required me to be in Indianapolis late one week and early the next, so I used the Martin Luther King, Jr. holiday weekend in between for a fun trip away from home. I mostly did things in Nashville, Tennessee, and Louisville, Kentucky, but I briefly stopped at Mammoth Cave in Kentucky for a short tour. I now wanted to see more of that cave, but I was still too scared of specialty tours like "Wild Cave," in which you don headlamps and squirm through tiny nooks and crannies, or "Violet City," which is lit by hand-held lanterns to simulate 19th Century tours.

As such, days before this trip, I purchased tickets on recreation.gov for two different two-hour tours: the Historic Tour and the Domes and Dripstones Tour. I arrived at the visitor center just after eight AM. Its huge parking lot was rapidly filling. It had been drizzling during my drive, and though the sky was clearing, the air was extremely humid, and the temperature was well on its way to a predicted high in the mid-90s. Fortunately, cave temperatures are in the mid-fifties all year.

The Historic Tour started at a shelter where the ranger guide gave introductory information and then led us to the cave's natural entrance. Although Mammoth Cave is now known to be the world's longest cave, with passages branching out all over the surrounding area, the section we were about to tour was the only part of it called Mammoth Cave until the 20th Century.

Many caves I have toured use engineered entrances with metal security doors surrounding them. I understand this is necessary to protect those caves from unauthorized entry and vandalism, but I loved that at Carlsbad and Mammoth, the natural entrances look natural from the outside since security devices are hidden well inside. We descended into that entrance via a concrete stairway, but our first primary image was not a metal door but a wide rocky mouth slobbering on us a bit due to the earlier rain.

After walking down into a long but unremarkable cave chamber, we gave the ranger our tickets and passed into an unquestionably remarkable chamber called The Rotunda. This was an enormous underground circular room with a diameter of 175 feet. This is a large room by any standard, but it is not quite the astonishing sight to a modern person who has been in a sports arena or convention center as it would have been to any American in the early 1800s when the cave was discovered. The ranger said this would likely have been the largest enclosed space those early cave visitors had ever seen.

While the enormous size of the Rotunda inspired the cave to be named Mammoth, there must be a common misconception that the cave is named for wooly mammoths. Four people asked a ranger where they could see the wooly mammoth bones. The rangers said there was no evidence of mammoths ever living in this cave, so there were no wooly mammoth bones to be seen.

In the Rotunda and the next room we entered, the ranger described the cave's first major industry: mining bat crap. Mammoth, like most caves, has long been home to bat populations, and their behinds left behind enormous deposits of excrement called guano. Bat guano contains nitrates that could be used to make potassium nitrate or saltpeter, a mineral used in making gunpowder. During the War of 1812, the United States needed gunpowder fast. Some of the saltpeter used to make it came from Mammoth Cave.

The miners in those days were enslaved African Americans who had to descend into the cave and shovel bat guano into vats. Surface water was moved into the cave's depths via wooden pipes and poured into the guano-packed vats so it could leech away needed minerals. Hand-powered pumps then moved the nitrate-containing water back to the surface for processing saltpeter. Even though guano mining in Mammoth stopped 150 years ago, astonishingly, many original wooden pipes and vats remained intact.

After guano mining ceased, the cave was sold in 1838 to a man named Franklin Gorin, who turned it into a tourist attraction. Unfortunately, Gorin used enslaved people as tour guides. One guide named Stephen Bishop became the first to discover many of the cave's features. Today's Historic Tour is essentially the same tour route early visitors would have taken, and many cave ceilings have the names of early visitors scrawled on them in black letters.

We saw many long-famed features. A bridge took us across the Bottomless Pit, a one hundred feet deep vertical shaft. While that was farther than I wanted to fall, it did not look bottomless with modern lighting. It probably did look bottomless when only torches and candles lit early tours. Fat Man's Misery was a narrow, winding passageway requiring anyone of normal width to walk sideways. Even as a fat man, I did not find it too miserable. However, we next went through a section with a short ceiling called Tall Man's Misery, which required uncomfortable squat walking. Doing that was miserable for me.

Aside from those interesting passageways, this cave tour was just a natural empty tunnel through rock that lacked the beautiful speleothems I had so enjoyed seeing in other caves. Those are formed because rainwater seeps into the rock above the cave and dissolves minerals out of it—typically limestone. The water then drips into the cave, and dissolved minerals can be re-deposited slowly, where they build features in a cave void. The ranger explained that the very dense sandstone covering the top of this part of the cave does not allow much groundwater to penetrate it.

When we passed two human-built brick walls, a visitor asked about them. The ranger responded that they were once restrooms for use by tourists, but he then said they developed plumbing problems and that when the National Park Service got the estimate for fixing those issues, "We decided y'all could hold it."

When a man on the tour tried to be funny and said he needed to go right now, the ranger pulled out a plastic bag and said, "You can use this, but you have to carry whatever you put in it for the rest of the tour." The man chuckled and said he could return to the surface without doing that.

We descended into the cave until we were 300 feet below the surface, then headed back up via steep inclines and a staircase. All told, we walked two miles underground. Upon exiting, we walked on a mat soaked in a soapy substance. Many Mammoth Cave bats suffer from the white-nose syndrome mentioned in the Carlsbad chapter. These mats prevent a fungus causing it from leaving the cave on tourists.

The two tours I purchased had a four-hour break between them, so I ate lunch in Cave City, a touristy town east of the park. As I returned to the park, just past the east entrance was a short trail to the opening of Sand Cave, the site of the Floyd Collins tragedy. I had seen a documentary about this and decided to check it out.

All are now known to be part of a single 400-mile-long cave, but in the 1920s, numerous openings to Mammoth Cave were considered separate caves and in various private hands. The owners competed for tourist dollars in what became known as the "Kentucky Cave Wars." The Collins family gave tours of one called Crystal Cave, but few tourists came since it was farther from the main highway than others. In 1925, Floyd Collins decided to explore and widen Sand Cave, which had an entrance nearer to that highway.

A rock fall started when Collins set off dynamite in Sand Cave. That fall trapped his ankle, and he could not escape. Once his plight was discovered, numerous rescue attempts were made, and Collins' ordeal became a news story. The quiet path I walked had been a media circus with reporters, sightseers, and merchants selling food and souvenirs. One tiny reporter won a Pulitzer Prize for repeatedly crawling into the cave to interview Collins. Sadly, all rescue attempts failed, and Collins died after seventeen days.

For more above-ground hiking, I then drove to the western end of the park and hiked to an overlook giving a view of a crook in the Green River called Turnhole Bend. Then, I walked a trail to Cedar Sink, which went through hills and then to a sinkhole that formed when the cave roof collapsed. On this trail, you could see a cave stream exit the cave into the sinkhole, emerge to the surface, and return underground.

Upon returning to the visitor center for my second cave tour, I dripped with sweat despite having only hiked two miles in the hot, humid air. I chuckled that I could use a shower while walking to the visitor center for my next tour and wished I had not said that when a full-on downpour started. It was still raining, though not so intensely, when the ranger arrived to lead us on the Domes and Dripstones tour. After an introductory speech, we boarded a bus that took us a few miles to a place once marketed as "the New Entrance."

This "new entrance" did not look natural. It was covered in a metal structure resembling the exterior of a doomsday prepper's bunker. It was never a natural opening. It was a human-created entrance made via drilling and dynamite by an oilman named George Morrison in 1924 so that he could compete with other nearby cave tours. Morrison initially struggled to grab tourists since he did not have Fat Man's Misery, the Bottomless Pit, or the other famous features of Mammoth Cave. Thus, he explored until he found a cave locale that ultimately did lure visitors. It was called Frozen Niagara, a large area covered in speleothems.

On our way to Frozen Niagara, the ranger led us down a series of staircases that descended vertical shafts called "domes." This tour was only three-quarters of a mile in length compared to the two-mile Historic Tour, but it required traipsing on 500 stairs. Even the horizontal channels took longer for the group to pass through because they were generally narrower than passages on the Historic Tour.

Finally, we reached a room with stalagmites, stalactites, and dripstones in spades. These paled in size compared to what I had seen in Carlsbad Caverns, but they were still beautiful. The namesake feature, Frozen Niagara, was a 75-foot-tall and 50-foot-wide array of parallel stalagmites draping down from a "shelf" in the cave's wall that was stunning to behold even if it looked more like a fringed curtain than a waterfall.

Before exiting, I paused before some well-lit cave formations to snap a selfie. Just after I hit the camera button, I noticed a bat flying directly toward my head, and I ducked with a quickness I did not know I possessed. While I am not scared of bats per se, I did fear needing precautionary rabies shots if one bit me.

After the bus took us back to the visitor center, I felt like walking above ground since the rain had stopped. Trails led from the visitor center to various points, so I walked a two-mile loop that took me through a forest and to the River Styx Spring, where an underground stream exits the cave and becomes a creek.

While leaving the park, I decided that despite my love of caves, the guano mining equipment on the Historic Tour most impressed me. The thought of extracting the excrement of flying mammals to make gunpowder was bizarre enough. It was more amazing that wooden vats and pipes were still there two centuries later.

How terrifying it must have been for those miners toiling long hours shoveling bat feces in a dark cave lit with only torches or primitive lamps. That would be enough to drive a person to a mental breakdown. Then I wondered if that was the origin of the phrase "bat shit crazy."

FORTY-FOUR
CHANNEL ISLANDS NATIONAL PARK
OCTOBER 12, 2014

AS I BOARDED a boat to California's Channel Islands National Park, I had baseball on the brain because the day before, my beloved Kansas City Royals went up two games to none in the American League Championship Series. It seemed like I might finally cash in on a promise my parents had made twenty-nine years earlier.

In 1985, the Royals won the World Series. I was a passionate Royals fan then, the way only a ten-year-old can be. I collected Royals baseball cards, studied Royals stories in the *Kansas City Star* as if each was sacred scripture, watched every televised Royals game, and listened to the rest on the clock radio in my bedroom.

I was trembling with excitement before my family's television in the sixth inning of Game 7 of the 1985 World Series because the Royals had an eleven-run lead and were just nine outs from baseball immortality. At this point, my parents announced it was bedtime and switched off the TV. I desperately wanted to see the Royals championship made official and the ensuing celebration, so I wailed in protest. That was all for naught.

When I tease my parents about this today, my mother asserts it was not her job as a parent to be my friend but to keep me safe and teach me right from wrong. While I concede that premise, I doubt going to bed ninety minutes later just one Sunday in 1985 would have endangered me or rendered me a delinquent.

At that time, my parents did not offer me any rationale for wresting my opportunity to watch the Royals win a Major League crown to match the one on their logo. They tried to quiet my protests by telling me the next time the Royals were in the Series, I would be older and could stay up for the last out then.

After I moved to Chicagoland for a job in 1997, I liked to embellish this story to needle the then long-suffering Cubs fans by claiming I had sobbingly told my parents, "This could be once in a lifetime. The Cubs haven't won a World Series since 1908!" I did not say that to my parents, mostly because I was not that clever at ten, but also because I never expected extended futility from the Royals. As 1985 ended, the Royals had been to the World Series twice and made the playoffs seven times in ten seasons. I assumed I would cash in on that promise to stay up for the end of another Royals trip to the World Series before I graduated high school.

In 2014, however, I was a cynical 39-year-old who had watched 28 Royals seasons go by without a post-season appearance, let alone a World Series. No team had a longer active streak without making the playoffs, and they were not narrowly missing. The Royals once lost 100 games in four out of five seasons, becoming a national joke. The parody newspaper, *The Onion,* ran stories like "Dying Boy Brought in to Cheer Up Kansas City Royals." A Royals playoff berth seemed less likely than a Washington Generals winning streak.

Friends suggested—some jokingly and some seriously—that I adopt a more successful team. The White Sox were great in the mid-2000s, and since I was living in Chicagoland, jumping on their bandwagon would have been easy and rational. Sports fandom is just not rational. There was no reason I should care about ludicrously well-compensated young men playing a game with arbitrary rules that I had never been any good at playing. Yet, I was a fan. The roots of that irrational fandom for me were planted in my childhood on the team nearest the place I was born and raised, so I faithfully followed the Royals to ups and downs, mostly downs, and annually attended one of their games in Chicago.

The Royals had a decent season in 2013, and when they looked like legitimate playoff contenders late in 2014, my cynicism receded. I began to believe. When they finished the regular season in Chicago—with me in attendance—the Royals qualified for the postseason as a Wild Card team. They next beat the A's in a nail-biting, 12-inning, 9-8 Wild Card Game and swept the heavily favored Angels in the American League Division Series. Suddenly anything seemed possible, baseball or otherwise.

Long before, I planned a Columbus Day weekend trip to Channel Islands National Park. I regretted that now because I was exhausted. My October business travel schedule was filled with consecutive trips to Orlando, Indianapolis, and Newport, Rhode Island. My beloved Royals also kept me up late at night with baseball games. Still, I had non-refundable airfare and a National Park project to finish, so I forged ahead.

To make matters worse, I woke with a nasty cold the morning of my flight to LA. After arriving at LAX, I called my friend Ben Lea, a librarian at USC whom I had met when he was working as a librarian at my alma mater. He came to Rolla after I had graduated, but he started coaching UMR's quiz bowl team. We soon became friends at various trivia tournaments. He had relocated to LA several years ago, so I had not seen him since his wedding and was looking forward to catching up with him. We had earlier planned to meet.

Ben answered my call, and after exchanging pleasantries, through which I sniffled and coughed, he said, "I just heard on the news that they are screening all O'Hare passengers for Ebola."

An Ebola outbreak in Africa was prompting panic in the United States at the time, but I had seen nothing unusual at O'Hare, so I replied, "Really? I left there six hours ago and didn't undergo an Ebola screening."

After I had another coughing spell, Ben replied, "So… you were just coughing but weren't screened for Ebola? Well, it was good catching up with you." He hung up the phone.

Ben called back, clearly pleased with his joke, and we made plans to meet at a barbecue restaurant for dinner. The Royals were playing the Orioles that night in the first game of the American League Championship Series, and I made it clear that wherever we ate, I needed to see that game. Ben loves baseball as much, if not more, than I do, so he needed no convincing to watch the game even though his favorite team is the White Sox.

Ben is also a quick wit, so watching baseball with him can provide added entertainment. Ben and I once attended a White Sox-Cubs game together, and when a Cubs fan hurled an insult his way, Ben replied, "In the last 95 years, the Sox have *thrown* more World Series than you've won."

The Royals beat the Orioles in extra innings that night, to my delight. I then had dinner with Ben.

The following day, Ben and I went to the California Science Center to see the Space Shuttle Endeavour and an exhibit of artifacts from the ancient Roman city of Pompeii. Seeing Endeavour was great since I had never seen a space shuttle in person. They were the symbol of space exploration and the frontiers of science in my youth, so seeing one was thrilling, but the exhibit itself was frustrating. The shuttle was in a giant shed, and we could walk around it, but they still needed to construct a way for us to get high enough to see inside.

The Pompeii exhibit was affecting and sobering, but not sobering enough to stop Ben and me from posing for a silly souvenir picture with fake swords at the end of it. Pompeii was an ancient Roman city destroyed and buried in ash from an eruption of Mount Vesuvius in AD 79. Its ruins have been studied and excavated since the mid-1700s. Because Pompeii was a busy town buried unexpectedly, excavations uncover daily objects like combs, games, and other accouterments of everyday life that are less likely to be found in burials. The hot ash also created ghastly body-shaped casts of some of the victims. Some of both were on display.

A lighter moment occurred when we entered one exhibit room, and a sign with an arrow on it said to proceed in that direction for the Erotic Bypass. From fine print, we learned there was a room with art found in Pompeii featuring erotic images, and the bypass could be taken by those whose eyes were too young or sensitive to view such a thing. Ben and I did not take the bypass.

Just before the erotica room, there was a glass display case featuring some ancient Roman plumbing equipment, including pipes and valves. Although my career derailed into packaging, I had a chemical engineering degree, and much of that curriculum involved the mechanics of moving liquids. Thus, seeing 2,000-year-old Roman plumbing equipment looking scarcely different from modern equivalents—although we are less likely to make such things from lead these days—diverted me for several minutes.

When I emerged into the erotic art room, Ben had already been there a while and asked, "Where were you?"

"I was checking out these cool ancient plumbing pipes and valves!" I gushed.

"Mr. White, it speaks volumes that you looked at plumbing instead of proceeding directly to the erotica."

"Given the correct information, I could calculate how long it would take to move those volumes through a given valve," I replied before adding with a smirk, "Besides, people tend to describe their privates as 'plumbing,' so it's essentially the same thing, right?"

"No. Vast oceans of no," Ben responded and resumed inspecting the ancient Roman artwork.

In the afternoon, we returned to Ben's house to watch the Royals beat the Orioles once again. We finished the day eating dinner with his family at a Mexican restaurant, where I learned Ben's mother-in-law had worked at a middle school once attended by Royals' starting third baseman Mike

Moustakas. "If only you had taught him how to lay off a pitch outside the strike zone or beat an infield shift," I quipped.

Ben was still recovering from back surgery, so he could not hike with me. Thus, I bid goodbye to him that night. The next morning, I drove to Oxnard and boarded a boat to Channel Islands National Park. There are eight Channel Islands in the ocean near Los Angeles. The most famous one is Catalina, a resort area not in the National Park. The five northernmost Channel Islands have remained mostly undeveloped and became a National Park in 1980. Like Biscayne, this park's primary mission is to protect the ocean surrounding the islands since it is rich in marine life. Many seabird species also use these islands as nesting grounds.

Getting to the islands requires a boat. I had booked a day trip from the official park concessioner. There were various day options, but I chose one for Anacapa Island, the island closest to the mainland. It was said to have spectacular vistas, and its proximity to the mainland meant less time on a boat and more time hiking.

In retrospect, the boat ride was more exciting than the hiking. Marine life was visible the whole trip. We passed within feet of seals and sea lions. We saw scores of flying fish shoot out of the water and dart below the surface again. We watched a whale spraying. The highlight was our encounter with a pod of dolphins, who swam up to the boat, often looking right at us. Some dolphins even seemed to surf the boat's wake.

As we approached the island, I saw a gorgeous stone arch on its south end. Named Arch Rock, it was a free-standing arch with a wide opening. Although primarily gray and brown, its top was a bright white, making me wonder if it had a layer of limestone on top. Nearer to the island, though, I noticed the bevy of birds atop it and realized the white layer was just bird crap, reminding me of my "white mangrove" incident in Biscayne.

The island itself topped out 200 feet above the ocean surface, had cliffs on all sides, and was flat on top apart from a hill on its south end topped with a lighthouse. From the dock, we climbed to the island's top via 157 stairs. The boat crew said a ranger would start a guided tour in an hour, so most passengers just milled around the visitor center, but I was impatient and walked the 2.5-mile trail system on my own.

There was nothing too exciting atop the island. It had no fresh water, so there were no canyons, large animals, or waterfalls. There were no trees here, and only scrubby plants grew on dry earth. The only plants more than a few inches tall were leafless, three-foot shrubs related to sunflowers that would have green leaves and large, yellow flowers in spring but were bare and leafless in October. The only colorful plant on this day was a ground-hugger with red-tipped leaves and white flowers. Just past the island's campground, I was surprised to see a volunteer work crew busily ripping these plants out of the ground. They explained it was an "ice plant," an invasive species crowding out the island's native plants.

The island's major attractions were thus scenic viewpoints from which one could look down the island's steep slopes to see its rocky shore below. The first two were worth the trip. One looked down on Cathedral Cove, a semicircular inlet on the east side of Anacapa with jagged rock spires jutting from the blue water. Dark strands of kelp visibly swayed in the ocean to the rhythm of white-topped waves lapping at those spires.

Inspiration Point, often featured on park postcards and brochures, was justifiably the park's most famous vista. From it, I could see the steep slope down to the sea on the north side of Anacapa. Beyond the island's tip was a string of several smaller islands—all just steep-sided mountains sticking directly out of the sea. The other islands seemed to form an infinite arc, and since the sky had become thick with low, white clouds, their ochre-hued peaks seemed to jut directly into the heavens. It was stunning.

The following viewpoints were beautiful but anti-climactic compared to the two masterpieces. Most memorable was Pinniped Point, where I saw dozens of seals and sea lions gathered on the rocks below. Although over one hundred feet below me, I could hear them barking loudly. After the main trail looped back to the visitor center, a spur trail led up the hill to the lighthouse. I decided to check it out but could not get to the lighthouse's base. A sign warned not to pass a certain point because the lighthouse periodically made a loud tone, and getting closer during that sound could result in hearing damage.

After returning to the visitor center from the lighthouse spur trail, I realized I had hiked the island's entire trail system and still had two hours before the return boat left. I had not yet entered the visitor center, so I walked into it and saw a Fresnel mirror once used in the lighthouse. The most interesting factoid I learned on museum signage was that someone tried to raise sheep on this sparsely vegetated island before its National Park days. I was skeptical that an island without freshwater lakes or streams could support a flock of sheep, but the NPS said the sheep got sufficient water by licking morning dew off each other's wool. After leaving the visitor center, I walked the trails again, but in the opposite direction this time for novelty's sake.

During our two-hour boat ride back to Oxnard, the clouds prevalent earlier in the day cleared, and the intense sunlight made the water gleam a brilliant blue...almost Royal blue, I thought with a gleam in my eye. Before returning to the mainland via another ride filled with thrilling marine wildlife sightings, the boat took us for closer looks at those noisy seals at Pinniped Point and Arch Rock.

I did not have long to reflect on my day in the Channel Islands as I flew back to Chicago the next day and flew to Florida the next morning for another business trip. Two exciting things happened while I worked in the Sunshine State. My nephew count had increased to four because my sister Jennifer gave birth to her second child, Henry. The Royals swept the Orioles, winning their first AL pennant since 1985.

The crazy Royals ride of 2014 ended weeks later when they lost the World Series to the San Francisco Giants. I was disappointed, but it was a thrilling Series that went the full seven games. The Royals were in it until the very last out. I was also thrilled that my parents were true to their word. Twenty-nine years after the previous Royals World Series appearance, this time, they let me stay up until that last out.

FORTY-FIVE
DRY TORTUGAS NATIONAL PARK
DECEMBER 15, 2014

ONLY THE DRY TORTUGAS, seven small islands seventy miles west of Key West, stood between me and the completion of my goal. There used to be eleven islands in Dry Tortugas National Park, but with sea levels rising, only seven Tortugas were still dry. I was only going to visit two of them.

My Dry Tortugas day would start with a boat trip from Key West to the four-acre Garden Key, the park's largest island by area. A concessioner daily makes a 70-mile, two-hour trip to the island each morning and returns to Key West in the afternoon. This trip cost $170, which made a tightwad's heart skip a few beats, but the ride included complimentary breakfast, lunch, and use of snorkeling equipment during the time we spent on the boat and the four hours we would spend on the island.

My boat trip was on Monday, so after arriving in downtown Key West at noon on Sunday, I walked around the city intending to see some of its sights. I was startled to see brightly colored chickens roaming sidewalks as pigeons do in Chicago. While most of my afternoon was spent strolling near water, enjoying the sunshine, and evading chickens, I toured two historic sites.

One was a house on a naval base that President Harry Truman used as his "Winter White House." The other was a large home that once belonged to Ernest Hemingway and his second wife. The latter proved more memorable with its lavish décor and antiques, many of which were seating for thirty cats. Many had six toes since they were descendants of a six-toed cat that had been a Hemingway family pet. Probably not coincidentally, the Hemingway house was the only place on Key West I did not see free-range chickens.

After walking around the city and downing a seafood dinner, I checked into a Fairfield Inn. These are bargain hotels among Marriott's various chains. All in which I had previously stayed were identically ugly boxes on the outside. This one, however, was an old converted motel, which seemed charming at first. The novelty wore off before I made it to my second-floor room because I had to drag my roller bag up a flight of outdoor stairs instead of taking the usual indoor elevator. I also had to shoo two hens away from my door.

To ensure I boarded the boat in the morning, I asked the hotel for a 6:30 AM wake-up call. That proved unnecessary, for I woke at 5 AM to a loud "cock-a-doodle-doo" from a rooster outside my room. After leveling a litany of foul curses towards that loud-mouthed fowl, I dressed and drove to a dock in Key West.

Due to some ill-timed reading, I boarded the tour boat with extreme trepidation. While planning this trip, I remembered once reading Sarah Vowell's *Assassination Vacation,* a great book describing her travels to sites associated with presidential assassinations. In it, she discussed visiting Dry Tortugas because some Lincoln assassination accomplices were once held prisoner on Garden Key. Having forgotten the details, I wanted to re-read the relevant passage the night before my tour in case there were key spots I should see in the park.

This proved a mistake because Vowell's park description was good, but she also described in detail that highly choppy seas affected the boat she took, and that caused her an epic bout of seasickness. The boat described in that book was the same one I was about to board. My literary-induced queasiness subsided soon as the sea was fortuitously calm on both ends of my trip. I retained both complimentary meals without issue.

Hoping to see marine life from the boat as I had while going to the Channel Islands, I started the trip standing on the deck. After twenty minutes, I had seen only a few flying birds, and, despite the sunshine, it felt chilly once the boat hit its 35-miles-per-hour cruising speed. Defeated, I soon retreated to the enclosed cabin and its heated seating area, where I watched informational videos the boat crew played on large TVs, like a snorkeling how-to guide and a documentary on NPS preservation efforts.

The crew announced we had entered National Park waters about an hour into the ride. Soon after, we caught our first sight of Garden Key and the hexagonal, four-tiered red brick building covering most of it. Fort Jefferson on Garden Key was the last of a series of masonry forts the United States built on the eastern seaboard to improve its coastal defenses in the early 1800s. Construction of this one started in 1846, and the place still needed to be completed fifteen years later when the Civil War started, mostly due to its remote location. An NPS brochure said this fort contains 16 million bricks—I took their word for it and did not check their count—and each was carried here by wooden sailing ships from Pensacola, Florida, or New York City.

Fort Jefferson was at least complete enough during the Civil War to serve its military purpose. During that conflict, it housed 1,700 people, mostly Union soldiers but also civilian support staff, some military prisoners, and enslaved people. Its top level was an artillery platform with enormous cannons that could bombard enemy ships. The lower levels were there to support and defend the big guns on top.

Bizarrely, even though on an island this far out at sea, the fort was encircled by a moat contained on the seaside by a low brick wall. The moat ensured an attacking ship, if it made it past the cannon barrage, could still not gain direct access to the upper levels of the fort with ropes and ladders. The crew would have to disembark and cross a moat while facing gunfire from troops in the lower levels.

The boat crew recommended that we start our island visit with a stroll on the top of the 0.6-mile-long moat wall. I did just that as soon as I disembarked. The moat wall stuck up above the water about a foot and had a smooth, paved top about as wide as a city sidewalk. From it, I saw seawater inside and outside the moat that was calm, clear, a shimmering aquamarine color, and teeming with brightly-hued fish. The fort covered most of the island, but small sections of white sand beaches extended past its walls. Some sported mangroves and palm trees. Many passengers walking the moat exclaimed that this place was paradise.

I next shifted into history nerd mode and made a second circuit focused on the fort. It had three levels. The topmost one had no roof. The lower levels had open arched ports from which weapons could have been fired. The bottom-level ports, directly across from me as I walked the moat wall, were covered with Totten shutters. These were designed in the early 1800s to open automatically when a cannon behind them was fired and re-closed automatically once the cannonball was away. This minimized the time that soldiers firing cannons were exposed to enemy fire, so Totten shutters were a major innovation in their day.

After crossing into the fort's interior via its drawbridge over the moat, I followed a series of signs that direct visitors on a self-guided tour. The route started on the fort's lowest level behind those shutters I had just seen. Period cannons were installed behind some of the shutters. Many other shutters were empty of cannons, but the metal grooves in the floor on which cannons could pivot were still there.

It was soon obvious that the fort's main architectural theme was a vast collection of arches. The ceilings above gun ports were arched. The corridors between ports were arched. There were so many arches that it could have been called Arches National Park had that name not already been taken. Many interior arches had icicle-like rock formations hanging from the ceiling or jutting from the floor that looked like cave stalagmites and stalactites. This made sense when I noticed the concrete here used coral as filler. In a similar process to the one in Carlsbad Caverns, acidic water was slowly dissolving lime from that coral and drip-by-drip, re-depositing it.

The tour route then took me to the parade ground inside the walls, a grassy field dotted with palm trees and smaller brick buildings like the forge where cannon balls were made. Next, I was directed to a stairwell that took me to the fort's second level, where there were few artifacts, but it was a stunning setting as the large open arched ports served as red frames for views of the shimmering blue water outside.

The top level was open with no ceiling. A metal lighthouse jutted above the floor. Ten enormous cannons were behind a low wall, mounted as if ready to fire. A ranger near the lighthouse told me most of the fort's small cannons had been removed by a marine salvage company as scrap metal soon after it was decommissioned around 1900. Fortunately, these big guns were original to the fort because they were too high and heavy for scrappers to remove. Recent restoration efforts restored them to their former glory.

Half the cannons were Rodman guns, 25-ton behemoths capable of firing 300-pound cannonballs three miles. The ranger said they were inaccurate, though, so the bigger danger to attacking ships would have been the five smaller Parrot Guns, which were more accurate due to having rifled barrels. During the Civil War, the Union blew gaping holes in the similarly designed Fort Pulaski, near Savannah, Georgia, by using rifled cannons. Rifled cannons like Parrott Guns thus obsoleted brick forts. By the end of the 19th Century, brick coastal forts had lost their military utility and were closed.

Fort Jefferson was used longer than some due to its remote location. It became a prison for Lincoln assassination conspirators and other convicted criminals following the Civil War. Its final use was as a coaling station for ships going to Cuba during the Spanish-American War.

After leaving the fort and eating my complimentary lunch on the tour boat, I made my next planned walk on another of the park's islands, Bush

Key. It has no buildings and is still a proverbial "desert island." Bush Key and Garden Key are just feet apart and connected by a sand bar, so visitors can often walk or wade between them. I could get there without getting my feet wet on this day.

There is no trail on the island, so hikers must walk on the narrow strip of white sand and gravel ringing its shore. The island's center was just a long, narrow hump topping out three feet above the current sea level, lushly covered with small plants and trees. Gentle waves lapped the sand beneath my feet, and a pelican floated just feet from me. Walking in this more natural setting felt more like a National Park. I was glad to experience it since hiking on Bush Key is off-limits much of the year because various tern species nest there. Another animal that nests in the Dry Tortugas, sea turtles, inspired their name. Because many turtles were on them, the discoverer of these islands, Ponce de Leon, named them Las Tortugas, Spanish for "the turtles." "Dry" was later added because "dry" was an old-time sailor term for an island without fresh water.

Having walked everywhere one could walk on these two islands, I needed something else to do as ninety minutes remained before the boat left. Sensing my lunch was sufficiently settled for swimming, I resolved to snorkel. I chickened out when given a chance to snorkel at Biscayne and was still anxious about it, but free gear could be borrowed, and it was a calm day. If I was ever going to snorkel, this was the time.

After changing into swim trunks, I borrowed snorkeling gear and walked to South Swim Beach on Garden Key. I felt self-conscious about being shirtless since I did not have a beach body despite losing weight with lots of walking for four years. Then again, had I walked here shirtless in 2011, I would have likely been mistaken for a beached whale, and Greenpeace would have rolled me into the water. Mere mild self-consciousness represented a triumphant increase in self-confidence for me.

Before stepping into the ocean, I reviewed the snorkel mask and tube I had been issued. The mask formed a seal around part of my face, leaving my eyes and nose in an air pocket so I could look around freely. The tube had one end that goes in the mouth and another that extended above the water's surface so I could breathe through it while underwater. Unfortunately, it was impossible to seal the mask to my face while wearing my glasses, so for me everything underwater was destined to seem blurry.

After tentative practice runs, I snorkeled a few hundred feet to the ruins of a coaling dock once used to fuel ships headed to the Spanish American War. A grid of metal posts driven into the ocean floor is all that is left, but the boat crew said this was a good place to snorkel since coral grows on the posts. The coral was here as promised in beautiful and sinuous shapes. Scores of brightly colored fish swam among them. It was delightful at first, but only for a few minutes. I soon recalled that the snorkeling how-to video shown on the boat ride to this island had warned of many aquatic creatures here that could sting, like certain jellyfish and the ominously named "fire coral." After that memory, any motion in the water I detected here prompted paranoia that a jellyfish was maneuvering to pummel my epidermis with misery-imparting molecules.

Additionally, distractions while I snorkeled, be it real fish or imagined jellyfish, often disrupted the constant mental effort required to keep me breathing through my mouth. While my conscious mind pondered the source of a detected movement, my brain would return to nose-breathing autopilot. Soon after, I would lose my breath, panic, flail like a crazy person, and finally, with conscious thought, re-direct breathing to my mouth. After half an hour, I decided snorkeling frustrations outpaced snorkeling pleasures. I returned to the beach, shed the gear, then swam without a snorkel until it was time to clean up and return to the boat.

During the ride back to Key West, the tops of my feet felt as if they were on fire, and I feared they had been stung by some nasty creature while I snorkeled, but when the tops of my feet uniformly assumed the color of a canned beet, I realized they were sunburned. While I had doused myself in sunscreen multiple times on Garden Key, I had just worn sandals all day, and it had never occurred to me to put sunscreen on my feet.

Not even scorched feet diminished my euphoria and triumph at completing my goal. A nearby family chatted with me for a while, and I took the opening to brag. They seemed genuinely impressed. Smirking, I

MY NATIONAL PARK DIET

concluded, "I should have brought a 'Mission Accomplished' banner to hang on this boat."

Instead of showing documentaries about the National Park on the boat's televisions during the ride back, the crew played a cheesy 1980s comedy movie, *Captain Ron*. My eyes stayed on the screen, but my mind drifted back to two small boats the NPS displays on the ground floor of Fort Jefferson that Cuban immigrants had used to reach the Dry Tortugas. After the 1950s Communist revolution in Cuba, the U.S. established a "wet foot/dry foot policy." Cuban citizens trying to reach the US who were intercepted at sea were returned to Cuba. However, intended immigrants who landed on U.S. soil could stay there. The two tiny boats on display in the fort each brought more than ten Cubans to this park over potentially dangerous ocean waters.

The Ken Burns documentary that inspired my goal insisted that National Parks were manifestations of American democracy, both in how each park resulted from democratic processes and in how the United States decided its most notable natural wonders should be owned by all of its citizens together. After experiencing these wonders, I passionately agreed with that view.

For the Cubans who made risky trips to the Dry Tortugas in those two boats, this National Park represented democracy more literally. For them, landing in this National Park meant a chance to live in the United States and have freedoms and opportunities not available in their home country.

Their risky, life-changing journey put my meager achievement in perspective. I was only feeling triumphant about a series of vacations. Completing my "National Park Diet" should not make me feel triumphant but grateful. Grateful my country has so many amazing natural wonders to see. Grateful I lived a life before I started this National Park Diet that afforded me opportunities to visit them. Grateful that the work of many Americans, past and present, had protected those wonders as National Parks or built roads, trails, and infrastructure that made them easily accessible even to fat—albeit now slightly less fat—nerds like me.

FORTY-SIX
CLOSING MY NATIONAL PARK DIET
FROM LATE DECEMBER 2014 TO JANUARY 2015

AFTER RETURNING HOME from the Dry Tortugas trip, my focus shifted to confirming how much weight I had lost with my National Park Diet and hurriedly completing another project: a photo book of my National Park pictures that I had been designing on the website Shutterfly.

The first morning I was at home after that trip to Florida, I checked my weight on my bathroom scale, wearing nothing but my glasses just as I had done when I first had the idea to start my National Park Diet. I weighed 296 pounds that day, or 52 pounds less than I had when I started that project. I was giddy to see that number. I checked my weight multiple times a day for over a week to make sure everything had been right on my first check. My weight did not change during the rest of December 2014. Walking many miles in Barrington, Illinois, and in many other places, for four years had also helped me do this. Still, I truly believed my detailed plan and obsession with visiting the National Parks had most helped me reach my starting weight loss goal.

While I had heard of Shutterfly from ads, making such a photo book about my National Park trips did not occur to me until my time at

MY NATIONAL PARK DIET

Mammoth Cave's visitor center. I had been handed a slip of paper with a code that day. It said I could get a small discount on buying a photo book I made on their website. I decided to use it.

Initially, I thought I would haphazardly slap in some favorite photos from my four years of National Park trips and place them in no specific arrangement. Soon after starting to make the Shutterfly photo book, I went wild with a far more detailed plan.

My finished book had an 11"x 14" page size, a hardcover, and 60 total pages. I had a page of photos for each of my 47 National Park visits. A few of my favorites, like the Grand Canyon, Yellowstone, and Glacier, required two pages. On each full-page entry, I noted the date(s) of my visit to that National Park, an outline map showing that park's location, and some of the best pictures from my visit there. I put each picture in a little white "frame" labeled with a text caption to make them look like the old-time postcards I was collecting. I also made pages of pictures from some favorite non-National-Park spots in my four years of travels, like Monument Valley.

On the first page of my Shutterfly book, I wrote quite a brief essay about my trips that is far shorter than this book, so there is no need to reprint that here.

I bought five copies of the photo book from Shutterfly. One was for me, one was for my parents, one was for my sister Jennifer, one was for my sister Melissa, and one was for a grandparent. Mine stayed in Chicagoland upon arrival. I sent Jennifer's to New York. The other three traveled in my car to my hometown of Clinton, Missouri, where I was heading at the end of December for the holiday season and to celebrate my 40th birthday with some family members.

When I gave my parents a copy of my Shutterfly book, they genuinely enjoyed it. My mother even insisted I sign it, and I was happy to oblige. Melissa and her family seemed to enjoy perusing their copy.

The last one went to my paternal grandmother, who was then my only surviving grandparent. That was ironic in one sense as she was the grandparent I had liked least in my childhood. She made mean comments about my weight whenever she saw me, so I generally would not have wasted any of my money on printing another Shutterfly book to give her due to her repeated past comments. Then I thought she would be nicer to me if she saw my picture book about my successful National Park Diet, with which I had lost just over 50 pounds. She kept her common practice the same when she got her copy. After looking at the pictures in my book, she commented, "You are so fat in all of these pictures that you should have used a slimming lens."

I stayed in Missouri with family for seven days, the last of which was my 40th birthday. That was a big milestone. People had asked me for days if turning 40 would send me into a mid-life crisis. I kept saying that would not happen.

On my birthday, while I celebrated with my family with a nice lunch, cake, and some birthday gifts, my Uncle John called. He told me to have a happy birthday but then began an aside about how at age 40, this was the strongest, most alert, and most healthy I would ever be in my entire life. From here on out, he concluded, it would all be downhill.

That dampened my birthday fun a bit.

My mother further heightened this unwelcome realization of passing time and my advancing age when she handed me a brown paper bag that held things like elementary school grade cards, newspaper clippings about my high school quiz bowl games, and envelopes of school and class pictures. Mom was on a downsizing kick and announced that if I did not take these things right now, she would throw them out.

I took the bag. Just a few hours later, I perused the bag's contents. While I did so, one of Melissa's sons, then six-year-old son Alex, took an interest in it. He reached into the bag and looked at several things. He last grabbed an envelope that had what was left of my sophomore-year high school pictures. He extracted a wallet-sized one and asked if he could have it.

"Sure, you can have it, but why do you want it?" I asked.

Alex replied, "So I can remember what you looked like when you are dead."

Okay, **_now_** I was having a mid-life crisis.

FORTY-SEVEN
MY UNFORTUNATE EPILOGUE
2015 - 2023

MY SEVERE ACCIDENT while hiking in Shenandoah National Park on May 24th, 2018 has damaged my life. As I write this epilogue, I have not been to a National Park since that accident happened because it caused serious damage to my brain and my body that left me disabled. I added this epilogue to a book attempt I first wrote in 2016 to explain what happened to me in 2018 and to try and emphasize how important it is to stay safe in National Parks.

Why was I there that day, and what accident happened? I will get there after a few lead-up pages.

In 2015 I kept walking often and gained no weight, but I did not lose more pounds. I had plateaued at just under 300 pounds. Nonetheless, I so enjoyed my four years of visiting National Parks that I wanted to keep them a part of my life. Since I had a good job and many other things I enjoyed doing, I did not set a new goal to visit a specific number of National Parks in a specific amount of time. I just wanted to see parks I had visited again when possible or visit other National Parks I had never visited for the first time.

MY NATIONAL PARK DIET

I made various business or personal trips in 2015 to locations near five National Parks I had visited before, so I briefly revisited my favorite areas in each of those parks. Admittedly I was more focused that year on watching the Kansas City Royals win a World Series for the first time in 30 years. It cost a lot, but I traveled to watch the first game of that World Series in Kauffman Stadium, 21 rows behind the Royals dugout.

During my four years of National Park visits, I became so obsessed with the parks that I started reading many books about their history, how the parks were run in the modern era, and the great work park rangers so often did to keep visitors safe or rescued when needed. My reading and collecting books about National Parks continued in 2015 and the years beyond, so I learned many new things about them.

When possible, I visited places run by the National Park Service that were not named National Parks. I had been to such places as the Gateway Arch, the Statue of Liberty, Gettysburg, and the memorials in Washington DC long before starting my four-year National Park visitation goal. I had enjoyed visiting them and often had not even realized before my visits that the NPS ran those places. In 2015, I wanted to visit more of them whenever I could. As I write this epilogue, I can say I have visited over 170 places run by the National Park Service, but that is not even half of the over 400 they run.

Since I knew that 1916 was the year the National Park Service was created, both from reading books and seeing the Ken Burns documentary, late in 2015, I began checking to see if there were some special moments for the centennial of that event in 2016 that I could attend. The exact day of the centennial was on August 25th. In time I decided that day would not work well for a vacation from work. Some official NPS centennial ceremonies were happening that day, but I gave up on trying to be at one.

Instead, I decided to pay a slightly off-kilter personal tribute to the centennial of the creation of the National Park Service by taking three vacations from work in 2016 that I would use to put me back in 17 of the earliest parks I had visited from 2011 to 2014. All of these were chosen because I could see places in those parks I did not see during my first visit since I weighed a lot less than when I first visited and could hike farther.

Eight more parks would be added to how many I visited in 2016 due to suddenly not having a job at the place where I had done brilliant engineering work for 19 years. During those years, I did so much amazing work on the technical design for the packaging materials of Gatorade and a few other food and beverage brands. Some of my work led to patents, cost-savings, packages consumers loved, and minor improvements to package recycling. During those years, I was first employed by Quaker Oats. Later, post-buy-out of that company, my employer was PepsiCo. I was told on August 4th, 2016 that my position was being eliminated on August 5th. I was handed a severance package and escorted out the door.

Months before that job loss happened, I had planned to drive to Minneapolis, Minnesota, to watch the Royals play the Minnesota Twins on a Saturday night in August. I was doing that to say I had seen the Royals play a game in each of the home ballparks of the five teams in the American League Central division. I had long planned to meet Fargo native Jason Schwengler at the game. He was an old friend from my trivia game days. He had tried to convince me that after the game, I should take a chunk of the next week off from work to visit Fargo. I told him I sadly could not do that since I had too many vacation days from work already set on making long National Park trips.

Suddenly without a job, I told Jason I no longer needed vacation days to go to Fargo. After the game, I spent about a day and a half in Fargo. Before I left Barrington to drive to a game and a visit to Fargo, I decided to revisit more nearby National Parks during that trip. I packed massive loads of clothing and hiking gear in my car. I planned where to travel, where to hike in parks, and spend nights in hotels well in advance. I would spend a day re-visiting the three National Parks in states containing the word Dakota, three days in Glacier, two days in Yellowstone, and sadly, only a few hours in Grand Teton.

On that same week-and-a-half trip, I visited several more places run by the National Park Service that were not officially named National Parks.

Most notably for me, I managed to be in Minnesota's Pipestone National Monument on August 25, 2016, the official centennial day of the creation of the National Park Service. I was pleased to be anywhere run by the National Park Service that day and found Pipestone fascinating. I had never even heard of it before I planned to be there that day. Pipestone has a lovely waterfall on site, so I would have enjoyed the place for seeing that if nothing else, but red pipestone in the National Monument's name refers to a stone long taken from that area by Native Americans for making peace pipes. I was fascinated enough by rocks and history to find things I enjoyed learning in this spot.

After that trip, my primary focus shifted to finding a new job, but in October, I made another trip involving National Parks since I would not be skipping work time. In a week and a half, I revisited the Great Smoky Mountains and Congaree. For the first time, I visited many other places run by the National Park Service that I had never seen before in the southeastern United States.

When I could, I started spending my free time late in 2016 writing the book on these pages…before the epilogue begins, obviously…on my 2011-2014 National Park Diet. I love to read and even collect books, so I had long had the silly dream of writing a book and getting it published long after I retired from my many busy hours of engineering work. Suddenly without a job, I decided to give writing a book a try just for fun. I did not expect it to be great, published, or fly off shelves. I just wanted to experience writing a book instead of writing detailed research reports or PowerPoint presentations about technical design and engineering.

While other ideas were considered, I ultimately decided to write a memoir on my four years of National Park trips since it was a shorter story to tell than most other parts of my life. The trips were recent in my memory, I had taken notes on every trip, and I posted multiple pictures with captions of everywhere I had been on Facebook. When my book attempt was complete, I thought it was so well written that it could get published and sold. I was not expecting book sale money like Stephen

King or J. K. Rowling get for their books, but I thought it might sell enough to break even. I tried to find a publisher or an agent, but none wanted it.

While I probably would not have found a publisher no matter how long I looked, I started a new job at Mallinckrodt Pharmaceuticals near Saint Louis in mid-January of 2017. My life became quite busy, and I gave up on finding a publisher by spring. I had to move to a new metropolitan area, sell a house I had owned in a town I had loved, and learn about the pharmaceutical products for which I would be working on engineering the packaging instead of Gatorade or other beverages.

The house I decided to rent upon moving for the new job was not ready for me to move into for a week and a half after I started working my new job. For that reason, I spent the days before I moved into my new rental spending nights at Robert Wright's house. He brought my attention to the fact that Missouri was celebrating the centennial of the start of its state park system. People visiting all of them in 2017 and getting a stamp in a Missouri state park passport chronicling their visit to each state park would win a free backpack and an entry to a drawing for a state park vacation. I decided to complete that myself, so most of my vacation days in 2017 while on the new job took me to state parks I had never visited in the state where I had been born and raised. I won a free backpack by doing this but did not win the drawing.

When I had a business trip to Las Vegas in September, I decided to take a couple of days off on the same trip to visit the north rim of the Grand Canyon, parts of Zion I had never seen, and make repeat visits to Great Basin and Death Valley. The Gateway Arch in Saint Louis was promoted to National Park status that year. I had visited it many times in the past, but I went there more than once in 2017 pleased that I was living and working in a metropolitan area that had a National Park.

Early in 2018, I considered taking vacations to National Parks that I had never visited…such as the ones in Alaska or Hawaii. That changed when I remembered that the first vacation strictly for fun I had ever taken as an adult with a full-time professional job was in the summer of 1998 to

Washington, DC, back when Robert Wright was living and working in that area. I spent a week of that vacation crashing at Robert's apartment at night and visiting memorials and most Smithsonian museums.

Purely as a personal tribute to how much fun that early vacation had been for me, I decided to make my first vacation of 2018 a week-long visit to that area 20 years after my visit in 1998. That trip was scheduled to be ten days long as it included Memorial Day weekend. I planned to spend half those days in DC at Smithsonian museums and at NPS-run sites and memorials. The other half would be spent visiting places the National Park Service ran in eastern Virginia. Many of those had ties to history, like Jamestown and Yorktown.

Even though I had been there twice before, I decided Shenandoah National Park should be on my itinerary. I visited part of that park in 2012, as already mentioned. In 2014, I went to the wedding of James Quintong, a friend of mine from my trivia playing days, at a site near Shenandoah. I decided while there to take a few days off from work to visit a few places near there that I had not seen, like Thomas Jefferson's Monticello. On one vacation day, I hiked trails in Shenandoah that I had not walked on my previous trip. I finished with a second hike on Bearfence Mountain since I had so enjoyed hiking that trail on my first trip to that park.

Adding Shenandoah to my 2018 trip to DC and eastern Virginia was driven by two ideas. First, I just loved the idea of being able to say my vacation led me to a return visit to a National Park. Second, I mentioned before that I liked the idea of driving the entire length of Skyline Drive in a single day the first time I went there, but I had not accomplished that in either my 2012 or 2014 visits. I decided to do that in 2018 by only hiking my four favorite trails from my two earlier trips to Shenandoah. Otherwise, I would focus on driving the full length of the often slowly moving Skyline.

Robert Wright was a native Virginian, so I tried to convince him to take that trip with me. He once expressed some interest but ultimately decided not to go, so I went alone. Just in case things went wrong, I sent a highly detailed list to my family of everywhere I planned to stop every day of that entire 10-day trip, including all my hikes in order, my flight numbers, my hotel reservations, subways I would ride in DC, and my rental car reservation.

While I remember everything from the early days of that trip and my first few hours of driving and hiking in Shenandoah on May 24, 2018, I remember absolutely nothing about my hike on Bearfence Mountain and the two months that followed. All I know is that others found that I fell more than 30 feet off the top of that mountain. That fall broke multiple places in the bones of my leg, back, and skull. I was left unconscious from that fall for many days, and my brain was so damaged that I was a medical mess for several months.

As such, I have no way of knowing why I received no help from anyone on-site at Shenandoah. My family, especially my mother, Deanna White, quickly determined something terrible had happened to me as I had not been answering calls or texts or posting pictures and comments on Facebook as I had earlier in my vacation. They spent hours tracking down where I must be. They were so frustrated that on phone calls, the National Park Service and Virginia state law enforcement both refused to look for me or assist in a rescue.

The only reason I am now alive is that Bradley Baldwin, the husband of my sister Jennifer, drove their family's car from Brooklyn to Shenandoah, found my rental car with help from the rental company, and thus found where that car was parked. That showed on what trail I must have had the accident. He did a detailed search of Bearfence Mountain trail and found where I had fallen. He then had to walk back down the trail and hike through the brushy area where I had fallen because that was not part of an organized trail. He then called for a team to provide medical help that took me to the University of Virginia hospital in Charlottesville.

For two months, I was in that hospital needing surgeries and having severe issues with my brain. I have no memory of my time in that hospital. I only know what family members have told me about it. They soon learned I was not being treated well in that hospital in so many ways. In late July, my family had me moved by flight to the much better treatment I received at Research Hospital in Kansas City, Missouri.

Starting in early August, my brain improved enough that I have my first post-accident memories in a room in Research. I could communicate again but not that well, as I had serious conversational aphasia. I could not even read a book without going dizzy. I was at risk of brain seizures. I had lost peripheral vision in one eye due to damage to a part of my brain from the fall. I needed surgery to install an acrylic skull plate to the part of my skull that had been crushed and damaged beyond repair.

After months of treatment, I was eventually better enough to leave the hospital and live in my parents' home. By mid-2019, I had made minor improvements. I could read a book, conversational aphasia happened quite rarely, and I took prescribed pills preventing brain seizures.

The biggest joys of my life in the past were all gone and showed no signs of ever returning. I had many physical pains resulting from the injuries to my bones that physical therapy helped reduce somewhat but could not eliminate. I had not lost my memory, but I was much slower than I used to be in pulling out facts stored in my brain. I had once been quite a good player of trivia games, but I was now slow in getting a clue response out of my mouth before a contestant said it while I was watching an episode of *Jeopardy!* on television. My doctors repeatedly told me that working a job or driving a car was unsafe for me.

Thus, engineering, trivia tournaments, hiking in parks, and the rock concerts on which I had spent so much of my time for decades were all now gone from my life. Two more places I had visited during the days I did hike were promoted to National Parks during these years—Indiana Dunes and White Sands—so I could at least claim I had retroactively added two National Parks to my list of visits. On the other hand, New River Gorge in West Virginia became a National Park during this time, and I have never been to that one. I can no longer claim I have visited every National Park in the contiguous 48 states.

It took some agonizing time to make it happen, but doctors had classified me as disabled quite early during these years so I could eventually be on Social Security disability. Eventually, I was better enough to live alone, but I needed to stay in my hometown in Missouri close to family members kind enough to drive me when needed to doctor visits or local shopping.

While I keep telling myself daily that it is better to be alive than dead, I find my current life boring. I try to find safe and entertaining things that I can do. I can still read books, listen to music, and watch television or movies in my house, so those are things I used to do. I can walk, but that is far more painful than it used to be. For that reason, I have abandoned hiking and bought an exercise bike I ride for 10 miles a day.

Late in 2021, I started writing this epilogue and did some personal editing and trimming on my 2016 book on my National Park trips, thinking the modern world of self-publishing books could get copies of my book printed. I did not expect to make much, if any, money for doing such a thing, but I so loved reading books. Having at least one book that I had written published and a copy of it sitting on my bookshelf would be a source of joy for me in my otherwise often boring life.

My neurologist at Research in November of that year asked me what I was doing at the time with my brain. I mentioned various things. After hearing my comment about trying to work on an earlier book attempt to get it self-published, he challenged me to write yet another book about my life before our next appointment scheduled for six months later. I took his challenge so seriously that I wrote an attempt at a book on my decades of playing trivia games. I became so focused on creating another book that, unfortunately, I did not touch this book again while writing that one. I finally came back to it.

I loved all my many early trips to National Parks, but I will never forget how badly the things that happened to me in a National Park in May of 2018 impacted my life. I only wrote this epilogue while refurbishing my previous attempt at a book on my four years of visits to National Parks to urge anyone who reads it and is inspired to take such trips based on what I wrote in 2016 to make sure your safety is always considered.

Accidents causing injury or death could happen in countless ways anywhere in the world besides areas inside National Parks. The news is so sadly filled almost daily with stories involving crime, vehicle crashes, and weather catastrophes. I am not trying to tell you in these pages that National Parks are the most dangerous places to be in the world or that they are the only places where something bad could happen to you.

Dangerous or deadly things can happen in a National Park, but some of those could happen almost anywhere, like a car crash or a fall. Others are only likely in true wilderness places, whether classified as National Parks or something else. I was unlikely to be attacked by a bear or mountain lion during my many years living in Missouri or Illinois, but such events are far more likely to happen near the Rocky Mountains.

It took until 2019 for me to understand this, but I learned from my accident in Shenandoah that rescue from disastrous events in a National Park could be harder to find than accidents in other places. If I had been hit by a car breaking traffic rules as a pedestrian in DC or had been in a car accident while driving along a Virginia highway in my vacation days in 2018 before I returned to Shenandoah, I may have ended such an accident with severe medical issues that left me in bad shape or even worse shape. The key point I am trying to make here is that law enforcement and medical emergency services would have been far more likely to arrive at an accident that I had experienced in such places and provide care to me or anyone else who have been hurt in it. That is because those accidents happened in a public place. Other people in those areas would have likely seen it and called law enforcement or an ambulance for attention to it even if none of the people in those accidents could ask for such help themselves.

Because my accident in Shenandoah National Park happened while I was walking a trail alone, knocked me unconscious, and made me unable to call for help, I received no rescue attempt from the National Park Service or any other government agencies. To be perfectly fair, the National Park

Service cannot have a ranger standing in every square foot of a National Park every second of every day looking for any accidents happening in that sector. Because I, unfortunately, have no memory of how and why exactly I fell from a trail in Shenandoah in 2018 that I had hiked twice before without issue, I have no idea if anyone saw it happen. I highly doubt anyone did see it. A park ranger seeing it as it happened is even more unlikely.

Members of my family found me and got me the medical attention I needed. The information I had sent them before my trip helped that happen. If I had just sent them a text saying I was traveling to DC and Virginia and then said nothing else, it is so unlikely they could have found me. That said, I had no way of knowing what bad thing would happen to me during my vacation and could not tell them what had happened after it did. Members of my family were all incredibly kind and hard-working to find me starting with the information that I had sent them, so they deserve the credit for finding me or for me even being alive now.

The National Park Service and Virginia law enforcement did not help my family do any of that. I have no idea how many requests for search and rescue operations such organizations must deal with each day. Some of those requests may come from folks like my family who have logical reasons and facts to think something bad had happened to someone they know in a specific park, but they have no direct proof of what had happened and where exactly it happened. Law enforcement or the National Park Service may wait a while to respond to such requests. They may think there is a chance the people asking them to investigate and start a rescue of someone they think had an accident in that National Park may not realize that person may have decided they did not want to respond or simply forgot to do so.

Going to National Parks alone may be bad for reasons like those. If I had not gone to that National Park entirely alone, I most likely would have had help much faster. Any friend or family member who had been with me in Shenandoah that day and had seen that accident happen to me with their own eyes would have immediately sought help for me in any way they possibly could.

That said, I went alone to 41 of the 47 National Parks I visited from 2011 to 2014. In all 41 of those, I had no issues or only minor ones that I found ways to work through. All those work throughs are mentioned in this book.

Would I have been happier if I had found one or more of my friends or family members who wanted to do everything I wanted to do in National Parks those four years, and we had found a way to do all of that together? Yes, I most likely would have been happier. However, because I found no friends or family members having the burning interest in going to National Parks that I had at that time, the many stories I tell in this book in the pages before this epilogue would likely never have happened. Before my accident in Shenandoah happened, I would have easily labeled trips to National Parks some of the happiest times of my life, even though so many of those trips were solo ones. I still tend to do that even though I feel a metaphorical gut punch when I think about how a bad trip to a National Park in 2018 has changed my life.

I have read many books about time in National Parks written by various authors, including John Muir's books. In those, I have read many stories about people who hiked alone in National Parks or places that would later become National Parks. They did much of this hiking in places that were not organized trails at the time they hiked there or in areas that still are not so organized. Some of the things they did sound borderline crazy to me. Such authors still somehow managed to make it through.

There is another thing to consider. Even if I had been hiking Bearfence Mountain with Robert Wright in May of 2018 and the same bad thing happened to both of us at the exact same time in the same place, there is no guarantee that both of us would have had a faster rescue. If we had both fallen off that trail and were severely injured in the same ways, there would have likely been no improvement.

I do not know enough to say whether you can safely visit and hike in National Parks alone. I did that so many times with no problems but nearly died the last time I did. It is probably always safer to visit and hike park trails with someone else, but that will not automatically make your time there utterly safe.

If you are visiting any National Parks alone or with someone else in the near or distant future, all I can say now is to take great care to stay as safe as you can while you are there. From 2011 until 2017, I found the National Parks such wonderful places to visit. I saw amazing things. I learned things I found valuable. I felt I understood things about my nation and nature that I likely would not have found outside a National Park.

If my accident at Shenandoah had never happened in 2018, I would only be saying in this paragraph that each National Park is worth visiting at least once and preferably seen much more than once.

Having your life made worse in a National Park is obviously not wonderful, so always read, consider, and make detailed plans to avoid such a thing happening before your trips to National Parks. Doing such things will hopefully keep those trips safe and wonderful.

AUTHOR'S NOTES

Everything in these pages happened to me at some point, but I cheated three times and moved three incidents. Two were from later repeat visits to two of the National Parks I made during the years mentioned briefly in my epilogue. I included those anecdotes in the chapters on my 2011 to 2014 trips to provide extra action in those chapters. In my story about visiting another National Park, I flipped the order in which I took the two tours. In full disclosure, I list each such instance here.

Guadalupe Mountains

I did not hike to Devil's Hall in 2012. That hike happened in 2016. In 2012, I instead hiked to McKittrick Canyon. Since the McKittrick hike was uneventful and Devil's Hall was initially more fun and later painful thanks to the cactus needle I accidentally managed to stick in my hand, I cheated and told that story here instead of the McKittrick hike.

Wind Cave

During both my first trip to Wind Cave in 2013 and my second trip in 2016, I found myself at one point stuck inside a car for quite some time surrounded by a bison herd. However, the one bison scratching its head on my rearview mirror was during the latter of those two trips. As mentioned in my epilogue, I returned to several parks on a trip in 2016 while without a job in my own car, not a rental. Thus, the bison scratching happened on my 300, not a rental car. That was just too good a story to pass on telling here.

Mammoth Cave

I took this cave's Frozen Niagara tour in the morning and the Historic Tour in the afternoon. For this book, I decided it was easier to recount the history of the cave I had learned about on these tours if I described the tours that I took in the reverse order from which I actually took them.

ACKNOWLEDGMENTS

First and foremost, thanks are due to all individuals, past or present, who have worked to create, expand, or improve the wonderful National Parks in the United States of America. My trips would not have been possible without their efforts. Also, thanks to Ken Burns, Dayton Duncan, and everyone else who made *Our National Parks: America's Best Idea*, the film series that directly inspired my trips. I have also read their book about the National Parks and still own a copy of that.

Assistance in further developing this book first came from Robert Wright and Ben Lea, who read early drafts and gave me helpful feedback.

Successful author Lisa Edmonds and professional editor Kirsti MacPherson, both of whom I know from events in my days playing in trivia games, explained the publishing process to me in more detail after I had no luck in finding a publisher for this book late in 2016 or early in 2017. I could not find a publisher even with their tips, but I appreciate their help. Kirsti also gave me some tips on editing my own writing. I am sure a professional could have done that far better than I did, but the tips helped a lot. I ultimately edited my own work for free.

While they did not directly influence my National Park trips, no one has positively impacted my life and character more than my wonderful parents, Walter and Deanna White. I am incalculably thankful for that.

My more talented sisters Jennifer Baldwin and Melissa Crawford, their husbands Brad and Johnny, and my four nephews Quincy, Alex, Clinton, and Henry all deserve my thanks as they are mentioned in these pages, provided free lodging to me during trips, and are fantastic people I am lucky enough to call family.

My gratitude goes to Robert Wright, Chris Taylor, and Ben Lea for their roles in my trips described on these pages. Even though I mentioned ignoring her recommendation in Lassen Volcanic, I did utilize many of Wenny Noha's other trail recommendations. Those enriched my other park visits. As such, she deserves my gratitude and far better treatment than my mocking of her insect-repellent shirts in these pages.

Many other friends and co-workers aided my trips with tips or ideas, like Steve Anderson, Michelle Bryson, Ward Cullum, Dolores Gorski, Rick Kraft, Phil Lawson, Eileen McGeady, Paul Nelson, Priya Parikh, Bill Racicot, Jason Schwengler, Dmitriy Shmagin, Charlie Steinhice, and Marc Wiescinski. I apologize to any other people who also helped me that I am now forgetting. I appreciate your help, even if I cannot remember it now.

Similar gratitude is due to every educator who taught me in the public schools of Clinton, Missouri, or at the University of Missouri-Rolla (now renamed the Missouri University of Science and Technology).

My acknowledgments once stopped there, but more gratitude now goes to my family that rescued me from the horrific accident described in my epilogue and the many medical professionals—especially those at Research Hospital in Kansas City—who have improved my damaged body and brain just enough to write another chapter in a book that I first wrote in 2016, edit it myself, and get it self-published in 2023.

PICTURE SOURCES

The eight pictures taken of me while I was inside a National Park from 2011 to 2014 that are on the outside jacket or front page of this book were all taken by one of my cameras.

Four of these were taken with my camera while on a tripod, I set to a timer, and then I had to move swiftly into the position where I wanted the picture to be taken.

The only two notable exceptions are as follows...

The picture of me leaning next to a piece of petrified wood on a trail in Petrified Forest National Park in 2011 was on my camera but I did not yet have a tripod. Robert Wright snapped that picture on my camera for me.

The picture of me standing in front of Delicate Arch in Arches National Park in 2012 was taken on my camera, but another hiker offered to snap a picture for me with my camera while I was trying to determine where best to place my tripod. Sadly, I did not know her before she took the picture, and I did not even learn her name. The picture was still taken with my own camera, but I did not even set the timer on this one or have it parked on a tripod when the picture was taken.

www.ingramcontent.com/pod-product-compliance
Lightning Source LLC
Chambersburg PA
CBHW071148060526
44107CB00147B/1402/J